RESTRUCTURING THE REGIONS

ANALYSIS, POLICY MODEL AND PROGNOSIS

by
David Wadley

ORGANISATION FOR ECONOMIC CO-OPERATION AND DEVELOPMENT

Pursuant to article 1 of the Convention signed in Paris on 14th December, 1960, and which came into force on 30th September, 1961, the Organisation for Economic Co-operation and Development (OECD) shall promote policies designed:

- to achieve the highest sustainable economic growth and employment and a rising standard of living in Member countries, while maintaining financial stability, and thus to contribute to the development of the world economy;
- to contribute to sound economic expansion in Member as well as non-member countries in the process of economic development; and
- to contribute to the expansion of world trade on a multilateral, non-discriminatory basis in accordance with international obligations.

The Signatories of the Convention on the OECD are Austria, Belgium, Canada, Denmark, France, the Federal Republic of Germany, Greece, Iceland, Ireland, Italy, Luxembourg, the Netherlands, Norway, Portugal, Spain, Sweden, Switzerland, Turkey, the United Kingdom and the United States. The following countries acceded subsequently to this Convention (the dates are those on which the instruments of accession were deposited): Japan (28th April, 1964), Finland (28th January, 1969), Australia (7th June, 1971) and New Zealand (29th May, 1973).

The Socialist Federal Republic of Yugoslavia takes part in certain work of the OECD (agreement of 28th October, 1961).

Publié en français sous le titre:

RESTRUCTURATION RÉGIONALE

*
* *

DT
W

88   03312

FOREWORD

The brief, as set out in the Preface, has been to examine regional priorities in the light of altered economic circumstances and prospects. The report is intended as a general statement to update and extend the "Reappraisal of Regional Policies in OECD Countries" that was prepared by the OECD Industry Committee's Working Party on Regional Development Policy and published in 1974. The report brings together the results of the Working Party's work since the Reappraisal was published and the contributions to the work made by its members as well as by experts in regional science working in the Member countries. It may be noted that the report considers differing theoretical and practical viewpoints, the intention being to present an incisive and balanced case in response to the brief.

The report has been written by Dr. David Wadley, Senior Lecturer, Department of Geography, University of Queensland, Australia. During 1984, while on sabbatical leave with the OECD in Paris, he worked intensively on regional policy questions and subsequently completed the report in 1985.

The Working Party has considered the report and has taken the view that it makes a valuable contribution to the subject, particularly in that it focuses on a number of issues which may prove indispensable to the effectiveness and efficiency of regional policy in a complex environment.

Given the interest in this report to all those concerned in one way or another with regional development policies and implementation, the Industry Committee recommended that the report be published on the responsibility of the Secretary-General, who agreed.

The views expressed in the report are solely those of the author and do not necessarily represent those of the members of the Working Party or of the OECD.

Also available

COSTS AND BENEFITS OF PROTECTION (September 1985)
(03 85 02 1) ISBN 92-64-12758-5   254 pages   £12.00   US$24.00   F120.00   DM53.00

CREATING JOBS AT THE LOCAL LEVEL (August 1985)
(84 85 01 1) ISBN 92-64.12748-8   106 pages   £6.00   US$12.00   F60.00   DM27.00

PETROCHEMICAL INDUSTRY: ENERGY ASPECTS OF STRUCTURAL CHANGE
(February 1985)
(58 85 01 1) ISBN 92-64-12683-X   162 pages   £9.50   US$19.00   F95.00   DM42.00

INDUSTRY AND UNIVERSITY. New Forms of Co-operation and Communication
(October 1984)
(92 84 04 1) ISBN 92-64-12607-4   70 pages   £3.50   US$7.00   F35.00   DM16.00

EDUCATION, URBAN DEVELOPMENT AND LOCAL INITIATIVES (February
1984)
(96 84 01 1) ISBN 92-64-12536-1   110 pages   £6.00   US$12.00   F60.00   DM27.00

Prices charged at the OECD Bookshop.

*THE OECD CATALOGUE OF PUBLICATIONS and supplements will be sent free of charge
on request addressed either to OECD Publications Service, Sales and Distribution Division,
2, rue André-Pascal, 75775 PARIS CEDEX 16, or to the OECD Sales Agent in your country.*

CONTENTS

LIST OF TABLES

LIST OF FIGURES

EXECUTIVE SUMMARY

1. Major changes have characterised the world economy since 1974 – the onset of floating exchange rates, oil price rises and ensuing inflation, and the growth of unemployment.

2. Such changes were accompanied by structural adjustment within and from the secondary sector of advanced nations. The OECD responded with a call for continuing "positive adjustment".

3. This process applies internationally as well as domestically. As the advanced countries rationalise "smokestack" and certain labour-intensive industries, such functions have gravitated to a group of newly-industrialising countries.

4. The rise of these newly-industrialising and other Third World nations is reflected in manufacturing and trade statistics and has been assisted by the development of multinational corporations.

5. In 1979, there were 11 000 such corporations in the world with 82 000 affiliates, of which 61 000 were in developed countries. Overall, multinationals appear to have outperformed domestic corporations in the 1974-83 recession.

6. In part this was achieved by the practice of portfolio management in which businesses could be readily acquired or divested.

7. Some regions thus experienced plant closure for reasons not necessarily related to the performance of individual branches.

8. Generally, international and domestic retraction characterised several traditional industries – textiles, steel, shipbuilding and automobiles. Severe employment repercussions ensued.

9. Often these sectoral failures created equally serious regional impacts in areas in which industry was localised.

10. Thus, "stranded" regions became more important, joining peripheral and congested areas as problem regions in OECD nations.

11. In this milieu, the "regional problem" requires re-interpretation and since 1974 has acquired distinctly political overtones.

12. To leftist writers, the low unemployment of the 1960s and the resultant wages push of the early 1970s destabilised the relations of capital and labour. Assisted by technological factors, capital became "hypermobile" and sought labour havens in developing nations under the auspices of the multinational corporation.

13. Given this process and an apparent lack of new market opportunities in developed countries, the regional problem is now different in that there is a much reduced supply of mobile plants to locate in assisted regions.

14. The changed situation renews the debate of whether mixed economies tend toward an internal spatial balance. The rationale of public intervention or non-intervention in regional development proceeds from the same question.

15. An imbalance/interventionist position remains the most popular among OECD countries as they seek to combat income differentials, regional unemployment and undesired internal population movements.

16. Regional policy has aims of both economic efficiency and sociopolitical equity. It can be strong or weak, centralised or decentralised in application. Policies can be macro or microeconomic, the latter involving capital or labour reallocation.

17. Much variation can exist in the economic and spatial targetting of programmes which since 1980 have become more restrictive in extent.

18. European evaluations have questioned the success towards distributional objectives of regional policy. In some cases, its cost-effectiveness has been in doubt.

19. Accordingly its rationale and execution must be re-examined.

20. Problems surrounding exogenous investment give greater emphasis to endogenous forms as a viable development strategy for many regions.

21. Moreover, the internationalisation of production requires the advanced nations to raise their technology levels or risk losing industry and employment.

22. Hence, from the regional viewpoint, a model can be proposed which ranks control and technology possibilities and associates them with regional strategy outcomes.

23. Countries relying on endogenous high technology development could be contrasted with those dependent on exogenous low technology production.

24. The former may generate sufficient growth to effect certain distributional aims of regional policy. The latter, lacking abundant development possibilities, may have to settle for solely aggregative (sectoral) aims.

25. Assuming constant technology, there are a variety of strategies which countries can use to further their distributional aims.

26. Endogenous development thus emphasises small and medium domestic enterprise with particular attention to its employment capacity, innovativeness and ability to adapt.

27. Enterprise zones constitute an interesting approach within urban policy, though British and American experience has revealed some pitfalls.

28. Direct public intervention though equity holding or nationalised lead firms has been tried in some European countries.

29. Finally, attention is turning from the secondary sector, which may be in decline, to service industries as a vehicle for endogenous regional growth.

30. Varying the level of technology in the model raises different considerations. Technological development can be interpreted via product or innovation cycles or a wave model of economic history.

31. Examination of the world's leading high technology complexes reveals several common features likely to interest regional policymakers.

32. First is initial advantage. Second is long-term government assistance. Third is local public or private initiative. Fourth is the desirability of a satisfying working environment.

33. Policymakers must thus judge whether their region can aim for the apparently most desirable posture: endogenous, export-oriented, product-based high technology.

34. Development issues include the academic interface as explored by the Working Party, the question of technological sovereignty, particularly if exogenous development is sought, and the relation of regional policies with those for national technological development.

35. These considerations can be elaborated in case studies of regional policy in OECD Member countries.

36. Japan is included as a case of a technology leader which is strongly pursuing distributional aims in regional policy despite their apparent impossibility in other nations.

37. Australia is investigated as offering an example of what can occur in a decentralised decision-making system when component entities compete for a reduced supply of investment.

38. From cases cited and other evidence, the prognosis for regional policy appears complex. Its context is likely to be dominated by ongoing international positive structural adjustment but implications of this process require further attention.

39. In respect of continuing technological progress, influences particular to the individual blocks of the OECD may generate centrifugal and centripetal forces in location.

40. The regional policy focus will have to accommodate higher risks in intervention and its foregoing emphasis on employment generation may be questioned.

41. It will further have to respond to realignment of national sectoral policies in which the issue of intervention has recently been extensively debated.

42. Thus integration of technology, industrial and regional policies will be important in both centralised and decentralised governmental systems.

43. The prognosis should be underwritten with ongoing policy monitoring and research both from OECD and outside sources.

44. This support is essential to provide some benchmarks in what seems likely to be a future of increasing heterogeneity in regional policy.

PREFACE

For the last decade and a half, the OECD has been concerned to monitor and, where possible, check disparities within Member countries which not only may create serious economic and social difficulties for people in disadvantaged areas but also hinder national growth. The Industry Committee's Working Party on Regional Development Policies (henceforth, the Working Party) is charged with providing to Member governments data on the nature and scale of regional problems and appropriate measures for dealing with them. Composed of senior regional policymakers of the 24 nations, the Working Party meets up to three times a year and has publicised its work in a series of OECD documents[1].

The first report gauged the extent of regional problems, outlined current policies and provided a comparative assessment of national experiences (OECD, 1970). A consultant's study next evaluated a wide range of approaches and techniques and identified general guidelines for regional development strategy given the changing conditions, priorities and constraints of Member countries (Emanuel, 1973). This heralded the *Reappraisal of Regional Policies in OECD Countries* (OECD, 1974) in which the institutions, requirement for resources and results of regional policies were studied.

The later 1970s saw several research initiatives resulting in publication. Proceeding directly from the 1974 report were two empirical volumes giving country-by-country cameos on regional problems and policies (OECD, 1976a, 1976b). Supplementary details in a standard format were provided in a shorter document (OECD, 1977a) which also noted the bearing of the western economic recession on regional policymaking. Also in 1977 there appeared two specific studies, the first on methods of measuring the effects of regional policies (OECD, 1977b) and the second on restrictive regional policies (OECD, 1977c). Similarly, in 1978, the service sector received attention as a vehicle of regional development (OECD, 1978a). The close of the decade ushered a series of country-based studies, production of which continued into the 1980s (OECD, 1978b, 1979a, 1980a, 1980b, 1981a). The overall situation was then summarised in the *Survey of Recent Developments in Regional Problems and Policies in OECD Countries* (OECD, 1982a). Comparative work of this type is now a perennial feature of the Working Party's activities.

Other recent projects have examined the efficiency of regional policy measures, first in terms of an inventory of central government initiatives and also in the context of positive adjustment and its related problems of instrument co-ordination (OECD, 1979b, 1983a, 1983b). In 1981 two enquiries were established, the more focused commenting on organisations to deal with regional problems in countries with federal constitutions (OECD, 1981b), while the broader one comprised a set of papers from various countries concerning research and policymaking in regional affairs (OECD, 1981c). In April 1982 OECD Ministers met in Stockholm to consider: the priority to be accorded regional development in a time of economic and budgetary difficulties; the problems of regionally concentrated industrial decline; and better use of local resources in development. It was recognised that relativities had changed considerably in a short time, demanding new levels of efficiency and effectiveness not only

13

from the private sector, but also among government policymakers. In acknowledgement of the many specific reports or country-studies since the mid-1970s, the need was felt for a general statement which would update and extend the *Reappraisal* undertaken by the OECD in 1974.

The brief of the current book is thus to examine regional priorities in the light of altered economic circumstances which, in general, have exacerbated existing difficulties and are providing a new set of problems for policymakers. The view put here is that the potential scope for a country's regional policy will increasingly be determined by processes of structural change in the international economic environment. These processes demark the range of options open to policymakers who, in the case of some nations, may have qualified ability to manœuvre; they are the backdrop to not only regional but ultimately sectoral economic policy. The issue for OECD countries today is the degree to which their sectoral policies, as determined by comparative advantage, are proactive or merely responsive to the international milieu. Moves toward the former and arguably more desirable position have recently produced a variety of micro responses, though their efficacy as long-term tools of regional policy in the face of global change is uncertain. National comparative advantage will likely remain the arbiter of success. Hence, regional policymakers will need to pay greater attention to the development of the world economy and national relativities in the future.

This report falls into three main parts. The preliminary analysis examines the recent crisis of advanced nations in terms of the shocks and synchronisations which emerged in the world economy after 1973. Problematic international shifts in production and trade can be partly interpreted through the rise of the multinational corporation (Chapter I). Chapter II shows how sectoral and regional declines have necessitated the development of a different typology of regions and fostered new perspectives on the "regional problem". The third chapter classifies the context and tools of regional policy and points to their mixed record of success in recent years.

The second part of the report involves the construction, elaboration and assessment of a model of regional development. It suggests that in the new economic environment of reduced mobile investment, certain aims of regional policy should be more accessible to countries reliant on endogenous, higher technology forms of growth. Aspects of endogenous development are then reviewed (Chapter IV). The bearing of new technology on regional development is examined in Chapter V, leading to selected case studies in Chapter VI which test the model and highlight a range of recent regional policy experience.

The third part is the prognosis of regional policy undertaken in Chapter VII. It deals with the context, focus and integration of future initiatives and their support through ongoing research. Directions are suggested for the studies of the Working Party and other analysts.

While the seven chapters so outlined reflect certain broad standpoints, the aim has been to present a balanced rather than a prescriptive case. In part this has been approached by attempting to blend academic insights with the practical experience of members of the OECD Working Party. It is recognised that the resultant work is only one point in the continuing debate over regional policy and that it must remain less than fully inclusive. Various operational constraints have predetermined an emphasis on English language sources and fieldwork has been strictly limited. Certain omissions characterise what has been achieved and they, like remaining errors, rest with the author.

On a brighter note, the project incorporates the assistance of many organisations and individuals. Acknowledgement is due first to the University of Queensland in Brisbane, Australia which released the author for twelve months' study leave and provided basic research funding. Further support was afforded by the Queensland Department of

Commercial and Industrial Development, also of Brisbane, Australia. Library and other facilities were made available by the Centre for the Study of Public Policy, University of Strathclyde in Scotland, and by the departments of geography of the London School of Economics and Queen Mary College, University of London and the Université de Paris I (Sorbonne). Much help has been derived from the SCANFILE bibliographic bulletins generously sent by the Headquarters Library and Information Service of the Commonwealth Scientific and Industrial Research Organisation in Canberra, Australia. A study tour to Japan in the course of the work drew help from the Ministry of International Trade and Industry (MITI) in Tokyo and the Oita Prefectural Government. Similarly, useful information was supplied by the British Department of Trade and Industry (Economics Division) in London, the Joint Economic Committee of the United States Congress in Washington, DC, and the federal Bureau of Industry Economics in Canberra, Australia. Permission to publish Figures 3.1 and 5.1 was offered respectively by Philip Allan Publications Ltd., Oxford, England and the New York Times newspaper, New York. Thanks are extended to all who have contributed to the work.

NOTES

1. The following résumé draws on Ezra (1982) which should be consulted for full details of OECD work on regional policy to 1982.

Chapter I

A CHANGED ECONOMIC ENVIRONMENT

Written during 1984 and 1985, this report is set against a backdrop of economic circumstances vastly different from those of a decade earlier when the OECD's (1974) *Reappraisal of Regional Policies* was compiled. Such conditions, which have greatly complicated recent regional policy and form the backdrop for present initiatives in Member nations, are examined in this chapter. The first issue is the structural development of the world economy over the period: it is the macro environment of all national spatial initiatives. Then comes a discussion of the shifts in global production and trade which followed the changes described. Part of the cause is found in the emerging role of the multinational corporation which is now a force to be considered in many regional programmes.

GLOBAL STRUCTURAL CHANGE

The General Milieu

Though each of the decades since 1945 has had its own particular characteristic in world economic relationships and trade policy, the end of the Second World War introduced for many OECD countries a long cyclical upswing which continued almost without interruption for the next quarter-century. After the recovery and reconstruction of the 1950s, nations began to experience relatively favourable growth. The ending of European balance of payments restrictions in 1958 and formation of the OECD in 1961 were signs of increasing international co-operation in a decade of creation and emergence. The formation of economic communities and dissolution of former colonial empires coincided during the 1960s with an industrial boom of significant proportions (Golt, 1979: 29). Such conditions provided fertile ground for the growth of corporate multinationalism which, in a sense, became a form of organisation supplanting the former colonialism.

Despite the progress, various economic difficulties were foreshadowed. The nascent strength of western Europe was becoming difficult to accommodate within the rigidity of the Bretton Woods pegged exchange rate system. Domestic policies in the United States associated with the conduct of the Vietnam war and the Great Society programme produced other instabilities and, by the end of the 1960s, advanced economies featured higher levels of inflation, an ongoing decline in real rates of return and greater costs of growth resulting from popular demands for improved lifestyles, environment and social welfare.

All these and other pressures necessitated a change to the exchange system. After 1971 the convertability of the United States dollar as a reserve currency was abolished and floating rates were instituted with strong implications for processes of industrial change and international financial stability (Hesselman, 1983: 200). The decade of the 1970s became that of a polycentric world (OECD, 1980c: 20) in which political and economic power was redistributed from traditionally dominant to other nations, particularly in the Pacific Basin and Middle East. The greatest challenge to stability emerged in 1973 when the OPEC (Organisation of Petroleum Exporting Countries) cartel quadrupled the price of oil. This was the first of a series of rises continuing throughout the decade.

In terms of real gross domestic product, economic growth had been faltering among certain OECD countries even before the oil price shock (Table 1.1). It was effectively arrested after 1974 as a string of nations recorded negative movements. In that year the western world entered a deep recession characterised before too long by stagflation, a new phenomenon in which relatively high inflation and unemployment went side-by-side. As shown in Table 1.2, the OECD achieved double-digit inflation in terms of increases in the consumer price index during 1974 and 1975 and again in 1980 and 1981. The mid-1970s were marked by strong wage demands often unrelated to gains in productivity. These demands coalesced with the cost-push inflation caused by the oil price hike and widened the gulf between employed and unemployed. Public policy for deflation characterised OECD economies in the later 1970s, differing degrees of success being achieved (Table 1.2). Only a few managed to contain the growth of prices to levels regarded historically as respectable: in the meantime, relegation of employment from its place as the first target of economic policy was having its own impact.

Unemployment as a percentage of the total labour force varies among countries but has risen overall since 1980 (Table 1.3). Wage demands have encouraged the substitution of capital for labour. This trend was abetted on one hand by interest in new technologies as a solution to the energy crisis and, on the other, by significant advances in computing and control systems which allowed a large range of operations to be automated (or robotised) for the first time. Allied with the onset of mass unemployment (now around 35 million in the OECD bloc) have been absolute and relative declines in the secondary sector of many countries. Trends implicit in Table 1.4 spark discussion of a new economic revolution in OECD nations in which labour is shed not from agriculture as has historically been the case in advanced economies, but from manufacturing (OECD, 1983c: 24). The problem now is that its absorption into the service sector is less certain than before because many services, despite their labour intensity, face the same pressures for capital-labour substitution as exist in manufacturing. Their position is also directly affected by slow-downs in public spending and reduced growth of the government sector (Townsend, 1983: 42).

Positive Structural Adjustment

Over the last decade, these inter-sectoral shifts have been recognised as part of the process of "structural adjustment". This phenomenon is not new and occurs all the time at levels of the sector, industry and firm: it involves reallocation of resources from less to more productive uses in order that organisations may remain efficient, competitive and profitable. Its stimulus may be changing demand patterns, technological development or greater competition, and the adjustment may manifest itself in birth and death, expansion and contraction, modernisation, innovation, diversification or a range of other business alternatives.

Conventional economic theory holds that growth and positive adjustment are closely related since the costs of failing to adjust are measured in reduced productivity, competitiveness and profitability with the inherent risks of stagnation, decline and demise. The costs of actually adjusting are lessened if action takes place in an expansive economic milieu in which there is high mobility of resources and an easy functioning of market mechanisms.

18

Table 1.1. **Annual percentage changes, real gross domestic product OECD countries, 1969-1983**

	1969	1970	1971	1972	1973	1974	1975	1976	1977	1978	1979	1980	1981	1982	1983	60-68	68-73	73-79	79-83	60-83
United States	2.8	-0.3	3.1	5.4	5.5	-0.6	-0.7	4.9	5.2	4.7	2.4	-0.2	3.0	-2.3	3.5	4.5	3.3	2.6	0.9	3.1
Japan	12.3	9.8	4.6	8.8	8.8	-1.0	2.3	5.3	5.3	5.0	5.1	4.9	4.2	3.0	3.0	10.5	8.8	3.6	3.8	7.1
Germany	7.5	5.1	3.1	4.2	4.6	0.5	-1.7	5.5	3.1	3.1	4.2	1.8	-0.1	-1.0	1.3	4.2	4.9	2.4	0.5	3.2
France	7.0	5.7	5.4	5.9	5.4	3.2	0.2	5.2	3.1	3.8	3.3	1.1	0.3	1.6	0.5	5.4	5.9	3.1	0.9	4.1
United Kingdom	1.3	2.2	2.6	2.1	7.6	-0.9	-0.9	3.7	1.2	3.5	2.0	-2.6	-1.3	2.3	2.5	3.1	3.1	1.4	0.2	2.1
Italy	6.1	5.3	1.6	3.2	7.0	4.1	-3.6	5.9	1.9	2.7	4.9	3.9	0.1	-0.3	-1.5	5.7	4.6	2.6	0.5	3.8
Canada	5.2	2.6	7.0	5.8	7.5	3.5	1.1	6.1	2.2	3.9	3.4	1.0	4.0	-4.2	3.0	5.6	5.6	3.4	0.9	4.1
Total of above countries	5.1	3.1	3.5	5.4	6.2	0.3	-0.4	5.1	4.0	4.2	3.3	1.1	2.0	-0.5	2.5	5.1	4.7	2.7	1.3	3.7
Austria	6.3	7.1	5.1	6.2	4.9	3.9	-0.4	4.6	4.4	0.5	4.7	3.0	-0.1	1.1	1.0	4.3	5.9	2.9	1.2	3.8
Belgium	6.6	6.4	3.9	5.3	6.2	4.5	-1.9	5.5	0.6	3.2	2.5	3.2	-1.1	1.1	0.0	4.5	5.7	2.4	0.8	3.6
Danemark	6.5	2.3	2.4	5.4	3.8	-0.7	-1.0	6.5	2.3	1.8	3.7	-0.4	-0.7	3.6	1.8	4.6	4.1	2.1	1.0	3.1
Finland	9.6	7.9	1.8	7.5	6.5	3.2	0.6	0.3	0.4	2.3	7.6	6.0	1.5	2.5	2.8	3.9	6.7	2.3	3.2	3.9
Greece	9.9	8.0	7.1	8.9	7.3	-3.6	6.1	6.4	3.4	6.7	3.7	1.6	-0.4	—	0.0	7.3	8.2	3.7	0.3	5.4
Iceland	3.1	7.8	12.7	6.5	7.9	4.0	-0.5	3.5	5.8	3.9	4.1	4.1	2.2	-1.3	-5.8	4.1	7.6	3.5	-0.3	3.9
Ireland	6.1	3.5	3.4	6.4	4.7	4.3	2.0	2.2	6.8	5.8	3.4	3.7	1.6	1.2	0.5	4.2	4.8	4.1	1.8	3.8
Luxembourg	8.9	2.2	4.3	6.2	10.8	3.6	-6.1	1.9	0.6	4.5	4.0	1.7	-1.8	-1.1	-2.5	3.1	6.5	1.4	-0.9	2.7
Netherlands	6.4	6.7	4.3	3.4	5.7	3.5	-1.0	5.3	2.4	2.5	2.4	0.9	-0.8	-1.6	1.3	4.8	5.3	2.5	-0.1	3.4
Norway	4.5	2.0	4.6	5.2	4.1	5.2	4.2	6.8	3.6	4.5	5.1	4.3	0.3	-0.6	1.5	4.4	4.1	4.9	1.3	3.9
Portugal	2.1	9.1	6.6	8.0	11.2	1.1	-4.3	6.9	5.6	3.4	6.6	4.1	0.5	3.5	0.3	6.6	7.4	3.1	2.1	5.1
Spain	8.9	4.1	5.0	8.1	7.9	5.7	1.1	3.0	3.3	1.8	0.2	1.5	0.2	1.2	2.0	7.5	6.8	2.5	1.2	5.0
Sweden	5.0	7.2	0.9	2.3	4.0	3.2	2.6	1.1	-1.6	1.8	3.8	1.7	-0.5	0.4	1.8	4.4	3.9	1.8	0.8	2.9
Switzerland	5.6	6.4	4.1	3.2	3.0	1.5	-7.3	-1.4	2.4	0.4	2.5	4.6	1.5	-1.2	0.0	4.4	4.5	-0.4	1.2	2.6
Turkey	5.3	4.9	9.1	6.6	2.0	12.5	10.1	10.8	5.1	3.2	-1.7	-0.3	4.5	5.7	3.0	5.8	5.5	6.6	3.1	5.5
Smaller Europeans	6.6	5.7	4.1	5.3	5.5	3.7	0.1	3.9	2.3	2.3	2.7	2.2	0.2	0.8	1.3	5.1	5.4	2.5	1.1	3.8
Australia	6.5	6.1	5.7	3.7	5.4	1.8	2.5	3.2	1.0	2.7	4.3	1.6	4.1	-0.8	-1.3	5.0	5.5	2.6	0.9	3.8
New Zealand	8.0	2.0	3.8	4.8	6.4	6.2	-0.4	2.1	-4.4	0.7	-1.7	3.2	2.8	0.4	-0.5	3.0	5.0	0.4	1.5	2.5
Total Smaller	6.7	5.7	4.3	5.1	5.5	3.5	0.3	3.8	2.0	2.3	2.7	2.2	0.6	0.6	-1.0	5.1	5.4	2.5	1.1	3.8
Total EEC	5.7	4.8	3.4	4.1	5.8	1.6	-1.2	5.1	2.4	3.3	3.4	1.0	-0.3	0.5	0.8	4.4	4.8	2.4	0.5	3.4
Total OECD – Europe	5.9	4.9	3.6	4.4	5.7	2.2	-0.9	4.7	2.4	3.0	3.3	1.3	-0.1	0.6	1.0	4.6	4.9	2.4	0.7	3.4
Total OECD less US	6.9	5.7	4.0	5.3	6.4	1.6	-0.1	4.8	2.9	3.4	3.7	2.1	1.2	0.8	1.7	5.5	5.6	2.7	1.5	4.1
Total OECD	5.4	3.5	3.7	5.3	6.1	0.8	-0.3	4.8	3.7	3.9	3.2	1.3	1.8	-0.3	2.2	5.1	4.8	2.7	1.2	3.7

Source: OECD (1984c: 44) and unpublished data, OECD.

Table 1.2. Annual percentage change, consumer price indices, OECD countries, 1969-1983

	1969	1970	1971	1972	1973	1974	1975	1976	1977	1978	1979	1980	1981	1982	1983	60-68	68-73	73-79	79-83	60-83
United States	5.4	5.9	4.3	3.3	6.2	11.0	9.1	5.8	6.5	7.7	11.3	13.5	10.4	-6.1	3.2	2.0	5.0	8.5	8.6	5.4
Japan	5.2	7.7	6.1	4.5	11.7	24.5	11.8	9.3	8.1	3.8	3.6	8.0	4.9	2.7	1.9	5.7	7.0	10.0	4.5	6.9
Germany	1.9	3.4	5.3	5.5	6.9	7.0	6.0	4.5	3.7	2.7	4.1	5.5	5.9	5.3	3.0	2.7	4.6	4.7	5.1	4.1
France	6.4	5.2	5.5	6.2	7.3	13.7	11.8	9.6	9.4	9.1	10.8	13.6	13.4	11.8	9.6	3.6	6.1	10.7	12.2	7.4
United Kingdom	5.4	6.4	9.4	7.1	9.2	16.0	24.2	16.5	15.8	8.3	13.4	18.0	11.9	8.6	4.6	4.0	7.5	15.6	11.2	8.7
Italy	2.6	5.0	4.8	5.7	10.8	19.1	17.0	16.8	17.0	12.1	14.8	21.2	17.8	16.6	14.6	4.0	5.8	16.1	17.7	9.7
Canada	4.5	3.4	2.8	4.8	7.6	10.9	10.8	7.5	8.0	8.9	9.2	10.2	12.5	10.8	5.9	2.4	4.6	9.2	10.1	5.9
Total of above countries	5.0	5.7	5.0	4.3	7.5	13.3	11.0	8.0	8.0	7.0	9.3	12.2	10.0	7.0	4.5	2.7	5.5	9.4	8.7	6.0
Austria	3.1	4.4	4.7	6.3	7.6	9.5	8.4	7.3	5.5	3.6	3.7	6.4	6.8	5.4	3.3	3.6	5.2	6.3	5.6	4.9
Belgium	3.8	3.9	4.3	5.4	7.0	12.7	12.8	9.2	7.1	4.5	4.5	6.6	7.6	8.7	7.7	2.8	4.9	8.4	7.7	5.5
Denmark	4.2	5.8	5.8	6.6	9.3	15.3	9.6	9.0	11.1	10.0	9.6	12.3	11.7	10.1	6.9	6.2	6.3	10.8	10.5	8.1
Finland	2.2	2.8	6.5	7.1	10.7	16.9	17.9	14.4	12.6	7.8	7.5	11.6	12.0	9.3	8.3	5.6	5.8	12.8	10.5	8.3
Greece	2.4	3.2	3.0	4.3	15.5	26.9	13.4	13.3	12.1	12.6	19.0	24.9	24.5	21.0	20.5	1.9	5.6	16.1	22.8	9.8
Iceland	21.9	13.6	6.6	9.7	20.6	42.9	49.1	33.0	29.9	44.9	44.1	57.5	51.6	49.1	86.7	10.5	14.3	40.5	59.5	26.8
Ireland	7.4	8.2	8.9	8.7	11.4	17.0	20.9	18.0	13.6	7.6	13.3	18.2	20.4	17.1	10.5	4.0	8.9	15.0	17.0	10.0
Luxembourg	2.3	4.6	4.7	5.2	6.1	9.5	10.7	9.8	6.7	3.1	4.5	6.3	8.1	9.4	8.7	2.3	4.6	7.4	-8.1	5.1
Netherlands	3.6	3.6	7.5	7.8	8.0	9.6	10.2	8.8	6.4	4.5	4.2	6.5	6.7	6.0	2.8	3.6	6.9	7.2	5.7	5.6
Norway	3.1	10.6	6.2	7.2	7.5	9.4	11.7	9.1	9.1	8.1	4.8	10.9	13.6	11.3	8.4	3.9	6.9	8.7	11.2	7.1
Portugal	7.0	6.3	8.3	8.9	11.5	29.2	20.4	19.3	27.2	22.5	23.9	16.6	20.0	22.4	25.5	3.2	8.4	23.7	20.8	12.5
Spain	2.2	5.7	8.3	8.3	11.4	15.7	16.9	17.7	24.5	19.8	15.7	15.5	14.6	14.4	12.1	6.6	7.1	18.3	14.3	11.0
Sweden	2.7	7.0	7.4	6.0	6.7	9.9	9.8	10.3	11.4	10.0	7.2	13.7	12.1	8.6	8.9	3.8	6.0	9.8	10.9	7.0
Switzerland	2.5	3.6	6.6	6.7	8.7	9.8	6.7	1.7	1.3	1.1	3.6	4.0	6.5	5.6	3.0	3.4	5.6	4.0	4.9	4.2
Turkey	4.8	7.9	19.0	15.4	14.0	23.9	21.2	17.4	26.0	61.9	63.5	94.3	37.6	32.7	28.8	5.8	12.5	34.4	47.5	20.7
Smaller European	3.7	5.3	7.3	7.5	9.6	14.0	13.0	11.7	12.7	13.1	12.4	17.1	13.3	11.9	—	4.3	6.7	12.8	—	—
Australia	2.9	3.9	6.1	5.8	9.5	15.1	15.1	13.5	12.3	7.9	9.1	10.2	9.7	11.2	10.1	2.2	5.6	12.1	10.3	6.8
New Zealand	4.9	6.5	10.4	6.9	8.2	11.1	14.7	16.9	14.3	11.9	13.8	17.1	15.4	16.1	7.4	3.3	7.4	13.8	14.4	8.7
Total smaller	3.6	5.2	7.2	7.3	9.6	14.1	13.3	12.1	12.7	12.5	12.0	16.3	13.0	11.9	—	4.0	6.6	12.8	—	—
Total EEC	4.2	4.9	6.1	6.1	8.4	13.0	13.0	10.5	9.8	7.0	9.1	12.3	11.1	9.8	7.3	3.4	6.0	10.4	10.3	6.9
Total OECD – Europe	4.0	5.1	6.6	5.5	8.6	13.3	13.2	10.9	11.1	9.3	10.6	14.3	12.1	10.5	8.2	3.7	6.2	11.4	11.5	7.5
Total OECD less US	4.2	5.4	6.2	6.0	9.2	15.3	12.9	10.6	10.4	8.1	8.9	12.5	10.5	8.8	—	3.7	6.2	11.1	—	—
Total OECD	4.8	5.6	5.3	4.7	7.8	13.4	11.3	8.6	8.8	7.9	9.8	12.9	10.5	7.8	5.3	2.9	5.6	10.0	9.4	6.4

Source: OECD (1984a: 84) and unpublished data, OECD.

Table 1.3. Unemployment as percentage of total labour force, OECD countries, 1960-1983

	1960	1970	1971	1972	1973	1974	1975	1976	1977	1978	1979	1980	1981	1982	1983	60-67	68-73	74-79	80-83	60-83
United States	5.4	4.8	5.8	5.5	4.8	5.5	8.3	7.6	6.9	6.0	5.8	7.0	7.5	9.5	9.5	5.0	4.6	6.7	8.4	5.9
Japan	1.7	1.1	1.2	1.4	1.3	1.4	1.9	2.0	2.0	2.2	2.1	2.0	2.2	2.4	2.6	1.3	1.2	1.9	2.3	1.6
Germany	1.0	0.6	0.7	0.9	1.0	2.1	4.0	4.0	3.9	3.7	3.3	3.3	4.6	6.7	8.2	0.8	0.8	3.5	5.7	2.3
France	1.2	2.4	2.6	2.7	–	2.8	4.1	4.4	4.7	5.2	5.9	6.3	7.3	8.0	8.0	1.3	–	4.5	7.4	–
United Kingdom	1.3	2.2	2.8	3.1	2.2	2.2	3.2	4.8	5.2	5.1	4.6	5.6	9.0	10.4	11.2	1.5	2.4	4.2	9.0	3.6
Italy	5.5	5.3	5.3	6.3	6.2	5.3	5.8	6.6	7.0	7.1	7.5	7.4	8.3	8.9	9.7	4.9	5.7	6.5	8.6	6.2
Canada	6.4	5.6	6.1	6.2	5.5	5.3	6.9	7.1	8.0	8.3	7.4	7.4	7.5	10.9	11.8	4.8	5.4	7.2	9.4	6.3
Total of above countries	3.3	3.1	3.6	3.7	3.3	3.7	5.4	5.4	5.3	5.0	4.9	5.5	6.3	7.8	8.1	2.9	3.2	4.9	6.9	4.2
Austria	2.4	1.4	1.2	1.0	1.0	1.1	1.7	1.7	1.5	1.7	1.7	1.6	2.1	3.1	3.9	2.0	1.4	1.6	2.7	1.9
Belgium	3.3	1.8	1.7	2.2	–	2.2	2.4	4.2	5.6	6.3	6.8	7.1	7.5	9.6	11.2	–	2.1	4.6	8.9	3.9*
Denmark	1.9	0.7	1.1	0.9	0.9	3.5	4.9	6.3	7.3	8.3	6.0	6.5	10.3	11.0	–	1.6	1.0	6.1	–	–
Finland	1.4	1.8	2.1	2.4	2.1	1.6	2.1	3.8	5.8	7.2	5.9	4.6	5.1	5.8	6.1	1.5	2.5	4.4	5.4	3.1
Greece	6.1	4.2	3.1	2.1	2.0	2.1	2.3	1.9	1.7	1.8	1.9	2.8	4.1	5.8	–	5.2	3.7	1.9	–	3.8*
Iceland	–	–	–	–	–	–	–	–	–	–	–	–	–	–	–	–	–	–	–	–
Ireland	5.6	5.8	5.8	6.3	5.9	5.6	6.4	7.8	7.6	7.1	6.1	6.1	8.9	10.7	13.7	4.9	5.7	6.8	–	6.1*
Luxembourg	–	–	–	–	–	–	–	–	–	–	–	–	–	–	–	–	–	–	–	–
Netherlands	0.7	1.0	1.3	2.2	2.2	2.7	5.2	5.5	5.3	5.3	5.4	6.0	8.6	11.4	13.7	0.7	1.5	4.9	10.0	3.5
Norway	1.2	0.8	0.8	1.7	1.5	1.5	2.3	1.8	1.5	1.8	1.9	1.7	2.0	2.6	3.3	1.0	1.8	1.8	2.4	1.7
Portugal	1.9	2.5	2.5	2.5	2.5	1.7	5.5	6.3	7.4	8.0	8.1	7.6	8.1	7.3	–	2.4	2.5	6.2	–	5.4
Spain	2.4	2.5	3.3	2.8	2.5	3.0	4.3	4.8	5.6	7.5	9.3	12.3	15.0	16.6	18.0	2.3	2.7	5.8	15.5	5.5
Sweden	1.7	1.5	2.5	2.7	2.5	2.0	1.6	1.6	1.8	2.2	2.1	2.0	2.5	3.1	3.5	1.6	2.2	1.9	2.8	2.1
Switzerland	–	–	–	–	–	–	0.3	0.7	0.4	0.4	0.3	0.2	0.2	0.4	0.9	–	–	–	0.5	–
Turkey	9.2	11.9	11.9	11.6	12.1	12.8	12.9	13.6	11.9	12.3	13.6	15.0	16.3	17.7	–	9.5	11.5	12.9	–	11.8*
Smaller European	3.9	4.4	4.6	4.6	4.6	5.0	5.9	6.6	6.5	7.2	7.7	8.7	10.3	11.6	–	3.8	4.5	6.5	–	5.5*
Australia	1.4	1.6	1.9	2.6	2.3	2.6	4.8	4.7	5.6	6.3	6.1	6.0	5.7	7.0	9.8	1.9	2.0	5.0	7.1	3.6
New Zealand	0.1	0.2	0.2	0.4	0.2	0.1	0.2	0.4	0.3	1.7	1.9	2.2	4.5	3.5	–	0.1	0.3	0.8	–	0.8*
Total smaller	3.7	4.1	4.3	4.3	4.3	4.7	5.8	6.3	6.3	7.0	7.5	8.4	9.8	11.1	–	3.6	4.2	6.3	–	5.3*
Total EEC	2.3	2.4	2.6	3.0	2.7	2.9	4.2	4.9	5.2	5.2	5.2	5.6	7.4	8.7	–	2.1	2.7	4.6	–	3.6*
Total OECD – Europe	2.9	3.2	3.6	3.7	3.5	3.8	4.9	5.6	5.7	6.0	6.2	6.8	8.5	9.8	–	2.7	3.4	5.4	–	4.3*
Total OECD less US	2.7	2.8	3.0	3.0	3.0	3.2	4.3	4.8	5.2	5.2	5.3	5.3	5.7	6.9	8.0	2.4	2.8	4.7	6.5	3.7*
Total OECD	3.4	3.3	3.8	3.9	3.5	3.9	5.4	5.6	5.5	5.4	5.4	6.1	7.1	8.5	–	3.1	3.4	5.2	–	4.3*

Note: * 1960-82 average.
Source: OECD (1984a: 84) and unpublished data, OECD.

21

Table 1.4. Employment in manufacturing as percentage of civilian employment, OECD countries, 1960-1982

	1960	1970	1971	1972	1973	1974	1975	1976	1977	1978	1979	1980	1981	1982	60-67	68-73	74-79	80-82	60-82
United States	26.4	26.4	24.7	24.3	24.8	24.2	22.7	22.8	22.7	22.7	22.7	22.1	21.7	20.4	26.8	25.8	23.0	21.4	24.8
Japan	21.3	27.0	27.0	27.0	27.4	27.2	25.8	25.5	25.1	24.5	24.3	24.7	24.8	24.5	23.7	26.9	25.4	24.7	25.1
Germany	34.3	37.4	36.9	36.4	36.1	36.1	35.2	35.1	35.1	34.8	34.5	34.3	33.6	33.1	35.3	36.6	35.1	33.7	35.4
France	28.2	27.8	28.0	28.1	28.3	28.4	27.9	27.4	27.1	26.6	26.1	25.8	25.1	24.7	28.4	27.9	27.2	25.2	27.6
United Kingdom	38.4	37.1	36.4	35.2	34.5	34.5	33.0	32.1	32.2	31.9	31.1	29.8	27.9	27.0	37.4	36.1	32.5	28.2	34.6
Italy	25.1	29.3	29.5	29.6	29.6	29.8	29.7	29.4	28.5	28.0	27.7	27.8	27.2	26.8	26.8	29.1	29.8	27.3	28.0
Canada	24.6	23.9	23.4	23.3	23.4	23.0	21.6	21.8	21.1	21.2	21.5	21.5	21.1	19.8	25.0	23.8	21.7	20.8	23.3
Total of above countries	27.4	28.9	28.2	27.8	28.0	27.7	26.5	26.3	26.0	25.6	25.5	25.1	24.6	23.7	28.2	28.4	26.3	24.5	27.3
Austria	32.1	32.7	32.6	32.6	32.9	32.2	31.4	31.0	31.1	30.8	30.5	30.6	30.2	29.4	32.5	32.5	31.2	30.1	31.8
Belgium	37.7	38.0	37.2	36.6	36.3	35.9	34.2	33.0	31.7	30.5	29.3	28.7	27.8	27.2	39.1	37.3	32.4	27.9	35.4
Denmark	25.1	22.8	21.8	21.4	21.9	21.4	19.7	19.6	19.7	19.6	18.9	18.4	17.9	17.4	24.6	–	–	17.9	–
Finland	27.9	28.7	29.2	29.4	29.3	29.0	28.3	28.6	27.7	27.1	27.3	27.8	27.2	26.0	26.8	28.5	28.0	27.0	27.6
Greece	11.6	16.0	17.2	17.5	18.3	18.5	19.0	19.1	19.4	19.1	19.4	19.6	19.4	19.2	13.1	16.5	19.1	19.4	16.4
Iceland	24.2	25.2	25.9	25.7	25.2	24.7	25.0	25.0	26.1	25.9	26.9	27.1	26.2	26.2	25.5	24.8	25.6	26.5	25.5
Ireland	17.2	20.4	20.4	20.4	20.7	21.0	21.1	20.8	21.2	21.1	21.2	21.2	20.8	20.5	18.3	20.2	21.1	20.8	19.8
Luxembourg	30.9	33.3	34.4	32.8	32.8	33.0	31.9	31.1	30.1	28.6	27.7	26.9	26.7	25.5	32.2	–	30.4	26.4	–
Netherlands	29.7	27.5	27.2	26.2	25.8	25.7	25.0	23.8	23.2	23.0	22.3	21.5	20.9	20.5	29.4	27.9	23.8	21.0	26.2
Norway	25.6	26.7	26.1	24.5	23.5	23.6	24.1	23.2	23.2	21.3	20.5	20.3	20.2	19.7	26.1	–	22.5	20.1	–
Portugal	22.6	23.7	24.1	24.5	24.9	25.5	25.1	25.3	24.3	25.4	25.8	25.5	24.9	25.6	23.3	24.1	25.2	25.6	–
Spain	20.8	24.4	24.6	24.9	25.4	25.6	26.6	25.9	26.0	26.2	25.8	25.7	24.9	23.8	22.5	24.5	26.0	24.8	24.2
Sweden	31.5	27.6	27.3	27.1	27.5	28.3	28.0	26.9	25.9	24.9	24.5	24.2	23.3	22.4	31.4	28.3	26.4	23.3	28.2
Switzerland	37.7	37.0	36.4	35.5	35.0	34.8	33.7	32.8	32.7	32.6	32.3	32.2	32.0	31.1	38.5	36.5	33.2	31.8	35.5
Turkey	7.6	9.8	10.0	10.2	10.5	10.7	10.9	11.0	11.1	11.1	10.8	10.7	10.9	11.1	8.3	10.0	10.9	10.8	9.8
Smaller European	20.9	22.3	22.3	22.2	22.4	22.6	22.4	21.9	21.7	21.5	21.2	21.1	20.6	20.1	21.7	22.2	21.9	20.6	21.7
Australia	30.7	26.4	26.6	25.5	25.7	25.1	23.3	23.3	23.0	21.8	22.1	21.8	21.3	20.7	29.3	26.4	23.1	21.3	25.9
New Zealand	26.4	28.8	25.4	25.4	25.7	25.6	25.0	24.9	25.4	24.0	24.2	25.2	24.4	24.6	27.4	26.9	24.9	24.7	26.2
Total smaller	21.6	22.7	22.7	22.5	22.8	22.8	22.6	22.1	21.9	21.6	21.3	21.1	20.8	20.3	22.3	22.7	22.0	20.7	22.1
Total EEC	30.2	31.4	31.2	30.8	30.6	30.7	29.9	29.4	29.1	28.7	28.3	27.8	26.9	26.3	30.7	30.9	29.4	27.0	29.9
Total OECD – Europe	27.3	28.6	28.4	28.1	28.1	28.1	27.6	27.1	26.9	26.6	26.2	25.9	25.1	24.5	27.9	28.3	27.1	25.2	27.4
Total OECD less USA	26.0	28.0	27.8	27.6	27.7	27.6	26.8	26.4	26.1	25.7	25.4	25.3	24.7	24.2	26.9	27.7	26.3	24.7	26.7
Total OECD	26.1	27.6	27.0	26.7	26.8	26.7	25.6	25.4	25.1	24.8	24.6	24.3	23.8	23.0	26.9	27.2	25.4	23.7	26.1

Source: OECD (1984c: 37).

Herein, the decline or death of firms will be more than offset by the creation of new ones and displaced labour can be re-employed without undue difficulty. Alternatively, in an environment of low expectations and growth, high unemployment and market imperfections, resources, particularly if they are marginal in nature, often remain unused. Uncertainly increases, business confidence, horizons and planning periods fall and investment is depressed. Cost competition may accompany the depressed demand, with investment devoted to enhancement of productivity rather than exploitation of new technologies or markets. In a setting of high risk, workers become less inclined toward vocational or spatial mobility, thus compounding the inflexibilities which now characterise the system.

Broadly, structural adjustment among OECD Members until the 1970s had revolved around a decline in primary and a growth in tertiary employment, though certain significant intrasectoral shifts had occurred within the manufacturing of some advanced countries. These transitions within a growth economy were relatively smooth compared with the discontinuous adjustments of the 1970s when the market mechanism was disturbed by the coincidence of various changes of a secular rather than cyclical nature. Serious imbalances emerged, some of which required major or abrupt action, though often this was undertaken too late to be wholly effective. Business reared in years of growth had scant experience of the new economic realities. The 1973 oil price rises aggravated incipient inflation and led often to restrictive monetary policies. High interest rates beset firms which, in any event, had reduced capacities to borrow. The second major oil price rise of 1979 (150 per cent) served only to disrupt any equilibria re-emerging after 1973.

In response to the structural problems that were besetting the advanced economies and inhibiting a return to growth without inflation, the OECD expressed a strong call for "positive adjustment" in sectoral and regional policies. Proponents of positive adjustment recognise the confluence of economic difficulties which beset advanced economies during the 1970s. Worse than the magnitude or abruptness of these events was a "diminished capacity and/or willingness of the economy and society in industrialised countries to respond to them" (OECD, 1983a: 7). Inflexibilities have grown up in recent years reflecting: attitudes and institutional developments which evolved in periods of full employment; the spread of public programmes with unintended adverse side-effects on incentives to work, save and invest; attempts by governments to preserve given production and employment structures; and, generally, the onset of slow rates of economic progress (Michalski, 1982: 6). Given an important interrelationship between economic growth and structural adjustment, sustained non-inflationary demand management needs to be supplemented by effective supply-side policies. Governments should note the essential functioning of the market system when they implement welfare, environmental and other social policies. Moreover, they need to enhance the flexibility and resilience of markets in the face of change.

Markets neither automatically ensure full employment and price stability, nor guarantee harmonious spatial development. They operate best in a context of stable political and social conditions. Inflation, however, introduces background "noise" that obliterates market signals. It reduces the capacity of market operators to invest, restructure and innovate. It slows down adjustment and is thus desirably avoided.

Stability, a keynote of success in macroeconomic management, depends on microeconomic flexibility which can only be achieved by ensuring that national product, as far as possible, is allocated under decentralised decision-making in the market. In practice, this may involve checks on hegemonic growth in the private or by the public sector. Micro must support macro policy in a "virtuous circle" and should not propose restrictions, subsidies or other instruments which distort the allocation of resources from industries and firms with the greatest potential for growth and employment creation.

23

Positive adjustment does not necessarily demand a diminution of intervention but, rather, that policies are efficiently designed, cost-effective, well-targetted and regularly reviewed. A policy mix for microeconomic adjustment would first ensure that the political, macroeconomic and social framework is favourable to private initiative and the market mechanism. The ability of market participants to plan ahead should be fostered by provision of medium and long-term structural projections. Temporary assistance can be offered to industries if their rapid contraction creates excessive social costs or if public assistance would ensure rejuvination and rationalisation. In general, though, preventive and anticipatory policies should be preferred to selective, defensive ones or direct government involvement in production. Finally, transparency is an essential prerequisite for policies that favour positive domestic and international adjustment (Eads and Graham, 1982). It not only helps policymakers and the public gain more complete information about the conditions of the market but also creates necessary counter-weights to organised producer groups that seek support for obsolescent structures.

An important outcome of the 1970s has been a refocussing on costs in commercial decision-making. In part this is expressed in a desire to reduce fixed expenses through the leasing of premises or equipment, externalising non-essential functions and engaging in subcontracting. It also emerges in the close attention accorded investment and location decisions. So much is complemented by the agreement among OECD governments that policies are required which will promote and manage structural change by enhancing the ability of market mechanisms to respond to supply and demand. Thus, actions of both the private and public sector with respect to structural change are likely to have not only sectoral but also spatial repercussions at levels from the international to the local. At the broadest scale, they have altered the production and trading relationships of OECD and other countries in phenomena variously termed "the new international division of labour", the "internationalisation of production" or the "new international economic order" (NIEO).

SHIFTS IN INTERNATIONAL PRODUCTION AND TRADE

Two economic theories help explain aggregate and some regional employment experiences of advanced countries over the last decade. First, continuing capital substitution in production can be interpreted by the equimarginality principle which states that, in order to achieve equilibrium, investment in any one factor (land, labour, capital or management) continues until returns from all factors are equal. In addition there is the Weberian theory of least-cost location. By this classical account firms maximise profits by minimising costs of the four factors of production. If a factor is sufficiently cheap in a region, relocation could be warranted as long as total operating costs to the firm are thereby reduced.

New Producers

"Structural adjustment" is no longer proceeding solely in an intranational context and production is now a global rather than a national affair. Aided substantially by the rise of corporate multinationalism and the internationalisation of financial markets, there has emerged "nothing less than a sweeping redivision of labour on a worldwide basis for substantial segments of industrial production" (McKersie and Sengenberger, 1983: 37). Within the OECD there have been major shifts from the United States and Europe to Japan but, just as significantly, new countries have amassed considerable manufacturing capacity and have entered competition with virtually all the established producers. This they have done on two bases; either, indigenous development of factories in selected industries or the development of branch plants of foreign corporations which may be oriented to serve host country or export markets.

Redeployment of world production has been facilitated by "technological innovation providing for the disaggregation of the production process so that labour intensive aspects of the production of complex products can be carried out in countries providing cheap and largely unskilled and semi-skilled labour" (Higgott, 1984: 64). An OECD report attibuted to newly-industrialising countries (NICs) the following dynamic features: a rising share of industrial employment, and an increase in real gross domestic product per capita relative to the more advanced industrial nations (OECD, 1979c: 19). In addition, such countries may offer low direct and indirect wage costs, limited or weak trade unionism, few or low labour standards, low energy and materials costs and restricted environmental controls. Their plant and equipment, invariably purchased from an advanced nation, is likely to be new (cf. Vickery, 1984: 132).

Apart from these producers, industrial and service producers within the OECD face competition from countries such as Israel and South Africa which are conveniently located to export to major world markets. Argentina, Chile, Brazil, India, Pakistan and Egypt now have several of the conditions required for rapid industrial growth. Increasingly outward-looking policies have been pursued since the 1960s by another set of nations including Colombia, Mexico, Malaysia, the Philippines, Thailand and Sri Lanka, some of which have established export platforms via free trade or enterprise zones. Finally, oil revenues have enabled various members of the OPEC cartel to invest in capital intensive, import-substituting forms of production. Fairly important capacities are expected to come on stream in the 1980s especially in petrochemicals, steel and motor vehicles. In light of all these developments, the OECD (1983c: 9) has written that:

> The internationalisation of the world economy is one of the most significant events of the postwar period ... Positive or negative developments in the world economy are likely to take place much more quickly than hitherto and to affect a much larger proportion of the world's population.

World Trade

Another way of appreciating the change is to examine world economic relativities (though available data concern almost exclusively the manufacturing sector rather than services). Belassa (1979a, 1979b, 1984) notes that during the 1970s developing countries assumed increasing importance as markets for exports of industrial nations and, likewise, as sources of supply for manufactured goods imported by industrial lands. It is widely recognised that there have been declines in the share of world industrial production for several major established competitors alongside gains for the newly-industrialising countries. The same picture emerges in world exports: the major trading nations have generally slipped while newly-industrialising countries have considerably improved their performance in relative terms.

Belassa's (1984: 3) definition of "industrialised" countries includes the United States, Canada, the European Economic Community (EEC), the European Free Trade Association (EFTA) and Japan. It does not matter that this grouping fails to correspond exactly with the OECD delineation since the story is generic in scope:

The developing countries ... increased their share in the extraregional imports of the industrial countries (as defined) in every commodity group between 1973 and 1981. While this share remained relatively low in engineering products (9.9 per cent in 1973 and 16.2 per cent in 1981), iron and steel (10.7 and 16.1 per cent) and chemicals (11.2 and 13.7 per cent), it increased from 39.8 to 45.2 per cent in textiles, from 63.3 to 73.8 per cent in clothing, and from 27.7 to 44.4 per cent in the other consumer goods category (Belassa, 1984: 18).

Belassa (1984: 29) follows the conventional theory of trade in suggesting that the two groups of countries have benefited from improved resource allocation, economies of scale and increased competition. Trade liberalisation would be of mutual advantage. In industrial countries, it would hasten ongoing structural change involving the exchange of capital for labour, the upgrading of the labour force and the expansion of research and development. Increases in productivity and higher growth rates could be expected. The importation of inputs that use largely unskilled labour also lowers the costs of production in advanced nations, thereby increasing export possibilities or leading to more effective import competition (Belassa, 1983: 272).

By this account and also in the view of the OECD (1983d: 31), the expanded world trade actually created net employment gains among the industrial nations studied. Elsewhere, Belassa (1984: 27) estimates that, given particular growth rates of their exports and imports, the industrial nations would experience "negligible" employment effects of trade increases in the period 1976-86. The International Labour Office has estimated that total elimination of barriers to imports from developing countries would lead to a 1.5 per cent decrease in manufacturing employment among advanced nations spread over five to ten years. By contrast, technological change associated with increases in productivity entails an annual displacement of labour of three to four per cent (Belassa, 1979b: 60-61).

In aggregate, then, it is too simple to claim that expanded world trade has occasioned job loss for any or all the OECD nations. After all, Belassa's analyses have concerned only manufactured goods and, as part of the exploitation of comparative advantage, the advanced nations should be enjoying considerable success in the export of labour intensive services – both as services *per se* and also to support the manufacturing exports.

Yet, in spite of the apparent advantages it should not be overlooked that newly-industrialising and other nations could be significant competitors of OECD countries. The 1975 United Nations Lima Declaration on industrial development would see developing countries' share of world manufacturing production rise from around nine per cent in 1980 to 25 per cent by the year 2000 (Robert-Müller and Robert, 1979: 9). Belassa (1984: 27) notes that negative employment effects cannot be ruled out since, on average, labour input coefficients are two-fifths higher for imports than exports in the trade of industrialised countries. Certainly, unemployment has risen in various sectors of OECD countries which specialise in import-competing and labour intensive production. Both the international redistribution of labour and ongoing technological change have thus had marked repercussions on advanced economies. Durable in nature, widespread in extent, they have proved a substantial challenge for regional (among other) policies. High unemployment and unused capacity in various industries and areas of developed nations also foster protectionist pressures including non-tariff trade restrictions, government restructuring or support programmes, world market sharing arrangements, "voluntary" export restraints and efforts to establish international cartels (Belassa, 1979b: 48; 1983: 259). Any of these devices can restrict economic evolution and most have been deemed inimical to the central task of the OECD which is to restore sustained, non-inflationary growth (OECD, 1983d: 18). With respect to this objective and also because of its sheer size and potentially significant role in regional restructuring and development, multinational enterprise is now attracting considerable attention in the work of the Organisation.

ROLE OF MULTINATIONAL AND CORPORATE ENTERPRISE

Conspectus

The OECD Declaration on International Investment and Multinational Enterprise of 21st June 1976 recognised that international investment has assumed increasing importance in the world economy, in large part due to the role of multinational enterprises. Co-operation among Member countries can improve the investment climate and enhance positive contributions which multinationals can make to economic and social development. Accordingly, Member governments stated their intention to accord foreign and domestic corporations equal treatment under their internal laws and administrative practices and to ensure that their regional authorities did the same. Co-operation in international direct investment was to be reinforced and measures were to be made as transparent as possible. A set of guidelines for the conduct of large firms was promulgated concerning general policies, disclosure of information, competition, financing, taxation, employment and industrial relations, and science and technology. The declaration and guidelines were reviewed in 1979 (OECD, 1979*d*, 1979*e*) and 1984 (OECD, 1984*b*, 1984*c*). The interest of the OECD's Working Party in multinational enterprise impact and conduct is summarised in the issues below.

By the 1970s the world economy was divided into units among which the movement of labour was severely restricted by immigration laws; that of goods and capital by tariffs and quotas; and that of portfolio capital by balance of payments considerations. The chief means of diffusing economic development was thus by the transmission of technology and management and this became the function of multinational enterprise (Johnson, 1973: 169). Throughout the 1960s, following and abetting the growth in world trade, foreign direct investment of leading corporations of OECD nations grew rapidly and became of increasing importance in the expanding and technologically-advanced industrial sectors. Despite the recession of the 1970s, international investment remained more buoyant than its domestic counterparts (OECD, 1981*d*: 12) and was seen as a source of economic growth by most nations. In a range of countries, the percentage of manufacturing activity accounted for by foreign-based firms increased and the same could be assumed for the service sector. Stronger penetration could indicate superior performance by multinational as opposed to domestic firms. So much can also be inferred from other evidence on multinationals' skill mix, capital intensity, technical competence and general concentration in growing or stable rather than declining industries. Other advantages of size concern the internalisation of financial markets (currency speculation and protection, exploitation of interest rates), the possibility of dumping, internal transfer pricing, the location of tax uptake and the ability through sectoral or spatial diversification to withstand economic downturns (cf. Robert-Müller and Robert, 1979: 6). By 1979, according to United Nations estimates, there were over 11 000 multinational corporations with 82 000 affiliates, of which 61 000 were in developed countries and the rest in the Third World. Of the 200 largest economic entities in the world, almost half are multinationals (Grant, 1983: 249).

In postwar years, as most markets underwent economic development, a traditional but not necessarily exclusive expansion programme among multinational firms was first export, then licensing, and finally local production under subsidiary control. There is some debate as to whether this strategy was "defensive" in light of trade barriers imposed by host governments which were pursuing import-substituting industrialisation; or "offensive" in that large firms found direct foreign investment profitable notwithstanding the various governmental constraints (Oman, 1984: 71-78). Whatever the truth, the continuation of the pattern is not assured. The preference for direct investment via wholly-owned subsidiaries is lessening in favour of "new" forms which cover reduced, minority and non-equity relationships such as joint venturing, turnkey operations, sub-contracting, licensing and management contracts. These arrangements are particularly apparent in mining and energy industries but also in manufacturing and services can offer initiating firms the opportunity to engage in operations for a set period as may suit their corporate product plan. The greater use by multinationals of reduced or non-equity forms of investment may again be a defensive reaction: firms seek to retain or ensure access to markets or raw materials in the face of host government restrictions on foreign ownership, increasing risks of expropriation or nationalisation and, more generally, a deteriorating "investment climate" due to state intervention, particularly in developing countries. Alternatively, it may be a strategic initiative representing better adaptation to changed conditions both in donor and host countries (Oman, 1984: 14-65, 71-78).

Facility Repositioning

Any view of multinational or, equally, large domestic corporations by regional planners must acknowledge their corporate objectives and, invariably, conglomerate structure. It is no longer adequate to assume that firms are interested in certain products or services for their own sake or will remain in a given field indefinitely. Now, many of the most advanced corporations may include essentially unrelated manufacturing or service operations in their divisional or subsidiary structures. The onset of strategic planning in the 1970s has afforded managers a very sanguine attitude to the various entities comprising the corporation, such that any could be readily rearranged, relocated or divested if it no longer meets corporate financial or other objectives.

The introduction of more strategic management practices has been a significant aspect of the multi-plant firm's impact in many regions. The presence of the large firm may have reoriented and, in some cases, opened up local economies. Inward investment could have expanded labour and hence product markets and had significant multiplier effects within or outside the region depending on the degree of "leakiness" involved. The establishment of technologies new to an area can also be a positive force, especially if they can be parcelled off in a spinoff process and taken up by local entrepreneurs. These are indeed some of the reasons for which regions welcomed multinational or exogenous firms in the 1960s and 1970s but, as soon emerged, the relationship of the firm to the local area was often attended by particular complexities.

The locus of decision-making power as between local and head offices has captured significant attention in recent OECD work and is of singular importance in regional development. A major issue is the role of communication and information technologies in effecting greater centralisation or decentralisation of decision-making. Decentralisation is favoured by some governments and should appeal also to regional bodies since it offers exogenous subsidiaries the opportunity to resemble domestic enterprises in their ongoing management and behaviour. Its proponents have argued that this pattern avoids cultural conflicts and produces a sensitivity to local trends and affairs which obviates sub-optimal performance at unit level. Such decentralisation may be implicit in the control-sharing arrangements discussed above.

On the other hand, centralisation appeals as a tool of strategic management, particularly in conglomerates. It may offer the chance for firms to reduce costs, boost overall efficiency and act upon changes in international comparative advantage. Control over strategy has consequences for those tactical decisions generally regarded as being more decentralised. Their parameters may well be determined in advance, reducing flexibility of the local plant. In recession, the incentive may be strong for headquarters to increase control over operating units.

The importance of such considerations emerges at the regional level when a decision is made to alter a plant's operations. In accordance with global structural adjustment, some corporations have closed plants in developed countries and relocated production in newly-industrialising or less developed nations. This is the most politically sensitive of a range of actions manifest in recession and, in some instances, governments have retaliated by withdrawing purchasing contracts or other concessions. However, it may be premature to jump to conclusions about the stability or otherwise of branch plants. From a substantial literature review, Erikson (1981: 146-49) sums up their pros and cons as follows:

i)   Branch plants can be easily established in leased premises with few overheads. From the managerial viewpoint, they may also be easy to close in times of trouble.

ii)   Multi-plant firms may be able to increase production efficiency through consolidation of facilities.

iii) Multi-plant firms are less likely to experience locational inertia than indigenous ones.

iv)   Existing branch plants are more likely to be efficient facilities so may be less subject to closure.

v)   Branch plants are better able to withstand recession because multi-plant firms can attract better managers, have pooled financial resources and benefit from economies of scale.

Cost elements and flexibility are critical in the long-run allocation of production to plants. It is necessary, first, to realise that sheer size is no guarantee of continued viability either for branches or corporations as a whole. Moreover, recession or not, the large firm will from time to time rearrange its activities in line with cost or demand changes, technological advance, competitor behaviour or government policy. The branch plant must establish a sufficiently secure position to justify its place in the corporation at large.

It is recognised that the general tendency, at least among the established firms, has been to eschew new investment and concentrate instead on productivity enhancement or cost competitiveness. A force underlying this redirection is greater risk sensitivity under prevailing economic conditions. Companies have attempted to eliminate inefficiences in their operations by modernisation or retooling and by moving toward more viable lines of production. Simultaneously, unprofitable entities are sold or closed. The overview achieved by many multinationals has enabled them to perceive conditions early and react rapidly, sometimes even anticipating pressures for change.

What disturbs most governments and unions are closures caused by circumstances outside the control of the local operation or those unrelated to its particular performance. Objections have also been raised relating to the rapidity with which closures have been made, leaving employees insufficient time to search for alternative work. Some nations and regions have doubtlessly suffered since 1974 under corporate policy and may take a more hard-nosed approach to development proposals in future possibly involving legislation (Gordus et al., 1981: 13). It is also likely that the actions of "offending" corporations will be remembered over the long-term, a consequence with which they are presumably comfortable. On the other hand, within any country and across groups of countries, the issue must be seen in an overall perspective. First, domestic single and multi-plant firms may also be closing premises or laying off workers for different reasons and there is no reason to make exogenous firms the scapegoat for what may be a general trend. Second, though data are unavailable in many cases, it has been suggested within the Working Party that the total employment record of foreign firms in individual countries may have been more favourable during the recession than that of the domestic sector. Even if the question of performance is never conclusively resolved for all OECD Members, it is the relativities of foreign and domestic firms that should properly be the centre of attention.

The emerging form of multinational corporations is difficult to discern, partly due to variations in age, foreign experience and company objectives. Much depends on the extent to which the corporation is run primarily as a producer of specific goods and services as opposed to the more entrepreneurial approach of regarding the business as a financial institution engaging in a number of ventures each offering different risks and returns. The former position is still probably the orthodox one and is supported by evidence of greater integration in multinational enterprises as reflected in the growth of intra-group trading and by the allocation of distinct roles to individual entities in the global materials sourcing and production system. Following rationalisation during the recession, some organisations appear more cohesive and integrated than before. Further, although standardization of production might facilitate plant transfer beyond the OECD block, other technological advances such as robotisation encourage a reverse trend. The possibilities for direct control over expensive equipment as well as the attractions of a well-developed market for services subcontracted *out* are powerful inducements for the large firm to keep operations in an advanced country or near to corporate headquarters. These two-way forces could have deleterious effects on the majority of OECD nations which as middle-sized industrial producers find themselves gradually forced out from either end of the production range. In general, though, future locational tendencies based on technology are indeterminate, adding to uncertainties attending other forces of international comparative advantage and geopolitics.

The above are a far from exhaustive list of issues involved in the current relationship of corporate and regional policy. Many, however, apply not solely to multinationals but concern any large multi-plant firm which operates across a series of regions. In effect, foreign ownership is one point in a spectrum of exogenous control.

CONCLUSIONS

This chapter shows the dynamic milieu of present regional policymaking in OECD countries. The series of economic shocks of the early 1970s capped by the rise of the OPEC cartel had significant and widespread effects and instigated global processes of change. Positive structural adjustment has been seen as one response and, to an important extent, is being effected in the activities of multinational and multi-plant corporations. In advanced nations, these actions relate no longer solely to investment: in the last decade retraction or divestment, combined with moves offshore to developing countries, have posed problems for regional policymakers.

Chapter II

A NEW REGIONAL CONTEXT

There are two aspects to the new context of regional policy in OECD countries, the empirical and the theoretical. Both are now examined. The first step is to consider the structural effects of the global changes described in the last chapter. Then selected regional repercussions are reviewed. These empirical outcomes have differentiated the landscape in OECD nations and have complicated and revitalised the ongoing debate on appropriate regional policy among theorists and practitioners.

IMPACTS OF ECONOMIC CONDITIONS

Though changes in the world economy and shifts in production and trade have had significant regional impacts, it is not possible from available sources to provide an inclusive coverage. There is no integrated database for OECD countries which discloses regional performance on major economic parameters. Nor is there presently a detailed classification of industrial and service employment by nation. Accordingly, the evidence here is fragmentary, and discussion indicative in intent. In concentrates on areas – principally in Europe – for which most information is to hand. Here the recession has been particularly severe (Robert-Müller and Robert, 1979: 13; Massey and Meegan, 1982) so effects can be observed at their fullest. The starting point is to consider sectoral data by industry and firm: regional data are then analysed.

Sectoral Effects

Several fields of production in advanced countries have borne the brunt of the recession – textiles, steel, shipbuilding and automobiles. Their experience in Britain, West Germany and France over the years 1970 to 1980 has been traced by McKersie and Sengenberger (1983: 14-27) and Jenness (1984: 30-33) (Table 2.1). In most instances, a pattern of employment loss, often of drastic proportions, is apparent. On the other hand, output indices may have continued to rise, indicating the now well recognised but worrying phenomenon of "jobless growth". The European textile industry, for example, shed 710 000 jobs and lost 4 000 firms between 1974 and 1980. Artificial and synthetic fibres have been particularly hard-hit. Restructuring has especially affected female workforces and has been spatially localised. The Commission of the European Communities considers that the textile industries of its Member countries could lose half their current employment during the 1980s, a count of roughly one million jobs. Import competition is seen as a primary cause.

31

Table 2.1. **Indices of production and employment, selected industries**
United Kingdom, Germany and France, 1970-83

Industry	Country	Measure	Year (Base 1975 = 100)			
			1970	1975	1980	1983
Textiles, Clothing, Footwear and Leather	United Kingdom	Production	n.a.	100.0	85.1	76.0
		Employment	n.a.	100.0	83.3	n.a.
	Germany	P	111.0	100.0	96.2	85.0
		E	n.a.	100.0	88.9	69.0
	France	P	98.7	100.0	96.4	88.0
		E	110.0	100.0	84.3	74.0
Iron and Steel	United Kingdom	P	133.0	100.0	74.4	75.0
		E	n.a.	100.0	66.8	75.0
	Germany	P	111.0	100.0	107.0	n.a.
		E	n.a.	100.0	85.0	51.0
	France	P	108.0	100.0	111.0	85.0
		E	96.8	100.0	75.0	67.0
Shipbuilding and Repairing	United Kingdom	P	n.a.	100.0	67.8	86.0
		E	n.a.	100.0	85.5	n.a.
	Germany	P	80.3	100.0	77.9	83.0
		E	n.a.	100.0	72.9	68.0
	France	P	n.a.	100.0	n.a.	n.a.
		E	93.2	100.0	94.5	98.0
Automobiles	United Kingdom	P	n.a.	100.0	85.9	74.0
		E	n.a.	100.0	91.6	n.a.
	Germany	P	99.6	100.0	121.0	148.0
		E	n.a.	100.0	121.0	117.0
	France	P	83.4	100.0	121.0	112.0
		E	86.1	100.0	104.0	93.0

Source: McKersie et Sengenberger (1983: 15-18) et OECD, *Indicators of Industrial Activity*, special computations.

The steel industry is described as being in "crisis" (McKersie and Sengenberger, 1983: 20). Among the ten European Community nations, capacity utilisation improved marginally from 56 to 60 per cent from 1982 to 1984 but, at the latter rate, trailed the world figure by eight percentage points (OECD, 1984d: 10). The workforce in steel in the ten countries tumbled from 800 400 in 1974 to 501 100 in 1983, a drop of 37 per cent. Germany and France weathered the storm with falls of 27 and 40 per cent respectively, but United Kingdom employment declined by 66 per cent (OECD, 1984d: 35).

Shipbuilding is an old industry with significant worldwide excess capacity. European and other nations subsidise production: Britain nationalised the remnants of its industry. "The resultant enterprise, British Shipbuilders, has been cut back steadily to the point where it constructs ships at only a few locations" (McKersie and Sengenberger, 1983: 24). These locations are pinpointed and regional implications discussed by Todd (1983: 356-59). Meanwhile, the German industry which lost 23 per cent of its workforce between 1975 and 1980 apparently remains threatened by further job loss.

The automobile industry, another durable producer, demonstrates all the essential causes and circumstances of industrial malaise in advanced nations: market saturation or

32

levelling; demand shifts; capital intensification in production; susceptibility to economic cycles; import competition or threat thereof; and product standardization or simplification allowing a greater diversity of sourcing arrangements. Beset *inter alia* by the repercussions of the energy crisis, British production was halved during the 1970s. Substantial government intervention and support has been required to maintain the industry and the national producer, British Leyland, has engaged in considerable plant closure and job-shedding. Experience in the German industry has been less drastic with modest employment and output growth. France well exemplifies the onset of jobless growth between 1970 and 1980.

The studies reviewed so far give the flavour of recent economic conditions and reflect the great difficulties which would be associated with intensive analyses over 24 OECD nations. The forthcoming discussion of regional impacts is accordingly constrained, even though its principal focus is again only Europe.

Regional Effects

Given gaps and time lags in official recording, scholarly meetings, current affairs weeklies and the financial press provide first approximations of the extent and impacts of the economic malaise (cf. Townsend, 1983: 60). For instance, in April 1984 a conference in Lille, France, attended by representatives of many regions in Europe heard that:

> Today the old certainties have disappeared; Europe has been submerged in a deep recession... Regions which were once strong and healthy have become diseased, and, partly as a result of having relied too much on (conjunctural) remedies, they are today on the decline. Faced with the serious difficulties assailing them today, the regions born out of the industrial revolution are very much alone. They can no longer rely on the benefits of economic growth being shared out; at the same time, the new technologies leave few chances to each region separately in the emerging new international economic order [Nord-Pas de Calais (Conseil Régional), 1984].

According to Camagni and Cappellin (1981a: 162), regional disparities in the European Economic Community diminished in the 1950s and 1960s as a result of the convergence of national economies and rapid productivity increases in peripheral regions. The 1970s, however, brought a reversal of foregoing trends due in part to increasing differences in exchange rates and sectoral price trends[1]. Data of the European Community extend the analysis by country previously provided in Table 1.3. Unemployment in the Community rose from 2.5 per cent in 1973 to more than 10.5 per cent in 1983, or around 12 million people. Growth in unemployment was marked after 1975 and accelerated again after 1980. Short-lived recoveries of output and employment were insufficient to offset the overall deterioration: the situation was worsened by sustained increases in the population of working age.

Absolute disparities in regional unemployment rates also increased after 1976 with the effect that regions in an initially unfavourable position experienced further deterioration, whereas regions with low levels of unemployment were less affected. As explained by the Commission of the European Communities (1984: 2.4/3-2.4/8), increases in unemployment over the years 1973-81 substantially below the Community average appear mainly in southern Germany, Luxembourg and northern and central Italy. Most seriously affected in terms of unemployment growth were regions in Belgium, the central and northern United Kingdom, Denmark, northern France, southern Italy and the Netherlands. Regions most affected by increasing unemployment generally featured relatively low levels of GDP per capita, lagging GDP and productivity growth and an incapacity to match strong labour force growth with employment creation.

Figure 2.1 describes the regional unemployment situation at April 1983 for European Community members save Greece. For the nine countries shown (all of which belong to the OECD), the average unemployment rate was 10.9 per cent with a standard deviation of 3.9 per cent. Bearing in mind that a "snapshot" of regional unemployment can be influenced by short-run or cyclical factors, it is apparent that the countries and areas worst affected include Denmark, parts of the Netherlands, Scotland, Northern Ireland, Eire, Wales and northern England, Corsica and Sardinia, southern Italy and Sicily. Areas featuring unemployment more than one standard deviation below the mean (i.e. less than seven per cent) comprised the Ile de France (Paris region), southern and central Germany and a limited part of northern Italy. These patterns reflect not simply the severity of the economic crisis but also the way in which countries or regions have reacted to it. In general, local economies featuring either agriculture and services (but *not* manufacturing) have escaped the worst impacts. The figures also reflect variation in the speed and strength of industrial redeployment among the countries concerned. Another important aspect has been the variability of growth in the labour force among regions. The Commission (1984: 2.2/1) records average rates of change over the period 1970-79 of from − 0.75 to 1.75 per cent per annum, equivalent respectively to a cumulative decline of seven per cent or an increase of 17 per cent over the entire period. To this diversity must be added that of workforce participation rates which varied among European regions in the order of 52 to 76 per cent.

The revelation of reasonably marked regional disparities should come as no surprise: they are the grist of textbooks and, in the European Community, can be seen also on a number of other parameters. As Keeble *et al.* (1982) and the Commission publication (1984: 4.4/7) show, there are great variations in regional accessibility ("peripherality"); regional infrastructure stock is variable; and so output measures diverge from one area to another. Superimposed on the traditional map of serious regional underdevelopment on the Community's western and southern peripheries is a set of other problems associated with economic crisis and industrial decline.

As far as output and productivity are concerned, the Community in 1984 held that regional disparities remain "as wide as ever". Differences of up to 50 per cent characterise GDP per capita among regions and are allied with similar, albeit smaller, differences in labour productivity (GDP per person employed). Evidently, therefore, imbalances have survived or thrived upon the troubled times since 1974. Among OECD nations, it is useful broadly to categorise regions in order that the different problems which they present can be generalised and adequately addressed.

REGIONAL ECONOMIC DISPARITIES

Traditionally, regional economic disparities have been ascribed to peripherality – distance from the main centres of population and economic activity – and/or to a high level of dependence on declining industries. Though these factors remain important in explaining variation within and between regions, gaps remain and recent academic research has concentrated on other effective elements. Both sets of causes are reviewed here as a backdrop to the categorisation of regions used in the report.

Figure 2.1. **REGIONAL UNEMPLOYMENT RATES, NINE EUROPEAN COMMUNITY NATIONS, APRIL 1983**

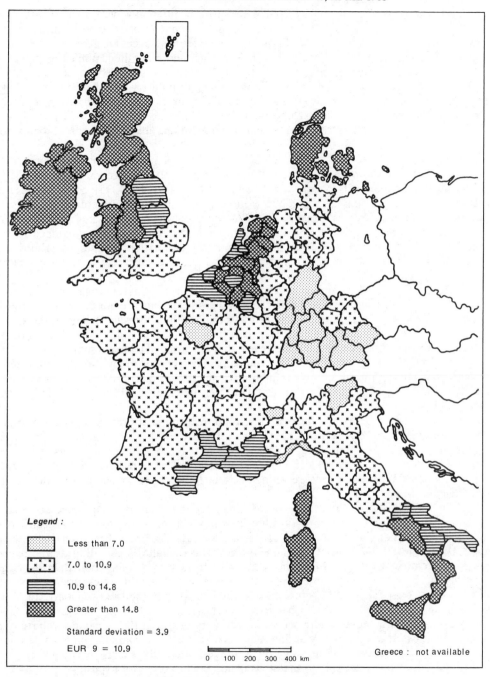

Legend :

Less than 7.0

7.0 to 10.9

10.9 to 14.8

Greater than 14.8

Standard deviation = 3.9

EUR 9 = 10.9

0 100 200 300 400 km

Greece : not available

Source : Commission of the European Communities (1984 : Map 2.4-2).

Explaining the Disparities

Peripherality can handicap development prospects in different ways: transport costs may be above average, resulting in higher prices and/or limited markets; transport links may be poor, creating delay and inconvenience; there may be reduced access to economies of scale; and sources of market information and customer contact may be limited. While the growth of advanced communications is offsetting these disadvantages to some extent, the peripheral region may succeed in attracting only a limited range of industry and, hence, it may have inherent structural weakness from the outset. To compensate, local industry may be considerably protected by distance from competitors. While this may underwrite its viability, a region is ideally served by strong intra-regional competition. This may be absent if only one or two enterprises comprise the local industry.

Industrial structure is a second major source of explanation of regional disparities though, as recently shown in the United Kingdom, its importance can vary from period to period [United Kingdom (Department of Trade and Industry), 1984: 35]. Structure is read first in the intersectoral sense (e.g. a concentration on agriculture, manufacturing or services) and then in the intra-sectoral sense (a preponderance of which branches of industry?). A classic structural problem is a regional concentration of declining industries matched with a failure to attract new ones. As the economic geography of a nation changes, structural and peripheral problems may become enmeshed: that is, regions formerly near the core can become more remote over time.

A third set of considerations covers the suitability of the regional environment, conceived largely in terms of socioeconomic infrastructure. These elements are not necessarily crucial apropos development prospects (unless below some absolute threshold) but are certainly permissive in scope. For instance, poor transport in or to a region can impose higher private costs on companies. It is possible, but unproven, that an outdated telecommunications system can be very inhibiting. More certain is that company managers and many entrepreneurs seek a rewarding social climate, not simply for themselves but also for their children (i.e. educational and other facilities). Similarly, the state of a local housing supply could be significant for both salary and wage earners.

Fourth is the incidence of exogenous control or ownership of firms in a region. Various possibilities were touched upon in Chapter I in reference to foreign corporations. Regional branch plants may lack autonomy and so have a reduced number of managerial and professional jobs which affects local industrial structure. The more advanced service needs could be supplied from a core area, resulting in a relatively poor range being available locally to indigenous firms.

A final set of factors relates to "birth" within an economy. The issues outlined above can, first, have an inhibiting effect on the birth of new products or processes – the propensity to innovate. Innovation is frequently a source of formation of new firms. In both these applications, the entrepreneurial climate is the key. It is thought that small firms and plants provide an employment backdrop more conducive to new firm foundation than do large entities. This may be because it is easier to obtain a necessary breadth of experience in small organisations. Other significant points may be the buoyancy in the local economy (to boost firms in their gestation period) and barriers to entry.

Any or all of the issues addressed could be instrumental in the economic welfare of a region. Most base their prosperity or find their disadvantage in a combination of causes. For this reason, classifications of regions which suggest mutually exclusive categories may oversimplify the real situation. On the other hand, one has often for expository purposes to reduce the potential plethora of individual regions in the OECD to just a few principal types. An example of this process follows.

Classifying Regions

Most typologies to date have been descriptive as opposed to statistical and reflect varying degrees of complexity. Glasson (1978: 197-202) views the United Kingdom in the frame of underdeveloped or sparsely populated; depressed industrial; and "pressured" regions. Brown and Burrows (1977) base their analysis of *Regional Economic Problems* around a classification of agricultural, (coal) mining, depressed manufacturing and "congested" regions. Calling for region-specific policies in Australia, Carter (1983: 15-17) delineated seven categories: the restructuring agricultural region; remote resource development region; urban-based resource development region; the restructuring basic manufacturing region; the environmentally-sensitive region; the warm-climate, coastal region; and the underdeveloped region. This grouping is probably specific to the nation concerned but illustrates the increased detail and sophistication which can be employed. Seven classes were similarly used in an OECD (1983e) study. A useful approach now is to recognise several categories exhibited in most classifications irrespective of their level of detail.

First, the OECD bloc, despite its generally advanced economic status, retains agricultural "problem" regions which, at one scale or another, usually feature peripherality relative to a core area. One type may be referred to as "backward", "lagging" or "underdeveloped" areas and can cover large parts of certain countries though resident populations may be small or scattered. One can add to this class remote, mountain and non-central areas which suffer lack of adequate communications, infrastructure or market access to participate fully in economic development. Many nations have either backward or remote regions or both. The former are represented in the United States, western Ireland, the highlands and islands of Scotland, the western and Massif Central areas of France, the northern Netherlands and parts of Scandinavia. Remote or mountainous zones exist in Germany, Austria, Switzerland, Portugal, the United States, Canada, Japan, Australia and New Zealand.

The reasons why regions lag behind include ecology, peripherality, lack of resources, and more favourable conditions for development elsewhere (comparative disadvantage). Population pressures combined with these factors may result in low incomes, high under or unemployment, low revenues and low productivity. Characteristic of adjustment problems is often a heavy dependence on the primary sector which reduces flexibility since the main products have low income elasticities of demand. Technology and information flows may be poor. Emigration is common, first from the land to larger centres and thence from the region itself. Some classifications at this point introduce another class of rural problem region: the depopulating one. In spite of longer term rises in individual earnings, the lack of alternative employment opportunities and inability to create necessary social and physical infrastructure promote continued emigration. This can be selective, taking the younger and more skilled members of the workforce who seek better chances elsewhere. The OCED (1983e: 33) has associated severe problems of rural depopulation with regions in Italy, France, Spain, Portugal, Norway and Finland.

Problems of the depressed agricultural regions are not necessarily soluble by market forces and their deficiencies in infrastructure and public services may lead to "vicious circles" in which backwardness begets backwardness or a widening of disparities with the rest of the country. Even the radical opening-up of such areas by freeways, rail lines or improved air services can be problematic in that then their erstwhile relatively isolated industries are exposed to concerted competition from more efficient producers elsewhere. Though regional policies have had some success in mitigating the worst inequalities, the Working Party in 1980 expressed the view that peripheral and depressed agricultural regions would need special measures for "a long period to come".

A second major set of depressed industrial or "stranded" regions has existed in certain countries for around half a century but since 1974 there has been an increase in their spatial extent and the intensity of their structural problems. Both shortfalls in demand and productivity gains through technological progress can create excess labour capacity. Depressed activity rates, low growth and levels of per capita income, and emigration are symptoms of the malaise. Areas can be peripheral to markets (following continued demographic adjustment within or among countries) and may suffer from an ageing infrastructure and workforce. Plant and equipment may be superannuated, intensive competition may be experienced from overseas producers and the social environment may be unsatisfactory. Pollution may further discourage investment.

Many factors in the situation go hand in hand. While the immediate problem may present itself in a lack of employment, analysts point out connections between the poor physical milieu, ossified management, deficiencies in the process of innovation, the gearing of labour forces to old industries in decline and insufficient opportunities in large, old companies for the onset of entrepreneurship. Critics would argue that entrepreneurship is hardly likely to be assisted by state intervention or nationalisation of ailing industries though this has been a common response since 1974. Likewise the apparent appeal of emigration should be tempered by the possibility of negative multipliers discussed later in this chapter. It also fails to address what may be an underlying need: that of a new industrial focus.

As far as purely structural causes are concerned, industrial depression arises for any of the following reasons (cf. Brown and Burrows, 1977: 121-22). A region might:

a) Show a systematic tendency in separate industries to do worse than other regions, so producing an aggregate shortfall (a "locational" effect);

b) Specialise in industries which are doing badly in a multi-regional or national sense (a "structural" effect);

c) Concentrate on industries in which its performance relative to other regions is consistently and inherently bad so maximising comparative disadvantage ("comparative advantage" effect).

Economic problems are invariably but not exclusively associated with concentrations of depressed industries reviewed earlier. Regions may have missed out on postwar opportunities to diversify their industrial base with newer, more prospective forms of production. Some key examples of regional adversity thus include:

a) In the textile industry, New England in the United States, northwestern and northeastern areas of England, the northeast of France and parts of Belgium and the Netherlands;

b) In steel, the Appalachian region of the United States, the Saar, Luxembourg, Lorraine and Ruhr areas on the Franco-German-Dutch border, Belgium, the north of England, southern Wales, various locations in Italy and parts of eastern Australia;

c) In shipbuilding, Clydeside in Scotland, northern England, and Liguria in Italy;

d) In motor vehicles, parts of the mid-western United States and the English Midlands (cf. Robert, 1984: 2).

As a final point, it is worth noting the emergence of economic depression in inner areas of what were once core cities of the industrial heartland. The problems created are largely the domain of urban policy but sometimes the impact can be regional in scope as the city's overall performance is reduced. Obsolescent housing, inadequate or abandoned industrial buildings and social deprivation are difficulties which may be exacerbated by emigration. As in the case of the other types of depressed industrial region, the operation of market forces without special action to redevelop the infrastructure or to encourage the relocation or establishment of manufacturing and services can accentuate the difficulties.

The third general class of problem region covers those "pressured" by rapid growth. Resources may be strained as will such infrastructure as transport and housing: there is likely to be excessive demand for labour. Pollution and congestion are common hindrances. Overall, past or continuing development introduces negative effects, though industries moving to pressured cities or regions expect to achieve economies of urbanisation or agglomeration. Regardless of a healthy situation in employment, income or the tax base, social dysfunction manifests itself in noise, excessive commuting and a range of other problems. Growth produces diminishing returns and marginal costs are eventually judged to exceed marginal benefits. This is accentuated in that congested regions may have siphoned needed development from the depressed areas, illustrating the interdependency of problems at a national level. Official action might be required to restrain or redirect new investment especially insofar as it is labour intensive. The classic cases of pressured regions include Paris and Ile de France, and London and southeastern England but, in Australia and elsewhere, it is often a goal in inter-regional planning to syphon excessive metropolitan growth to other (or, especially, peripheral) regions. Of course, this is now a more delicate process than before since it is difficult for authorities to discourage any new investment proposal whatever its locus. This becomes just one more facet of the multi-dimensional "regional problem".

THE REGIONAL PROBLEM

Early OECD regional publications in common with later textbooks stress that socioeconomic "imbalance" among areas constitutes the "regional problem". Evidence of its existence has been presented for capitalist countries but it appears in centrally-planned economies too. Indeed spatial imbalance has characterised advanced nations since the onset of the Industrial Revolution and, a natural outcome of change, may be a permanent feature of a dynamic economy.

The basic question is whether anything should be done about the situation. This issue is possessed of certain proprieties which have been only recently recognised and exposed. Weaver (1979: 182) writes that:

> It has long been proscribed to emphasise the political side of political economy. For regional planners, politics are typically anathema: at best a nuisance, at worst a dangerous foray into the realm of power and the irrational. Conversely, market exchange, the specialization of labour, and free trade have achieved canonical status, associated almost uncritically with progress and modernity.

In this light, it is probably fair to remark that regional planning has been a rather orthodox political issue, a redistribution which won greater or less support in countries in which it was adopted. This apparently comfortable situation is now questioned by commentators for a number of reasons. It is useful to review the theoretical issues at two levels. First comes an interpretation of economic processes which have produced today's problem regions. There follows a guide to the various standpoints possible in the debate. Finally, the practicalities facing regional authorities on a day-to-day basis are outlined.

Origins of the Problem

A feeling among a number of academics is expressed by the industrial geographer Doreen Massey (1979: 243) who writes that:

To see regional policy and regional problems as simply questions of spatial distribution is completely inadequate ... it will only be possible to get to grips with analysing what is happening now if an effort is made to go beyond essentially statistical techniques and distributional outcomes to understand the mechanisms behind the numbers. Second, the "regional problem" is not a problem produced by regions but by the organisation of production itself, neither is its solution simply a technical question.

To Massey, spatial inequity may be positively useful for unplanned private production for profit. It may preserve for longer than otherwise certain favourable conditions of production such as low wages or lack of militancy. She quotes a study by Secchi (1977: 36) which posited that the existence of growth and inequalities made the Italian economic system more flexible in terms of labour supply than it would have been in a better-balanced regional situation or, alternatively, that disparities gave the possibility of a higher rate of technical progress for a given investment rate than would have occurred under equalised development.

These points may pass undisputed by academic observers – Wilson (1979: 85), for example, has remarked that "it is tempting to infer that disparities represent a distortion that can be attributed to some general features of the economic system". So much is clearly the view of Marxist analysts who have become prominent in the regional policy debate since the late 1970s (cf. Peet, 1983). Arguing from the basic accounting processes of accumulation, they propose that market economies follow inherently crisis-ridden courses with successive recessions, upswings, booms, overheating, crashes and depression. State intervention is simply a safety-valve aiming on one hand at short-term demand management and, on the other, at long-term investment to promote economic restructuring for the sake of further accumulation. The latter is the province of regional policy.

As the milieu became more complex in the 1980s, Marxist authors began to write of the "devalorisation" of stranded regions, divestment being necessary to create conditions for profitable future development. In the meantime the state may invest in the devalorised capital (with public industries) using surplus appropriated from taxation. To the extent that public industries show low returns but provide inputs for more profitable sectors, state investment is a "redistributive mechanism by which the working class is forced to subsidise private capital even further" (Susman, 1984: 96). The ability of a population to sustain its economic security and social fabric is reduced to a reliance on a political state in which labour interests may be less directly influential in the work place. By this analysis, the result of state policies (in nationalised industries, housing and various employment programmes) is to bring the value of national labour-power more into line with the international division of labour. The dialectic thus consists of the vulnerability of regional populations to changes in profitability on a global scale: alternatively, state intervention tends to undermine the bargaining power of labour (Susman, 1984: 97-98).

The perennial contradiction pointed to by this type of analysis, expansionary capital versus antagonistic labour, is as well known as to require little comment except to reinterpret the wages push of the low unemployment era of the late 1960s and early 1970s as a "success" for labour which hastened the evolution of the capitalist system. Gibson and Horvath (1983: 178) argue that capitalist sectors enter periodic restructuring crises in which one variant becomes subordinated by or evolves into a newer one. They define a submode of production as "an historically specific articulation of capital-labour and capital-capital relations defined by a unique lever of exploitation and type of surplus appropriation". Thus in the latter half of the postwar period, the world capitalist economy shifted from a monopoly (i.e. national monopolists) to a global submode. This was brought about initially by the crisis in the monopoly submode (falling profit rates) which led to the restructuring and dislocations of the 1970s.

To Susman and Schutz (1983: 163), the multinational's structure proved more competitive for allocating and accumulating capital as well as for crisis avoidance (cf. Chapter I). With operating principles based explicitly on capital manipulation rather than product development, conglomerates and financial institutions today constitute the agencies of international capital. Capital is far more mobile than before ("hypermobile") so labour cost advantages can be exploited on a global basis. In response to such competition, relict monopoly capital in the former industrial heartlands is forced to impose severe limitations on wages in order to stay viable or "increase the rate of surplus value appropriated from their workforces" (Susman and Schutz, 1983: 165). Moreover, it may find it increasingly necessary to orchestrate the activity of small "competitive sector" suppliers. From an empirical analysis in the United States computer industry, the authors show that this latter process may require competitive sector firms to relocate to be even closer to dominant organisations. Such pressures would be particularly important in industries involving horizontal or diagonal competition (i.e. component assembly production). The implications for regional development are plain. Many areas could be seriously affected if transnational or monopoly firms seek locations most adapted to capital accumulation (perhaps offshore) and compel competitive sector firms to agglomerate there. For their part, Susman and Schutz (1983: 175) conclude that:

> Changes in the world economy have rendered all regions, including the old industrial regions, vulnerable to decisions made in remote centres of capital control and subject to a hypermobility of capital that defeats any serious local planning ... Our study suggests that the extent to which concentrated capital now dominates over regional development has, if anything, been underestimated.

One needs no particular experience in or sympathy for Marxist analysis to appreciate the relevance of this standpoint. It is applicable to peripheral regions and smaller, weaker nations whose bargaining power *vis-à-vis* large private economic entities may be limited. It raises the question of whether real policy automony can exist or whether sub-national and even national programmes can be little more than responses to changes dictated at the global scale. Such a consideration is a cornerstone for this study and conditions much of the discussion to follow.

Standpoints

From a comprehensive review, Armstrong and Taylor (1978: 21-24) find that there is no generally-agreed explanation of the occurrence of spatial disparities in growth. The position just canvassed is that regional disparities are among several major imbalances characterising capitalist economies. Another view holds that regions tend towards a long-run equilibrium (i.e. the components of the economy find an internal balance). It might draw as evidence the apparent convergence of United States regions over the last half-century (Vanhove and Klaassen, 1980: 106-08). The dilemma is compounded by the following points:

i) Most commentators agree that, at least for the present, imbalance is a fact of life. The question, following from the above perspectives, is whether it is temporary or permanent.

ii) Supporters of the two schools can adopt the same policy prescriptions for different reasons. An "equilibrium" adherent could support intervention to speed up long-run processes: an "imbalance" theorist could advocate it to stave off a long-run inevitability. For different reasons, both could recommend a *laisser faire* strategy.

iii) Equilibrium and imbalance theorists, as often as not, would take opposite policy prescriptions.

The various arguments are of perennial relevance in capitalist democracies which uphold the propositions that economic growth is good and everyone should share in it. They are of particular concern to two groups: people who perceive their geographical situation as disadvanted; and policymakers who may be charged with the "overall" development of a nation. Yet, evidence is lacking of a direct correlation between the extent of regional disparities and the means or intensity of ameliorative policies; moreover, there is possibly little relation between the comprehensiveness and form of policies in OECD nations with their levels of economic achievement depicted in Tables 1.1 to 1.4.

There are four possible standpoints to the regional problem. The first is a balance/non-interventionist posture which, if one can agree with the theoretical underpinnings, is internally consistent (cf. Holland, 1976: 236). It reflects a *laisser faire*, neo-classical view of economics. More problematic is a second outlook, balance/intervention. This has conceptual difficulties unless one can justify the provision of funds to hasten an allegedly long-term certainty.

The third possibility is imbalance/non-intervention. Herewith, policymakers could recognise the difficulties associated with imbalance but feel unable or unwilling to do anything about them. Instead, they would rely on "autonomous adjustment". It would also be possible to imagine a positive adoption of imbalance/non-intervention but this is again problematic in that it would involve placing substantial faith in comparative advantage and discounting negative economic or social externalities. Its occurrence is rather unlikely except in an idealised *laisser faire* world. In fact, the majority of OECD nations support a fourth (imbalance/interventionist) standpoint. Recently, the OECD (1983e: 8) remarked as follows:

> The theoretical justification for the incentive systems is that market forces alone, or in combination with non-regionally differentiated government policies, cannot be relied upon to bring about the desirable level or degree of industrial development in the disadvantaged regions... This is, of course, a controversial statement, since some economists hold the view that the desirable level of industrial development is the one that could be achieved through the operation of market forces, and that regional policies are themselves misconceived insofar as they seek to impose a state-determined pattern on the geographical distribution of industry. Governments that pursue regional policies reject this argument as one that overlooks the political, social and equity arguments for giving attention to the special problems of weaker or disadvantaged regions.

As confirmed at the 1982 meeting of Ministers of OECD countries responsible for regional policy, many Member nations hold that regional needs and disparities must continue to be taken into account in adjustment policies. Indeed, most participants felt the need to reaffirm the political and often an economic basis for regional development. It is to be more than simply "social assistance" involving marginal measures and is fundamentally concerned with structural transformation. All OECD nations thus pursue regional policies in one form or another.

Regional Policy in Practice

Whatever their views on its cause or prognosis, most practitioners face the reality of regional imbalances with a mandate from some authority to attempt to "rectify" them. This is given in acknowledgement that differences are unlikely to be resolved in the short-run and that "even if a *laisser faire* approach was eventually self-righting, the inevitable distress of the intervening period would probably necessitate some form of intervention" (Glasson, 1978: 202-03). In practice there may be three main political imperatives (Brown and Burrows, 1977: 18-29). Additionally, there have emerged since the 1970s some new and difficult practical questions upon which politicians will require first-hand socioeconomic advice from planners.

The first political concern is equality of income. Though differences among individuals usually exceed those among regions, spatial disparities may indicate a misallocation of resources which reduces output for the economy as a whole. Equally, low wage levels could indicate inferior skills, education, organisation or management. Apart from their tendency to become endemic over time, the differences imply that a rearrangement of productive factors would lift marginal outputs and so enhance total social welfare.

Second, following the 1974 recession, unemployment has become a central issue in regional policy. There are several considerations. Unemployment may arise due to a deficiency in aggregate demand for goods and services or to a fundamental mismatch between the demand for and supply of labour. The fall-off of aggregate demand in the last decade has aggravated latent structural problems and produced all too few regions capable of taking up labour slack. In these circumstances, the continued existence of structural (and even frictional) unemployment is unacceptable to policymakers. The desirability is self-evident of programmes capable of putting the right type of labour in the right place at the right time (i.e. simultaneously overcoming spatial as well as occupational mismatch). In this way output is realised from the gainful employment of otherwise idle labour, just as it accrues from having adequate labour to produce levels of output demanded by more buoyant markets in other regions.

The case against structural imbalances of labour (or, indeed, other factors of production) was highlighted in the mid-1970s by the onset of inflation. In this context, governments could not allow the demand for labour in regions to exceed a given threshold lest it generate an increase in money wages which subsequently triggered a wage-price spiral. In modern economies, with nationally-integrated unions and advanced communications, wage increments produce "flow-ons" through other regions and industries. These are inimical to deflationary macro policy and underscore the importance for regional decision-makers of monitoring labour shortage as well as surplus (cf. Armstrong and Taylor, 1978: 118-29). More recently, though, inflation has been checked in many OECD economies, leaving unemployment as the key problem. As McKay (1979: 293) observed:

> Given rising levels of unemployment it becomes increasingly difficult to argue that expansion in the peripheral rather than the "prosperous" regions will ease inflationary pressure and the claim that regional policy contributes to national growth by bringing into employment resources that previously made no contribution can be applied to employment creation in other regions.

Such arguments strike at the core of the difficulties faced by interventionist regional policy in the current environment. Nevertheless, as the United Kingdom delegation to the Working Party has argued, there is nothing in the situation which logically precludes the possibility of net economic benefits. For example, a better interregional balance in the supply and demand of labour could still facilitate increases in total output for a given degree of inflationary pressure. Similarly in countries in which governments are trying to reduce inflationary expectations, it is possible that fewer short-run structural labour adjustments may be required if unemployment is evenly spread rather than concentrated in localised pockets. It must be remembered that regional policy is aimed at the long-term and not at the trough of a recession. Since in most countries regional measures are largely associated with investment projects, the success of which depends on economic events over an extended time period, some weight has also to be attached to the possible recurrence of generally higher pressures of demand.

The third case for intervention is the potential for population loss due to emigration. The pathology of a community in decline is forcefully illustrated by McKersie and Sengenberger (1983: 29-31). Involuntary emigration indicates economic failure, creates social distress and is politically volatile at and beyond the local level. It introduces the possibility of negative multipliers which may be more or less serious depending on the operating elasticities and thresholds of regional businesses. If public bodies of the region in question are carrying debt, a greater burden is left for the remaining populace. Emigration can also be detrimental to the national economy if it creates an excess of socioeconomic infrastructure in the declining region, this situation representing a sub-optimal use of capital. All this is not to argue that regional decline is inadmissable: in certain circumstances it may augment structural adjustment or national welfare. The policy objection is essentially to unplanned or uncontrolled decline which can become difficult to thwart.

The past decade has seen significant impetus to radical movements supporting direct popular action for social or economic ends (cf. Carney, 1980: 41). A new rationale of regional policy in the 1980s is to allay nationalist or separatist pressures which have erupted in some OECD countries and elsewhere in the world. Glasson (1978: 204) takes the conservative but pragmatic position that:

> In democratic countries it is a sound policy to appease depressed areas because such areas if neglected for some time will invariably vote against the government. It the neglect extends over a long period, nationalist tendencies may develop.

By this reasoning, the dissolution of national entities is inherently undesirable. From the viewpoint of a parent state, this will most often be the case: in a finite and militarily strategic world, no country likes to lose territory or risk having an alien regime as a neighbour. On the other hand, separatist movements should not be denounced *per se* since they can in some cases allow a fairer expression of popular ambition and, as several examples from postwar Asia have shown, they can also be successful. In a global sense, results of indigenous initiative may outweigh those of "appeasement" and continued economic sub-optimality at the behest of a centralised regime. There is room in the regional policy debate of the 1980s for a dispassionate consideration of separatist claims, though this is unlikely to be provided by the parties concerned. The magnitude of the economic and political burden to parent states should always be borne in mind. Useful introductions to this topic appear in Armstrong and Taylor (1978: 172-81) and Firn and Maclennan (1979).

Questions of this type demonstrate the need to question textbook orthodoxy and standard approaches in managing the "regional problem". For example, Aydalot (1983: 7) has pointed to the potential importance of shifts in work attitudes and changing perspectives towards the quality of life which continued from the early 1970s to the current decade. One effect has been to create small regions in certain countries such as the United States or Australia in which "different" value systems obtain. Are these to be designated "problem" areas because they support alternative lifestyles, subsistence production or non-growth? The emergence of such movements has a long tradition but, in the present era, could be pioneering in the context of a post-industrial society. In the event, such communities may be no more "disruptive" than specialised retirement regions which also contribute little to national production. From this illustration, however, one suspects that the parameters in the "regional problem" could have changed. What seems of most significance now is an area's propensity to employ and/or ability to consume (cf. Blair *et al.*, 1984).

CONCLUSIONS

Not only the empirical but also the theoretical context of regional development has become more complex over the last decade or so. OECD nations are currently experiencing excess capacity of unheralded postwar proportions in labour and capital utilisation and are generally affected by austerity in their public sectors. Regional development, like other programmes, has to justify itself. The task is complicated by a lack of hard and fast theory which tends to make the setting of goals and objectives a "slippery" exercise. Additionally, new issues are looming which may require reappraisals of practice or values. From this nexus, the task of the next Chapter is to examine the broad framework of current regional policy as a backdrop to a theoretical conspectus in Chapter IV.

NOTES

1. The same authors equally point out that in the 1970s regional disparities *within* Community nations tended to decrease.

Chapter III

REGIONAL POLICY: NATURE AND PERFORMANCE

The immediate need is to define, categorise and evaluate the "regional development policy" discussed to date. Ten years ago, the OECD (1974: 77) wrote that:

> Regional policies are in an experimental stage, even in those countries where they have existed longest ... it is only over the last decade or so that the notion has gained ground that governments have both the duty and the power to guide ... change in the general interest, and not simply to intervene with palliative measures in particular places.

With extra experience and in the face of debates reviewed above, it is doubtful whether regional policy today can proceed with such disclaimers. Observers across the political spectrum recognise the costs of administering programmes and the need for any action to be both effective (doing the right thing) and efficient (doing the thing right). It is necessary for policymakers to recognise the role and limitations of different measures and to specify, target, calibrate and evaluate each correctly. Explanation here proceeds in terms of the context of regional policy which can be categorised into macro and microeconomic variants. Targetting is understood as the economic and spatial coverage accorded the various instruments. Finally, evaluation studies are reviewed in order to show the efficacy of regional programmes to date.

CONTEXT OF IMPLEMENTATION

Examination of the detail of regional policies usefully begins with a discussion of their frameworks. As the OECD has often explained, Member countries have a range of governmental systems and thus the ethos and delivery of regional policy varies considerably. No formula is necessarily the "right" one but, universally, practices must be adapted to changed economic conditions. This section considers the extent of intervention and the centralisation or otherwise of policy implementation.

Extent of Intervention

Economies range from totally *laisser faire* to full command situations and the emphasis on regional policy would normally accord with a government's posture along this spectrum. Many analysts view increased postwar activity in regional development as part of the growth in government involvement (OECD, 1983a: 30) associated with the onset of welfare states (OECD, 1981e). Yet there are subtleties.

As will be shown, government involvement can apply through macro but, more particularly, microeconomic policies. Measures can also be instituted by central or regional administrations. They can consist of incentives (carrot) or disincentives (stick). In this context, the permutations of possible regional policy (and problems of design) are manifold. First, it is necessary that macro and micro and central and regional instruments be aligned. Not a lot, however, is known about the relative strengths or cost effectiveness of the different policy options. Moreover, not all policies may be "transparent" with respect to their regional implications (i.e. so-called "non-spatial" policies). It is possible that a government could operate no overt regional programmes yet exercise various effects through indirect policies in other fields. Accordingly, to make any estimates of the extent of government intervention, it is necessary not simply to line up the very obvious microeconomic programs: the nature and strengths of both direct and indirect instruments should be gauged. "Strength" could perhaps be tapped in levels of spending in the case of incentives or extent of penalties in the case of restrictions.

The issue of a "desirable" extent of involvement in regional development will likely never be pinned down. Some governments may have to do little to assist progress towards objectives of redistribution, aggregate growth and public cost effectiveness outlined by Schofield (1979: 251). Others may try hard and achieve apparently little. Work on comparative regional policy has really begun only since 1975 in the publications of the OECD and the Centre for the Study of Public Policy at the University of Strathclyde in Scotland (Yuill and Allen, 1980-1984). Apart from the questions of mode and level raised above, there will be other problems among the instruments themselves. For example, is one more effective than another? Can one disincentive more than offset the effect of a handful of incentives? Inefficiency of policy could be as much a problem of design as implementation. Perhaps, in general, consideration of spatial implications of actions should take place higher in political bureaucracies.

Centralisation of Policy Control

The extent of government intervention in regional policy and locus of control are inextricably linked. In theory, control options range from fully centralised to fully decentralised. In practice, the unitary or federal nature of government conditions the framework.

Implicit in positive adjustment arguments is a fairly centralised control of policy. There is, first, little place for local political pork-barrelling, or feather-bedding of inefficient industry, however strong its sentimental attachment to a region. Strict selection of areas for assistance implies unitary control. Suggestions have also been made of checking regional imbalance by using macroeconomic fiscal policy in the form of general income and profit tax concessions to firms. These ideas would also require central authority unless regional governments are accorded such powers (cf. OECD, 1983a: 78).

Central control is perhaps the organisationally-efficient strategy in various fields of service delivery. Of manpower policies, for example, McKersie and Sengenberger (1983: 121) have argued that:

> Under the present conditions of low overall economic growth and considerable decline of key industries in many countries, the capacity for decentralised problem and conflict resolution has narrowed ... the solution is to be found by more centralised policymaking (i.e. policies on national and international levels in line with the more internationalised nature of competition).

This seems to be also the view of the positive adjustment school. While conceding that the potential efficiency of centralised regional policymaking could be impaired by failure sufficiently to involve local decision-makers, the writers counterpose the thought that local interests may disregard national objectives and interfere more massively with the working of the market system. "Competition on the basis of subsidies between sub-national authorities can lead to overbidding ... and may not result in any net gain in economic growth or regional balance" (OECD, 1983*a*: 81).

The question of devolution is extremely complex (Armstrong and Taylor, 1978: 172-80). Provocative insights can be drawn from a paper on "Values, Power and Policies" by Klein (1981: 176) who writes that:

> In the seventies, a clash has become apparent between two sets of values in most advanced industrial countries. On the one hand, there are the values of equity: the demands that resources should be distributed (both geographically and in terms of various indicators of individual need) equitably. This has led to greater centralisation, in that the state has increasingly played the role of the rationing agent. On the other hand, there has been an increasing revolt – if only at the level of political rhetoric – against bureaucracy and against centralising paternalism: the values of participation are increasingly being stressed. Interestingly, the anti-bureaucratic rhetoric tends to be the common currency of both New Left and Old Right, of both those who urge an advance to a more syndicalist organisation of work and those who demand a return to the market system.

Of the social (welfare) policy system, Klein (1981: 177) foresees more fragmentation in the 1980s. While periods of growth are characterised by a centralisation of credit, ones of economic crisis are more likely to feature the diffusion of blame. "That is, when governments can no longer hope to claim credit for the extra benefits made possible by economic growth, their strategy may increasingly emphasize decentralisation, if only to divert blame for shortcomings and inadequacies". Could this in part explain European experience which, notwithstanding the requirements of "positive adjustment", has apparently featured "a retreat by national governments from the regional planning front" (Hudson and Lewis, 1982: 5)? These authors see a new consensus emerging on ideas of regional self-management, decentralisation and devolution. Such tendencies are observed in Belgium, France, Italy, the Netherlands, Portugal, Spain and the United Kingdom as central governments concede more powers to local economic initiatives and create enabling legislation.

Regional discretion within a centralised administration might provide a workable compromise for the 1980s. Arguably, the greatest problems in future will still lie in federations which actively seek public intervention in economic development. Policy co-ordination has inherent difficulties in this situation not only in the domestic interregional sense but also from the international viewpoint if certain regions act unilaterally in problematic ways. In Australia, Wadley and Bentley (1981) pointed to possible consequences for rural development if metropolises were to begin concentrated industrial promotion programmes. More striking are recent observations from another federation, the United States, of what can occur when regional development control becomes highly decentralised.

In a paper reflecting certain ironies, Blair *et al.* (1984) discuss the "market for jobs". By this account, the guiding imperative for metropolitan and regional politicians is employment. Communities must increasingly compete to attract jobs and many now offer healthy subsidies to prospective enterprises. Through enterprise zones and a range of local incentives, jobs are "bought" at costs ranging from zero to more than $US100 000 each. Currently, prices (subsidies) and commodities (jobs) are poorly defined. In future, contracts will become more explicit: good jobs will fetch higher prices than bad ones.

Figure 3.1. TYPOLOGY OF MACRO AND MICROECONOMIC OPTIONS IN REGIONAL POLICY

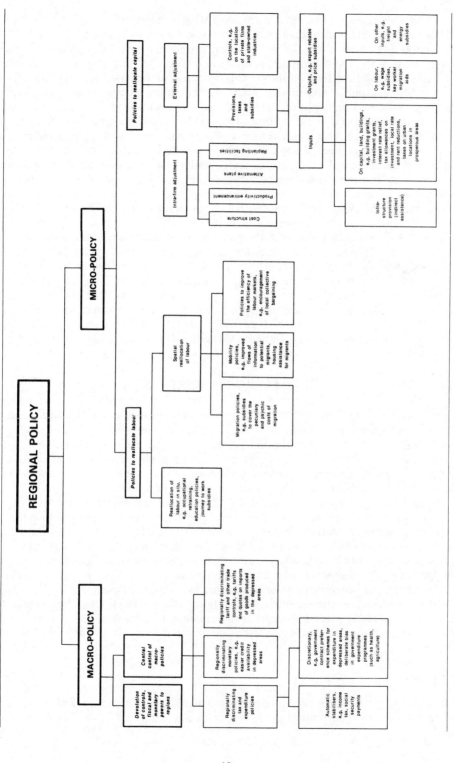

Source : Adapted from Armstrong and Taylor (1978 : 163)

So much places in the domestic microcosm what is happening now internationally as countries vie for the investment favours of multinational enterprise. In a further step, Blair *et al.* (1984: 59) add a new dimension to the term "mixed economy". Communities, realising that they along with private entrepreneurs are risk takers will increasingly become equity participants rather than settling for the secondary benefits of increased economic activity. The distinction between public and private enterprise thus blurs. A system that emphasized a fairly *laisser faire* and certainly decentralised regional policy produces by market bidding processes a socialised situation akin to that advocated from an entirely different perspective by Holland (1976: 251-76). This is an ultimate scenario for decentralised regional policymaking and well illustrates its potentialities and, perhaps at a higher spatial level, pitfalls. Positive adjustment proponents will surely find difficulty with it and so could central governments or local taxpayers. Yet one should not be surprised: the problems were foreshadowed over a decade ago by Emanuel (1973: 154-59).

This, then, is the overall context within which regional policy might be pursued. Its macro and microeconomic variants are set out in Figure 3.1 and discussed in following sections. Perusal of the chart reveals that though the intent of the measures may be similar, their natures are widely different. It is equally the case that their spatial impact can vary, macro policy being invariably inter-regional in character whereas micro policy can be both inter and intra-regional. A final important point relating to Figure 3.1 is that in federations there is no certainty that both types of economic policy will be available to either central or regional governments: each level may have one type or some incomplete combination of both. In general this tends to create special problems in the OECD countries with federal constitutions – Australia, Austria, Canada, Germany, Switzerland and the United States (OECD, 1981*b*).

MACRO POLICIES

Macroeconomic policies concern aggregate national income and expenditure and take three basic forms: fiscal policy which deals with government revenue (tax) and expenditure; monetary policy; and other national economic controls. It can be fairly argued that regional development in all countries will be shaped by macroeconomic policy whether or not this is recognised and encouraged by responsible authorities. It is also true that the extent of macro influence is only gradually being recognised by workers in the field.

On one hand it has been said that the spatial impact of recession is not uniform and that persistent disparities raise doubts about the ability of macroeconomic policy alone to create satisfactory economic conditions throughout a country (cf. Strong, 1983: 430). On the other hand, as Hesselman (1983: 197) has pointed out, "fiscal, monetary or exchange rate policies may have a greater impact on industry than policies explicitly designed to foster its structure or conduct". Finally, Manners (1981: 286) suggests that in the United Kingdom (and many other countries), macroeconomic priorities moved away from employment creation (which can be place specific) to the reduction of inflation (which is not). Considering that some nations pose macroeconomic instruments as their main regional policy tools, the need for and signficance of increased research into the various implications and effects scarcely needs underscoring.

Fiscal Policy

In countries in which a central government is able to exercise control over regional development, various opportunities exist via fiscal policy. First, regions will be influenced by ongoing automatic stabilisers which regulate the peaks and troughs of demand in the economy. Progressive income taxes, for instance, act as a brake on regions experiencing strong prosperity and provide the wherewithal for welfare payments to those in less fortunate circumstances. Though various other of these inbuilt transfer mechanisms could be cited, little of their impact may be known unless it is the practice of a nation's treasury to dissect incomes and expenditures spatially.

More transparent are discretionary measures relating to government revenue and expenditure which can be adjusted to provide concessions to peripheral or stranded regions *vis-à-vis* (or at the expense of) others. Tax provisions can be directed to both companies and individuals in an attempt to regulate the productive factors of capital and labour (and also entrepreneurship or management). That such discretionary measures could be gross in application is both an advantage and a drawback: by assertively tackling problems at one economic or spatial level, they may create others at a more refined scale. Moreover, their pertinence is affected by the claims of other policy goals and instruments.

Government expenditure is perhaps less problematic and more amenable to research. There is growing interest, for example, in regional implications of central government defence spending which for strategic reasons often favours remote parts of a country. Administrations may also set out fairly clearly their purchasing guidelines but this requires a research response on two fronts: where will products or services be *bought* and where will they be *applied*. As Armstrong and Taylor (1978: 169) point out, within a nation regional economies are open and can hence be "leaky". A spatially tailored purchasing policy can count on little success if spillovers are pronounced from region to region – and if some produce opposite effects from those desired. Yet, as much as examining input-output tables, researchers in many countries will also have to investigate the simple locational dynamics of purchasing policy since, overall, little is known of the government as consumer.

Monetary Policy

Control over the money supply and the setting of exchange rates may have a bearing on a country's regional development though this could be gross and difficult to discern. Adjustments to the money supply could alternatively stimulate or overheat regional demand depending on its condition at the time of the action but, in the current environment, they will always be restrained by the risks of inflation. Suggestions of a regionally-discriminating monetary policy, effected perhaps in credit provision, could be difficult to operationalise, would challenge the market's normal estimation of risk and would be subject to the same spillovers as described above. Manipulation of exchange rates is the other possibility but this is regarded normally as having sectoral effects depending on the placement of importers and exporters in the economy. These agents, however, also have a spatial locus and so regional repercussions can emerge. Again, these require much fuller investigation.

Other Measures

The third major means of macroeconomic policy involves tariff and trade controls which can have strong sectoral and regional effects. Tariffs against imported goods are common in OECD countries and are at least visible: they are joined by a series of more complicated instruments such as import quotas, "temporary assistance" and bounties on local production. The specific purpose of each may vary but the general intent is to protect – either infant industries till they reach take-off size, or declining industries until they "stabilize". Depending on the concentration of production, regional effects can be localised or diffuse.

Measures of this kind inevitably involve redistributions. Bounties and "temporary assistance", for instance, may require a disbursement from taxpayers (the exchequer) to firms (i.e. generalised source to specific recipient). More controversial can be tariffs which penalise exporting sectors for the welfare of import-competing enterprises. A classic redistribution is from capital intensive and highly efficient primary producers to labour intensive and not-so-efficient manufacturers. In this case (evidenced in a number of OECD economies) the primary sector pays a premium for manufactured inputs priced against domestic costs of production and there is a subsidy from agricultural to industrial regions. This may thwart some production at the agricultural margin (economically and/or spatially) but allow more manufacturing activity than would otherwise have been possible. In the domestic economy the efficacy of such redistributions is largely a normative matter but internationally, as economic theory points out, they are detrimental to free trade and the mutual benefits it can bestow upon nations. As stated before, OECD policy opposes such protectionism and thus the trade-controlling group of fiscal measures would find little favour as ongoing tools of regional development.

MICRO POLICIES

Whereas macro policies revolve around aggregate income and expenditure, microeconomic measures are principally intended to affect resource allocation by influencing the behaviour of particular economic entities. According to Figure 3.1 micro policy options revolve around the decision of whether to reallocate labour, capital or both. Simply put, the issue is whether to move workers to jobs or *vice versa* as a means of tackling structural unemployment. Though opinion on this issue has oscillated since the 1950s (Vanhove and Klaassen, 1980: 17), at least the micro alternatives are direct and attempt to regulate factor supply (as opposed to the generalised, demand-oriented macro policies). Thus, they are concerned with the structural elements (firms, households and individuals) rather than the economy at large.

Consider an economy in which firms offer lifetime employment to workers (as may occur in corporate business in Japan). Workers, perhaps with some company or public assistance, set up places of residence and a community. Economic conditions change. Will corporations now seek to relocate workers to new enterprises or adjust the established plants to undertake new functions? Which would be cheaper?

This idealised scenario has limited application in the advanced western democracies. Firms have few if any long-term obligations to workers and can relocate plants in a fairly free manner. Internal adjustment may be too costly, especially if it involves adoption of new products. In this light, regional decline is no more than the simultaneous unwillingness or failure of a group of firms to adjust *in situ* to changed economic conditions (cf. Thwaites, 1978: 446-47). The state, which may not have monitored the developing crisis, is left to sort out the resultant situation.

The contrasting possibilities above bring out McKersie and Sengenberger's (1983: 40) point that the first form of structural adjustment is internal to the firm and consists of introducing new products or technology or improving the utilisation of plant and human resources. From the viewpoint of the state (or individual regions), such restructuring is perhaps the cheapest type especially if it provides continuity of *in situ* employment. The alternative, as suggested, is external adjustment involving inter-firm or inter-industry reallocation of capital and labour. A table by the authors illustrates the different nature and implications of the two modes (Table 3.1).

Table 3.1. **Modes of restructuring**

Parameter	Mode of Restructuring	
	Internal	External
Nature of the Change	Changes in products and technology and internal reallocation of the work force	Drop in demand and a shift of capital and labour from the declining to the expanding industries
Pace of the Change	May be implemented more slowly	Reasonably rapid
Geographical Implications	Usually same locations	New locations
Source of Financial Assistance	May be generated from working capital or banks	Often outside sources especially government

Source: McKersie et Sengenberger (1983 : 42).

From this representation, the preference in public micro policy should be to encourage internal (private) restructuring. According to McKersie and Sengenberger (1983: 40):

Internal restructuring has gained in importance relative to external adjustment especially in Europe. In part this evolution is due to the process of growing concentration of industry, but also to the increased search for job security, employment stabilization and other elements of fixed costs of labour at the firm or plant level. Nevertheless, there remain important sectors in national economies where structural adjustment proceeds in an external fashion ... Thus, the current depressed industries with large-scale loss of jobs, like shipbuilding, textiles and automobiles, show relatively low overall potential of internal transfer of resources to new and different product categories; therefore, the changes are bound to lower their employment levels substantially.

Some industries feature both internal and external restructuring. In United States rubber production, for instance, there have been shifts to new technologies such as in the development of radial tyres; new methods of compensation (a move from piece-work to day-work); and moves towards full-shift utilisation of plant. The industry has gone from full unionisation to around 30 per cent non-unionisation. Meanwhile, some factories have been closed in a round of external restructuring.

In total, then, micro policy involves a fourfold choice: a focus on workers (labour) or jobs (capital) and a preference for internal or external restructuring. The types of programmes implicit in this matrix appear in Table 3.2. The remainder of this section examines these options. It should be borne in mind that, unless firms are prepared to pay the longer-term social costs of external adjustment, the internal techniques are preferable in reducing state involvement.

Table 3.2. **Micro policy options**

Type of Restructuring	Workers (Labour)	Target Jobs (Capital)
Internal	Human resource techniques	Enterprise viability
External	Labour market re-engagement	Regional development

Source: Adapted from McKersie and Sengenberger (1983 : 62).

53

Labour Reallocation

Labour reallocation is essentially the *laisser faire* solution to the adjustment problem. In an ideal economy, labour would be fully informed and perfectly mobile so that occupational and spatial mismatch would not occur. Perhaps the operation of guest worker schemes in times of economic growth is the closest approximation to the model yet seen.

In recessions, normal frictions to mobility are exaggerated, locking surplus workers in the more depressed regions. If, regardless of theory, they fail to move to regions of greater opportunity, intervention is possible in two directions. The first, as per Figure 3.1, is *in situ* enhancement of the workforce by public or private retraining, educational schemes or those involving subsidised activity of various kinds. If these measures are for various reasons ineffective, spatial reallocation to support external restructuring is the second alternative.

Armstrong and Taylor (1978: 183-84) agree that there may be several barriers to the necessary geographical mobility: *a)* interregional earnings differentials may not sufficiently reflect differentials in the marginal product of labour; *b)* even if they do, labour might not perceive them; and *c)* even if perception occurs, migration remains costly for the mover. The first hindrance can be tackled by policies to improve the efficiencies of labour markets, such as local rather than national collective bargaining which would allow expression of regional relativities. A location bonus payment for workers by government is another possibility though, as a macro policy, zonal personal income tax relief could be more direct.

The importance of providing both social and economic information for potential migrants is fundamental but not necessarily well handled unless the industrial policy agency has a good welfare and counselling arm. In the current climate, concern should be with the job security being offered in the recipient location. Stories of workers leaving a job to improve their lot only to find themselves out of work in the new location a few months later have been among the most savage of the recession.

The pecuniary costs of migration create high risks and may be insurmountable if potential migrants have long been jobless. As notable are the psychic costs which may fall disproportionately on the migrant's spouse and family. Attention to such costs behoves the sponsoring authority lest migrants and their families become sufficiently upset to require social or psychological rehabilitation. While regional or national customs have a commendable charm, they can also form significant barriers to newcomers and this should be recognised in any mobility programme.

Enough has been said to indicate potential difficulties with labour migration. Beaumont (1979: 66) suggests others which point to why this technique may be adopted by authorities as a second choice to capital mobility. Emigration can further sap economic vitality in a depressed region, introducing negative multipliers and increasing stagnation. Possibly the more skilled and able people move, leaving behind an unbalanced demographic and economic structure. Entrepreneurship may be sapped or exhausted, worsening regional adjustment prospects. Atop all this, the migrants could find insufficient infrastructure in the recipient region, so reducing the quality of available services or boosting inflation.

It would be unusual for an advanced country to have broad policies requiring the movement of people from one area to another. But, according to Glasson (1978: 208), "many countries include incentives to labour mobility in their tactics of interregional planning, although for political reasons the fact is not much emphasized". An unpublished enquiry by the OECD Working Party in 1976 showed that measures in force are aimed at encouraging mobility of persons who have difficulty in finding suitable employment in their own regions. Part of the problem may lie in the fact that schemes are administered by departments of employment rather than regional development. In the only published evaluation found, that of the United Kingdom Employment Transfer Schemes, Beaumont (1979: 77) concluded that labour mobility policies tended to produce low benefits rather than high costs, their chief shortcoming being that a high proportion of persons assisted would have moved anyway and that a large number of migrants do not remain long in the employment destinations. This experience is of obvious relevance to other countries and suggests the need for a fuller examination of labour reallocation policy design, including the functioning of the housing market (Manners 1981: 296).

Capital Reallocation

Microeconomic policies involving capital can be focussed on internal or external adjustment, respectively adopting aims of enterprise viability *(in situ)* or regional development (Table 3.2). It is a shortcoming of much literature on regional policy that the first option is underplayed since it may be the less costly. Key techniques are considered here at the outset.

McKersie and Sengenberger (1983: 63-70) list four ways in which adjustment can be facilitated before the state becomes involved in large-scale expenses of regional development. First, there are changes to the cost structure of existing firms for the sake of continued viability. A response which has become quite common in the United States is that of "rollbacks" of wages and fringe benefits to avoid job loss. Many of the 50 or so major instances have occurred in industries such as steel, automobiles or rubber which have faced severe economic problems. Workers have accepted rollbacks in preference to plant closure: the dilemma this creates for union leadership is obvious.

A second technique of internal adjustment to improve cost competitiveness is productivity enhancement. In the United Kingdom, United States and Sweden, among other countries, this has involved the dropping of demarcation disputes, movement to continuous operations, renunciation of premium pay, and other means of better matching the work organisation, deployment of labour and the technological requirements of the job. These approaches have proved quite successful in situations in which competitive problems have not been overwhelming.

The third strategy is the development of alternative plans for the continuation of factory operations (as suggested above). While this may be the imperative for some Japanese conglomerates, in countries such as the United States, Canada or the United Kingdom where such a commitment to long-term worker welfare is not manifest, the use of this alternative is rare. As McKersie and Sengenberger (1983: 68) remark:

> In most instances, management is not interested, nor does it feel that it is competent to enter into new lines of business solely for the purpose of keeping its existing work force occupied. Where this approach is, in fact, pursued, there seem to be a number of facilitating factors. For one, management feels a commitment to provide continuity of employment for the current work force and to remain in the local community. Second, management possesses an entrepreneurial spirit which means that it is willing to go out and look for new business and take the high risk of getting into new lines of work. Finally, some type of capital infusion must be available from retained earnings or from financial institutions.

The fourth "internal" possibility is the replanting of facilities in existing areas as has been done by various major automotive and rubber companies in the United States mid-west and as is often necessitated by space restrictions in Europe or Japan. Numerous factors could influence a firm's decision of whether to adjust or modernise plant *in situ*, relocate within reach of the existing workforce or, instead, move from a region altogether. The issue is raised as to whether, in a competitive milieu, firms owe employees or a community anything for a long-term labour record just as, in previous boom times, employees owed enterprises anything in restraining wage and other claims. Further debate may surround McKersie and Sengenberger's (1983: 70) point that "as far as union leaders are concerned, if they know that the new plant will be organised ... they are probably indifferent as to whether the new plant is in the old area or in some new area of the country."

Regional development supporting external adjustment of firms is the alternative major form of micro policy involving capital. It is the focus of the public sector response to localised decline and areal imbalance. It relies on the premise that certain economic activity is relatively "footloose" and, allowing for initial establishment costs, can operate efficiently in a wide range of locations. Relocating industry is the typically Keynesian response to the problem of inadequate demand for labour in specific regions (Armstrong and Taylor 1978: 187). As shown in Figure 3.1, capital reallocation programmes have several forms: controls, taxes, infrastructure provision, and subsidies and allowances.

Controls are policy measures typically associated with discouraging investment in certain types of region. They have the twin advantage of being of almost no direct cost to government and they are very effective in times of economic growth. Ignoring those required for local planning purposes, the main examples have been the use of licensing systems of industrial and office building in the United Kingdom, the special taxes and licensing in Ile de France and similar measures in the Netherlands, Italy and Japan (cf. OECD, 1978a: 39-40; Sweet, 1981: 20-68; Gudgin and Fothergill, 1984: 160). In addition to the situation in these nations, restrictive measures in Norway and Sweden were reviewed by the OECD in 1977. The publication (OECD, 1977c) also details the rationale for controls in areas which can be defined as congested.

A common feature of controls has been their appearance in unitary governmental systems and, with the exception of Italy, in spatial systems dominated by a single large agglomeration or by a contiguous agglomeration area. Their operation is likely to be hampered in federal arrangements which effectively would pit decentralised locations in one state against central or metropolitan locations in another (cf. Nicol and Wettmann, 1977: 92-97; 1979: 164, 221). As to effectiveness, a study of industrial movement from 1961 to 1971 in the United Kingdom found that controls affected both generation and distribution [i.e. stimulated movement in aggregate and also induced selection of assisted areas (Ashcroft and Taylor, 1979: 60-61)]. Overall, disincentives may be useful in achieving necessary degrees of spatial refinement in regional planning: firms do not adequately consider the advantages that they might derive from expanding somewhere other than in their immediate locality. But alternatives need to be made more palatable by some kind of positive incentives (Brown and Burrows, 1977: 191).

Recently, the rationale of controls has been severely challenged by the decline in economic growth and mobile investment. In the case for positive adjustment, it was argued that:

On the whole, the slow growth of the 1980s accentuates the negative effects of restrictive measures, while their positive effects may be less substantial. Slower growth means that the amount (sic) of projects available for transfer is reduced and that the social cost of abandoned projects due to restrictive measures is higher (OECD, 1983a: 80).

In May 1984 a conference attended by some members of the OECD Working Party in Tokyo was told by consultant Robert Howard that "control with persuasive or coercive steering in mind for economic reasons seems now ... to be much weaker than it was, or abandoned altogether", the latter being precisely what happened in the United Kingdom in 1981 (Gudgin and Fothergill, 1984: 160). While it is difficult both economically and politically to dispute the apparent logic in some of the positive adjustment claims in a time of dislocation (cf. Nicol, 1979), it is worthwhile remembering that controls are oriented to cope with long-run externalities of growth in core areas. Their removal may simply be trading a short-term advantage for a longer run problem, other things being equal.

Taxes applied at the microeconomic level can be used in a positive (concessional) or negative (restrictive) manner to shape industrial location. In the former mode, rebates or tax holidays operate in the same way as a subsidy whereas, applied negatively, they constitute a control. Tax concessions are offered by central or regional government: those not administered by regional developers may remain rather blunt in application. If based, as is usual, on profits, they constitute a variable source of revenue and cannot be valued in advance. Moreover, they are only of assistance to firms actually making profits! It is important, particularly in federations, to ensure that taxation provisions are congruent among different levels of government and that they also accord with the package of other subsidies and controls. As an example, in the current economic milieu, a payroll tax can be largely inimical to the aim of most authorities which is to encourage labour uptake.

Infrastructural provision has been a favoured policy of regional development in the United States, Australia and other countries which wish to limit government intervention in the conduct of private enterprise. It can encompass labour training (as discussed above): such a focus has been important in the United States Appalachian development plan, though Swedish vocational training and retraining is probably the worldwide exemplar (Brown and Burrows, 1977: 187). In the long-distance economies, work continues at a fairly fundamental level to provide transport and communications, the benefits of which more often flow to primary industries or mining than manufacturing or services. Elsewhere the concept of "infrastructure" may be extenuated so far as to include the development of public industrial estates in which land and buildings may be offered at highly concessional rates. This model casts the state as a venture capitalist and may require fairly careful selection of enterprises to ensure that sectoral aims are achieved and stable commercial complexes are built up.

The last set of options, subsidies and allowances, can be applied to inputs (either fixed or operating) or outputs and are regarded as particularly appropriate for the nurturing and assistance of new firms. They can be "one-off" (as in the case of a building investment allowance), temporary or permanent. Their effect is that of a regional currency devaluation achieved without the many problems which would apply if macro policy were used to the same end. The range of possible subsidies and allowances is well set out in previous works (OECD, 1974: 96-98). It is the focus of the Yuill and Allen yearbooks (Table 3.3). Still more information appears in OECD (1979b) and other OECD country-based publications. A prominent feature of incentive systems is the wide variety of forms and types, though there is no uniformity from one nation to the next. Of the 18 Members surveyed by the OECD (1979b), none offered the entire range. The most popular types, offered in the largest number of countries and involving the greatest public expenditure, were subsidised or guaranteed loans and capital investment allowances. Compared with European nations, North American countries and Japan offered relatively few types of assistance (OECD, 1983e: 6).

It is useful to look more closely at the pros and cons of these various incentives which have become the mainstay of regional policy (Allen et al., 1977). Soft or subsidised loans may be offered directly by the state or by financial intermediaries with the state as benefactor or guarantor. Loans are "softened" by reducing interest rates or delaying repayment of principal. They can cover varying proportions of project costs but seldom more than 70 per cent. The duration of a loan is normally tied to the life of an asset. One advantage of this measure is that

Table 3.3. **Main regional incentives** *(a)*, **13 European countries, 1984**

Country	Incentives	Incentive Type[1]				
		CG	IRS	TC	DA	LRS
Belgium	Interest subsidy		D			
	Capital grant	D				
Denmark	Company soft loan		D			
	Investment grant	D				
	Municipality soft loan		D			
France	Regional policy grant (PAT)	A/D[2]				A/D[2]
	Regional employment grant (PRE)					D
	Local business tax concession			A		
Germany	Investment allowance	A				
	Investment grant	D				
	Special depreciation allowance				A	
	ERP regional soft loan		A			
Ireland	Development grant – new	D				
	Development grant – services	D				D
Italy	Cassa grant	A				
	National fund scheme		A			
	Social security concession					A
	Tax concessions			A		
Luxembourg	Capital grant/interest subsidy	D				
	Tax concession			D		
	Equipment loan		D			
Netherlands	Investment premium	A/D[3]				
United Kingdom	Regional development grant	A				
a) Great Britain	Selective financial assistance	D				
	Office and service industries					D
b) Northern Ireland	Capital grant	A				
	Selective assistance	D	D	D		D
Greece	Investment grant	D				
	Interest rate subsidy		D			
	Increased depreciation allowance				A	
	Tax allowance				A	
Portugal	Financial assistance	A/D[4]	A/D[4]			A/D[4]
	Tax concessions			A/D[4]		
Spain	Regional investment grant	D				
	Official credit priority		D			
	Customs duty reductions			D		
Sweden	Location loan		D			
	Location grant	D				
	Employment grant	D				A/D[5]

Notes: *(a)* For number code explanations, see footnotes to this chapter.
D = Administrative discretion in award, rates up to a maximum.
A = Little or no administrative discretion in award, rates fixed.
Source: Yuill and Allen (1984: 72).

projects must be evaluated financially by a private or public credit institution which offers a regional authority more security in the use of taxpayers' money. Moreover it is not necessary to mobilise a large amount of capital at the outset. On the other hand, loans are not particularly transparent and their benefits may not be easy or quick to evaluate (Vanhove and Klaassen, 1980: 327).

Another option is the accelerated depreciation allowance. Tax concessions may be offered to firms in problem regions. "Free" depreciation spreads the allowance over the life of the asset, to be taken up at will by the recipient. An alternative is to inflate the purchase or initial year's allowance which may have decided advantages in net present value terms. Advocates of depreciation claim that it benefits the efficient before the inefficient and that it offers certain flexibility. Opponents argue that it benefits multi-locational as opposed to single plant firms and that some businesspeople are not sufficiently experienced to appreciate its implications (Brown and Burrows, 1977: 188-89). The allowances, moreover, are part of a national tax system and may have limited potential for targetting by regional policymakers. They also apply only when a firm is profitable. Within Europe, only Greece and Germany manage such schemes (Yuill and Allen, 1984: 72).

By contrast, investment or capital grants are widespread. They are normally offered for self-contained projects and, less frequently, for individual items of expenditure. Highly flexible in nature, they can be made available on a full or partial, automatic or discretionary basis. Yet, as Glasson (1978: 241) notes, capital subsidies have the advantages of usually being simple and explicit, of being a single rather than a continuing payment and of encouraging new investment in (highly visible) buildings, plant and machinery. The capital stock and ability to compete of a region are thereby enhanced. Yet much of the capital stock could be supplied from outside the assisted area and generate only a limited interregional spinoff. Capital intensive firms may require modest amounts of labour and draw inputs from extra-regional sources. "This, on the face of it, is an odd way to assist regions whose chief trouble is a surplus of labour ... benefits ... go mainly to proprietors and ... to the buyers of ... output, both of which groups of people are likely to live mostly outside the region" (Brown and Burrows, 1977: 189). Other disadvantages are recorded by Vanhove and Klaassen (1980: 326). Grants can be very expensive to the treasury, may have spread effects in the form of inflationary pressure on other regions, may have psychological overtones of a welfare handout but, most importantly, represent a bias toward capital intensive projects.

The obvious counter is to subsidise existing or new employment in support of capital reallocation for the apparent benefit of labour-intensive firms. While this might incorporate an income transfer from rich to poor regions, cut local production costs, and minimise spread effects, it also requires an interface of regional and manpower policies in which it may emerge that in labour matters the governmental employment authority is more experienced than its partner attending to area development (see, for example, the discussions in McKersie and Sengenberger, 1983: 48-54 and Jenness, 1984: *passim*). The efficacy of labour subsidies depends as well on the role of direct labour in a firm's cost structure and it may require a substantial sum to affect sales prices. Complex output and substitution effects of capital and labour need to be examined (Armstrong and Taylor, 1978: 190-95). A labour subsidy may additionally encourage labour hoarding and the shoring up of inefficient concerns. Then there is the query as to where the subsidy goes. Workers may bid up the money wage via union pressure, creating higher wages but no increase in employment. Alternatively, the subsidy could end up as profit, again doing nothing for employment. In sum, there are many sound reasons to challenge the simple and intuitive appeal of a labour subsidy which, at its worst, becomes no more than covert (non-tariff) protectionism. For all these reasons but, more likely, their actual and potential expense, labour subsidies alone have not been common in regional development though now some countries, notably the United Kingdom and France, are combining elements of labour and capital grants as part of an incentive package. As a final point, European Communities competition rules prohibit ongoing labour subsidies, a factor of importance for the ten OECD nations concerned.

59

TARGETTING

As demonstrated by Allen *et al.* (1977), regional policy design is seldom easy. A central issue, coverage, is multi-faceted but only the most significant aspects are detailed here. They concern economic (characteristics of firm and project) and spatial criteria (delimitation of regions for assistance).

Economic Coverage

Eligibility criteria by firm and project are a prerequisite to any development programme. Among the key ones are firm origin, size and type, and project size and type.

As regards the origins of companies, diverse viewpoints apply. The positive adjustment case disputes any discrimination between national and foreign investment in regional policy. Yet, to some policymakers multinationals have proved especially attractive because of their large investments often with flow-ons to other parts of the regional economy, their offer of new technology, their potential to revitalise local markets and their promised diffusion of new management techniques and employee training. But situations such as that described by Blair *et al.* (1984: 57) in which tailor-made deals have been arranged for foreign firms offering substantial employment "pose concerns for international co-operation and positive adjustment" (OECD, 1983a: 79). As well as advocates of over-proportional and exactly proportional aid for multinational *vis-à-vis* domestic enterprise, there is another group who would pay under-proportionally or not at all. Hayter (1982: 277-82) argues that regional policies seeking foreign investment simultaneously and necessarily discriminate against endogenous investment and can create "truncation" in the curtailment of local authority and restricted functional development regularly observed in branch plants. There is evidence to suggest that some multinationals have regarded governmental offers as extra benefits once basic viability is established in an area. International and interregional competition with investment incentives can prove costly both in financial terms and those of regional impacts (OECD, 1983a: 80). If, indeed, a regional authority does choose to attract foreign investment, its incentives should at least be of the right type and level and appropriately targetted (cf. Blackbourn, 1978: 125).

As opinion on multinational investment has polarised and the supply of footloose firms has shrunk, renewed interest has been shown in small and new business, particularly that representing endogenous enterprise. The latest United Kingdom plans, for instance, offer automatic grants which treat small companies more generously than large ones. Allen *et al.* (1977: 25) remark that there are no *a priori* grounds why particular incentives should carry specific size constraints and much is left to the discretion of the policy designer. Fiscal concessions, administered beyond the regional development department, are seldom other than universal in scope. Eligibility for more direct forms of regional aid frequently specifies minimum firm or project size but this may be merely for administrative convenience in reducing an otherwise prodigious number of applications. Larger projects will make more impact on development but the very largest may have to be excluded or referred to higher levels of government if their budgetary impact is overwhelming. However, maximum project size limits are posted by only three of 13 European countries (Denmark, France and Germany) (Yuill and Allen, 1984: 82-83). In general, authorities' interest is in project size, assuming that the firm itself is big enough to support the proposed venture. There is effectively no upper limit to firm size.

Firm type has not in the past been a major issue in regional development policy but may become more important in future. In most OECD countries, attention has largely gravitated to mobile investment invariably in manufacturing. This has been seen as a "locomotive" sector, with significant implications for up and downstream employment generation. Perhaps this focus was defensible given agencies' limited funding but it now sits uneasily with the contraction of secondary activity. Pressure for change is likely to come from sectorally-oriented critiques such as that of the positive adjustment school and also from the emergence of footloose and relatively labour intensive service industries which may be attractive targets in development programmes. Strongest evidence of this trend is the flood of civic interest since 1980 in provision of high technology and research and development parks for environmentally "clean" firms whose profits and payroll look good from the taxation viewpoint. A list of eligible services in 13 European OECD countries is shown in Yuill and Allen (1984: 74-75).

Initial investment, extension, modernisation, rationalisation, re-organisation and takeover are among project types which can be publicly supported. Not all may have positive employment implications. Each, however, has a particular profile of costs and benefits and will require a tailored selection of macro or micro instruments. In Europe, Allen *et al.* (1977: 21) have found that setting-up and extensions are almost always eligible. Other modes may attract assistance but with stringent side conditions. In 1984 the principal countries which aided all project types were Italy and Northern Ireland and both required stable or positive employment impacts (Yuill and Allen, 1984: 80-81). No substantial work on this aspect of coverage has been done by the OECD since 1979 (OECD, 1979*b*) but it is generally a rather stable part of regional policy. Any subsequent survey would well adopt the definitions of Yuill and Allen which reflect substantial conceptual progress in the 1980s. After Allen *et al.* (1977), these authors have additionally examined eligibilities down to the level of the item. These topics are rather specific and are overlooked here in favour of the wider question of spatial coverage.

Spatial Criteria: Delimiting Regions

While a typology (cf. Chapter II) outlines the sorts of regions one can anticipate in advanced countries, it says nothing of where such regions begin and end. A workable delimitation is essential for any administrative action and, if funding is involved, some consensus is desirable. Though Glasson (1978: 40-49) demonstrates the technicalities of delimitation, Armstrong and Taylor (1978: 149) point out that there is no unique way of classifying areas to be assisted. Even given that simple physical planning criteria have been satisfied (e.g. size of region, incorporation of hinterlands, recognition of topography etc.), there remains the question of the parameters to be used in delimitation. Though it may be desirable to take many factors into account, one is reminded that "a clear, unambiguous classification of areas is possible only if there is a single purpose for undertaking the classification" (Armstrong and Taylor, 1978: 151).

Delimitation is both practical and dynamic as illustrated in the German case (OECD, 1983*f*: 128-29). The objectives of regional policy were identified and the unit for its conduct was determined as the regional labour market. Across the nation, 170 of these Arbeitsmarkt-regionen were delineated on the basis of commuter intersections. Regions selected for assistance were determined according to three indicators: *a)* a "labour reserve quotient" (Arbeitskraftreserve-Quotient), a measure of excess labour supply; *b)* regional income disparity in relation to the federal average; and *c)* a measure of the inadequacy of infrastructure. These three indicators were weighted to give an overall score for each region and a cut-off was applied to designate assistance areas (Gemeinschaftsaufgabengebiete).

The relative absence of theory means that even textbook accounts of delimitation are pragmatic. Armstrong and Taylor (1978: 154) find favour with a draft method proposed by the European Communities in 1973 which derived its differentiating characteristics from the Communities' regional objectives and used multidimensional criteria. Armstrong (1978: 523) elsewhere argued the need for sensitivity even if a good "paper" solution is developed and this point is made additionally by the OECD (1983*f*: 129) with respect to the German formulation.

The spatial coverage of assistance measures can either be "broad banded" or "pocketed" (Allen *et al.*, 1977: 18-20). Broad delineation is inexact in that funds may go to areas characterised by neither great potential nor acute depression. Alternatively, it involves less "drawing the line" or "boundary hopping" (i.e. discrimination) and so is politically comfortable and more stable. "Pocketing" involves greater proof of eligibility and can create problems in dealing with multi-plant firms (i.e. at which plant they choose to establish their profits). Economic problems may be rapidly solved in tightly defined areas, requiring derating, and this tends to make the economic environment appear highly dynamic and rather uncertain for businesspeople.

In what proportion of a country should regional incentives be available? This issue was considered as recently as 1983 by the Working Party (OECD, 1983*e*: 20-21) with the following results. It was recognised first that incentives are designed to provide differential inducement to invest and promote employment or development in relatively disadvantaged regions. The issue for policy in current conditions is whether the emergence of high unemployment, low growth and social dysfunction weakens former distinctions between "more" or "less" prosperous areas, so requiring an adjustment or concentration of incentives towards the most handicapped areas. Some countries have, in fact, taken this step while others have introduced new incentives to cope especially with problems of industrial decline.

In the Working Party's view, no single rule of thumb is available to decide what proportion of a country should be eligible for regional incentives. If the proportion is significantly more than one half, the increasingly limited number of locationally "footloose" industries receives no particular direction, and investment is widely diffused. Cumulative or growth pole processes may not be invoked. The opposite approach is to "pocket" assistance in, say, one quarter of the area of a nation, accept the political fallout, and concentrate on building a limited number of viable centres or regions. This option has been selected after experience with the alternatives by some of the larger semi-peripheral economies.

Regardless of the proportions of area and population earmarked for aid, the delimitation of regions is dynamic. Geographic criteria in all major OECD countries were published in 1979 (OECD, 1979*b*: 60-90). The latest OECD data for 16 Member nations appeared in 1983 (OECD, 1983*e*: 35-36) and are updated in Table 3.4. It shows great heterogeneity among nations in terms of the percentage of population found within designated assistance zones. High ratios of land area may reflect a sparsity of population requiring assistance or high levels of urbanisation; conversely, it is desirable to keep relatively low the ratio of inhabitants assisted lest the intention be to have synonomous "regional" and national policy with the pitfalls mentioned above.

Other monitoring is undertaken by Douglas Yuill and Kevin Allen in the yearbooks on *European Regional Incentives*. Their coverage has extended to the ten European Community countries, Portugal, Spain and Sweden (thus excluding Norway, Finland, Switzerland, Austria and various small republics and principalities). These annual compendia provide copious detail in text and maps. In 1980, the editors reported a tendency towards widening spatial coverage as a response to high levels of national unemployment. Adjustments were marginal rather than wholesale. Only Denmark and the United Kingdom reduced coverage. For other countries to follow suit, a "complete review" of policy would be necessary and, even then, strong pressures would remain for marginal extensions (Yuill and Allen, 1980: 10-11).

Table 3.4. **Spatial coverage of regional incentives, selected OECD countries, 1983-84**

Country	Extent of Coverage
Austria*	Approximately 25 per cent of the population.
Belgium	Development zones. Start of 1984, 34.7 per cent of population.
Canada*	Designated regions. 93 per cent of the surface area holding 51 per cent of the population. A review of the regions eligible for industrial incentives is under way.
Denmark	General Development Regions. Start of 1984, 24 per cent of population.
Finland*	Development zones. Approximately 77 per cent of the land and holding about 45 per cent of the total population.
France	PAT zones. Start of 1984, 37 per cent of population.
Germany	GA areas. Start of 1984, 28.4 per cent of population.
Greece	Investment grant. Start of 1984, 58 per cent of population.
Ireland	The whole country is elibible although a distinction is made between Designated Areas (DAs) and Non-Designated Areas in terms of award maxima. Das cover approximately 50 per cent* of the territory holding some 28 per cent of the population.
Italy	Mezzogiorno. Start of 1984, 35.6 per cent of population.
Netherlands	The basic investment account premium (IPR) covers 33 per cent of the geographical area and 27 per cent of the population.
Norway*	No explicit designation of development areas. The maximum grant of 35 per cent is limited to the northern part of Norway, neighbouring municipalities of North Trondelag and Sogn og Fjordane; of 25 per cent in other specifically designated districts, and of 15 per cent elsewhere.
Spain	Large areas of industrial expansion. 52 per cent* of the national territory holding 36 per cent of the population.
Sweden	Designated regional problem areas. Start of 1984, 13.5 per cent of population.
Switzerland*	Mountain regions: 66 per cent of the area of the country holding 23 per cent of the population. Regions whose economy is at risk: 12 per cent of the area of the country holding 11 per cent of the population. These regions are partly included in the mountain regions (i.e. 69 per cent of their area and 50 per cent of their population).
United Kingdom	All problem regions including Northern Ireland. Start of 1984, 30.4 per cent of population.

* 1983 OECD data.
Source: OECD (1983*e* : 35-36), and Yuill and Allen (1984 : 78)

In 1981 the yearbook reported two opposing trends. There were *ad hoc* extensions in response to the deteriorating economic climate in particular localities of the United Kingdom, France and the Netherlands. The counterposing movement was "a widespread desire to reduce coverage and concentrate assistance on the areas of greatest need" (Yuill and Allen, 1981: 7). This was discerned in the United Kingdom, Denmark, Italy and Germany (see also OECD, 1983*f*: 129-30). It was recognised again, though, that it was very difficult politically to exclude areas from funding except after a full-scale policy review.

The 1982 situation was complicated as nations such as the United Kingdom and Denmark wrestled to effect their cutback plans. Some rationalisation was noted in Greece and the Netherlands but the general point emerging that year was that while new areas tend to be designated immediately, descheduling has to be staggered over a period of up to three years. "As a result, the coverage of the problem regions ... increases in the short-term, with any budgetary benefits of the cutbacks not normally being felt till towards the end of the transition period" (Yuill and Allen, 1982: 13).

In 1983 the spatial changes were described as "major indeed" (Yuill and Allen, 1983: 18). In only three countries (Ireland, Luxembourg and Portugal) was stability of coverage evinced: in each case, the entire nation was eligible anyway. Relatively minor changes applied in Italy and Spain but, after agreement with the European Commission, both Belgium and Denmark were able to effect spatial reductions or downgrading in their regional development assistance. A similar move was realised in Greece, while in the United Kingdom cutback plans developed from 1979 came to fruition. Restructured or rationalised arrangements are reported from France, Germany and the Netherlands but in Sweden a dramatic reduction was effected in a very short time, population coverage falling from 28.6 to 13.5 per cent and the areal spread from 77 to 62 per cent.

By 1983, therefore, only France, Greece, Italy and Belgium among among the European Community countries planned to have more than 30 per cent of their populations in designated problem regions. Whereas in 1980, the population coverage in European Community nations had been about one-third, it had now fallen considerably and was approaching one-quarter. On the other hand, pressure for *ad hoc* and sectoral adjustment was increasing and signs were emerging that the conventional problem area/non-problem area demarcation was under attack. This was seen as a serious threat to orderly development (Yuill and Allen, 1983: 24).

In 1984, the authors reported stability of spatial coverage in Ireland, Luxembourg, Italy, Sweden and the United Kingdom. Elsewhere cutback planning or implementation continued as "a major feature of regional incentive policy for a number of years now" (Yuill and Allen, 1984: 18). The rationale was apparently threefold: *a)* a desire among Community countries to effect cuts in public expenditure; *b)* the scrutiny devoted regional policy in a time of high unemployment; and *c)* the growing influence of the European Commission on area designation. On the last point, it was considered that the Commission now devotes more attention to regional than many other aspects of industrial policy.

Selectivity

As in social welfare policy (OECD, 1981*c*: 49-50), one of the important debates in the regional literature surrounds the selectivity of policy instruments – particularly incentives. Selectivity has two facets. Discrimination introduces overt selection in conditions or rates of award among areas, activities or project types deemed eligible for assistance. It is multidimensional and, at the margin, could become entirely individual in which case it would assume a "discretionary" character. This term is more usually applied to the decision of whether or not to award assistance and to vary the rate of the award. Discretion, therefore, constitutes a not fully predictable and potentially covert type of discrimination.

This issue is not new, having claimed attention in the OECD's (1974) previous *Reappraisal*. Here the Organisation warned that in a number of countries many automatic subsidies had been absorbed by firms without affecting appreciably either their overall position or major decisions on output, employment or expansion. They were, in fact, a simple financial transfer. On the other hand, such automatic transfers "at least pump money into a region and help to retain a higher degree of profitability than would otherwise be the case" (OECD, 1974: 105). While this outcome depends to some extent on the degree of leakage from a region, automatic measures do have certain distinct advantages. Their predictability is valuable in business planning and helps to bring decisions to a point. Their transparency is another positive aspect.

The alternative to offering automatic assistance is to foster some type of selectivity. Allen *et al.* (1977: 27-29) remark that discrimination can be difficult or costly to introduce. It is not favoured in tax systems administered outside the regional development sphere. It may have political constraints from the outset. If a scheme generates numerous applications, discrimination can be awkward to apply. The more delicate the necessary decisions, the greater the problems of implementation. Schemes can become unintelligible to recipients, a waste of their time and a marketing "lemon" for the proponent agency.

Discretionary schemes are, likewise, highly controversial. Supporters claim that they enable awards to be considered with the needs of particular regions and applicants in mind; they can be tailored "at the margin" to give just the right amount of aid and thus save public money. On the other hand, they are expensive to administer and may require concentrated case or general research. Decision processes are crucially retarded. They are not very transparent and may reduce business confidence in the existence of predictable ground rules which can justify the effort of applying for an award. Small firms which lack sophistication or expertise in the presentation of cases may be disadvantaged, as could the domestic *vis-à-vis* the foreign firm, the old project against the new and the small scheme as opposed to the large (Allen *et al.*, 1977: 32-33).

What do other commentators think? Three views warrant attention. First, Armstrong and Taylor (1978: 197-205) agree that economic policies are improved by greater selectivity. Apropos regional policy, they suggest a clearer differentiation: in the type of region to be assisted; between areas in the amount and type of assistance provided; and greater selectivity to the types of industries induced to relocate in depressed regions. On the last point, they argue that growth pole strategies have emerged as viable means of regional development but that they rely rather heavily on the selection of "locomotive" industries. These, of course, are the ones that should be differentially assisted.

Second, the positive adjustment school has put forward a rather complex case which deserves quotation. Basically, automatic and general assistance systems are preferred to selective and/or discretionary interventions. This is because:

> When aid is discretionary there is always some danger that, due to social and political pressure, funds are allocated to less productive firms, thereby prolonging the existence of inefficient structures and running the risk of stimulating over-capacities. In practice, discretionary procedures often penalise those productive firms which are ultimately more likely to promote investment and eventual employment (OECD, 1983*a*: 79).

Selectivity, it is argued, is alone insufficient to reorientate regional structures. If applied, it is greatly desirable to select negatively (i.e. grant regional assistance to all companies of the relevant area except those belonging to a particular activity which is already dominant and in excess capacity). In this way, diversification is augmented.

The third standpoint is that of Professor Franco Fiorelli of the OECD Working Party. He points out that:

> While it is possible in many cases to accept the practical preference for automatic measures ... (they) are all the more justified the greater the risk of arbitrary administrative decisions and the more comparable the production situation and/or objectives. Conversely, selectively is all the more justified the less the risk of arbitrary administrative decisions and the more clearly defined and transparent the existing or sought after targets of production differentiation.

Automatic incentives, he continues, are not of themselves neutral. Their value depends on actual regional conditions and their effects will be discriminatory depending on firms' combinations of productive factors. For example, a normative choice is involved as to whether an automatic incentive is to be applied to capital or labour.

Based on all these considerations, it is likely that the debate over selectivity will continue into the foreseeable future. The issue in discrimination is not so much with the fact as the form but with discretion the case is more tentative. Yuill and Allen (1984: 72) reveal that of 13 European countries' main incentive schemes, discretionary provisions apply to more than half (cf. Table 3.3) but, earlier, Allen *et al.* (1977: 33) reported that "in Europe it would seem ... automaticity is taking over from discretion". This was said to be because fixed rather than "up to" rates were being introduced and because, for reasons of their inherent complexity and work demands, discretionary decisions were becoming routinised. Another development of note was the publication of set conditions through which awards could be made available to all firms able to fulfil them. This is arguably a worthwhile and goal-oriented means of implementation. Its efficacy can be compared with that often emergent in a switch from statutory to performance zoning in local industrial planning.

EVALUATION AND PERFORMANCE

Many analysts in different countries have set out to establish the efficacy of investing public funds or effort in regional development and, as Schofield (1979: 251) points out, the assessment can proceed from three separate perspectives. The primary purpose of policy is the regional distribution of economic activity. Second is the aggregate efficiency within the economy (contribution to national output net of resource costs). Third is the financial impact on the national treasury (net costs).

Technically, assessments have been hampered by a series of problems which have made results less than ideally conclusive (Pinder, 1983: 89-91). To begin with, in what the United Kingdom House of Commons during 1973 described as "empiricism run mad" (see Glasson, 1978: 224), development programmes have sometimes proceeded against poorly defined goals which may change with successive governments. "Industrial policy is unlikely to be formulated with the aid of an explicit quantitative model; rather there is often only a vague framework in which the possible effects of policies are qualitatively assessed" (Hesselman, 1983: 198).

Next, it may be difficult to establish a counter-factual situation or isolate regional policy as the sole factor responsible for an area's economic performance. Lastly, analytical methods themselves have been subject to considerable controversy (Diamond, 1984: 36). All these factors complicate resolution of a problem which is inherently difficult enough: they may also reduce the confidence of observers and critics. A full exposé of techniques is beyond the scope of this paper and is available elsewhere (OECD, 1977*b*; Nicol, 1980, 1982; Ashcroft, 1982; Bartels *et al.*, 1982; Diamond and Spence, 1983). A few pointers are, however, in order.

Evaluation studies can be classified on several parameters. Partial evaluations examine the impacts of regional policy on measures usually relating to the spatial distribution of economic activity. Their sophistication can range from casual empiricism to detailed modelling. Comprehensive evaluations, in contrast, are concerned with costs and benefits either from the standpoint of the national economy or that of the sponsoring authority (the treasury). Within the partial studies, one can additionally differentiate micro and macro analyses. The former use questionnaire and interview techniques to examine the extent to which regional policy, among other factors, influences firms' decisions in relation to employment, investment and location. Macro studies separate the effect of regional policy from other variables and quantify its size.

Given this great range of approaches, some loose ends are to be expected in any determination of results. In general, studies relate to policies, not individual instruments. The present account begins at the level of policies, this, however, being only a springboard for investigations of the efficacy of individual instruments. All evaluation studies cannot be named: a survey is undertaken by Nicol (1980). Findings are simply summarised in two groups – those of continental European and United Kingdom studies. Their value is restricted to the extent that a number concern a period before 1980 or at least before the extent of the recent recession became apparent. The approach is to commence with partial micro and macro enquiries before looking at comprehensive ones (where available).

Continental Europe

Micro studies, irrespective of their spatial focus, have concentrated on a number of themes: locational determinants; the location or investment decision process; costs, performance or satisfaction at the new location; and hypothetical questions. A survey by Nicol (1980: 74) revealed 33 carried out in continental Europe, the great majority of which concerned locational determinants. Germany, France and Denmark contributed the bulk of all the work.

Locational determinants were thus the dominant theme of German research, two studies considering experience until as late as 1977. In general, the major factors influencing locational choice were the availability of site and buildings, labour, and transport infrastructure. Regional policy had apparently little ability to attract new investment or condition movement. Its role emerged as a secondary determinant: *within* a chosen region, it could persuade a firm to opt for an assisted area.

Nicol (1980: 83-84) examined eight micro studies which related to France. In most, the positive inducements of regional policy were accorded little weight and only disincentives in spatial choice were forceful in their "push" role, apparently by inducing a significant amount of plant location in towns 150-200 kilometres distant from Paris (Pinder, 1983: 96). Moreover, there is confusion as to whether regional incentives had an effect on the location decision of multinational plants. Perhaps, overall industrial rather than regional policy attracted overseas companies to France.

Of Denmark's six micro studies, four again concerned the location decision. In no case did a study period postdate 1975. From relatively small sample sizes of up to 108 firms, the conclusion emerged that regional policy did not play any significant role as a "pull" force or in terms of area attractiveness, even despite its strengthening in the 1970s. Access to the traditional manufacturing inputs – materials, labour, markets – captured most attention.

Clearly, studies from these three countries ascribe a limited role to regional policy. Two Italian investigations, however, conceded policy a greater impact in attracting both international and domestic investment to the Mezzogiorno. Though markets in the north may be the initial bait, differences in the cost of capital between north and south (as influenced by policy) can be decisive in the final analysis. On the other hand, four studies from the Netherlands (up to 1976) again downplayed regional policy in favour of labour or real estate considerations in the location decision. A rather similar pattern emerged in Belgian research of 1975.

Among continental European countries, there are relatively few macro and scarcely any comprehensive studies with which to support conclusions of those reviewed above. In Germany, macro studies rate the importance of regional policy somewhat higher than do micro studies but the efficiency of incentives in inducing additional investment is negative. The one French macro study indicated that policy effects had waned during the 1970s: as large companies considered Third World locations, labour cost differentials within France were also of correspondingly less importance. No macro studies were found for Denmark. In Italy, however, macro analysis has tended to support the conclusions of micro work. Focusing on various elements but in particular the role of grants, it views regional policy as having a positive impact in promoting southern locations. Dutch micro and macro workers take opposing views of the efficacy of policy. Among the latter, some would allow it quite a considerable effect (Nicol, 1980: 89). Overall, therefore, the picture from continental Europe is rather negative and more work is suggested to reduce conflicting evidence within and among the different approaches.

United Kingdom

British policy evaluation is the most advanced in the world and anaylsts have devoted more effort to the assessment of regional initiatives than any other type of adjustment measure (OECD, 1983*f*: 205). While Nicol (1980) reviewed a plethora of studies, an official and more up-to-date view is provided by the United Kingdom (Department of Trade and Industry) (1984: 87-123). Among the partial accounts, micro studies based on surveys have suggested that regional incentives play an important though not necessarily a dominant role in company location decisions. Commissioned enquiries of 1968 and 1976 both confirmed that regional incentives ranked behind labour availability as "major" factors in choice of location. In the latter survey, two-thirds of respondent companies noted them as key issues. For multinational firms, however, the locational choice appears differently based and a 1983 enquiry suggested market access as the most important factor in the decision to enter the United Kingdom. For foreign firms establishing in assisted areas, incentives played a role in two-thirds of cases.

Not only new location but also reinvestment has been surveyed in the micro approach. In this application, grants appear to have been crucial to the decisions of only a minority (usually less than 15 per cent) of firms. However, 40 to 50 per cent considered that their deliberations were in some way assisted or modified by the existence of incentives (e.g. plans amplified or brought forward or better equipment purchased): they became, in fact, an integral aspect. Attention has more recently turned to the impact of the government's factory building programme on start-up decisions of firms and, hence, the structure of regional economies.

Macro partial evaluation techniques have focussed principally on the effects of regional policy on employment but have also considered firm movement to assisted areas, investment, output, productivity, profits and wage levels (Diamond and Spence, 1983: 43-75). The employment studies use either standardization or explicit modelling techniques over a policy-off period (the 1950s) and a policy-on period in some cases covering years in the 1970s. These time frames create some methodological problems since the role of regional initiatives may become entangled with issues such as changes in transport infrastructure (e.g. motorway building), government policy towards nationalised industries, the development of North Sea oil, and simultaneous increases in unemployment and the capital intensity of manufacturing. However, results suggest that during the 1960s policy-on period and up to 1976, effects on employment creation in manufacturing ranged from 100 000 to 330 000 jobs. The variability in estimates is due to the different timespans and sectoral and geographic coverage of the studies. The impact is thus significant though the absolute size is unclear (Nicol, 1980: 59; Pinder, 1983: 92). More certain is the finding that policy, particularly in the north of England, Scotland and Wales, was in the period 1967-71 of greater value as compared with 1971-76 when the job creation rate was effectively halved (Marquand, 1980*a*: 47-49). Later enquiries have suggested that in these regions and northern Ireland, there was no addition to policy's cumulative impact on manufacturing employment between 1976 and 1981. Implicit in this result, however, are effects of recession and the normal process whereby jobs created by regional policy cannot be expected to last indefinitely (a so-called "plateau" effect). Also, it is relevant to note that, had policy been abandoned in 1976, there would have been a greater decline than was observed in the estimated absolute cumulative impact of policy by 1981. The abolition of a Regional Employment Premium in 1977 is likewise assumed effective.

Ongoing British partial evaluations, headed by Barry Moore of Cambridge University, produce separate estimates of the employment effects of regional policy on immigrant and indigenous sectors of manufacturing in the principal development areas [United Kingdom (Department of Trade and Industry), 1984: 100-03]. Without elaborating the methodology, it suffices to note that the new techniques generate higher estimates of policy effectiveness than conventional methods. By 1981 policy is claimed to have created some 445 000 jobs in all assisted areas and effects over the period 1976-81 appear in a more favourable light. When a multiplier of 1.4 for induced service employment is applied, a grand total of 630 000 new posts is estimated. The British Department accepts this as an upper figure and acknowledges other academic studies providing lower range estimates of 250 000 manufacturing or 350 000 manufacturing and service jobs. It also admits that policy appeared less effective in the late 1970s than in the late 1960s.

Explicit modelling has been a key technique in the partial macro studies concentrating on firm movement. An unpublished 1983 enquiry by the Cambridge team estimated over 900 policy-induced moves from 1960-71 and a further 500 from 1972-81. Other analysts' counts are more conservative, one positing 500 moves from 1961-71 while another suggests 500 moves to northern England, Scotland and Wales over the entire period 1960-77. Quoting the Cambridge evidence, Pinder (1983: 93) advances that controls were responsible for 45 relocations per annum as opposed to six attributable to investment grants. Such figures can, of course, be disputed in a debate which leads off into the efficiency of individual instruments (cf. Diamond and Spence, 1983: 52-55, 65-69).

As the majority of expenditure in British regional industrial policy since 1960 has been on investment incentives, impacts on the distribution of investment are of considerable interest. While earlier studies were very sensitive to the technique used, a Departmental account to 1980 puts forward in general that the share of national manufacturing investment enjoyed by northern England, Scotland and Wales increased markedly after 1960 and appeared responsive to the changing strength of policy. Over the period 1975-80 investment in these areas was on average 5.8 per cent higher than their share during the policy-off period allowing for the effects of industrial structure.

Comprehensive evaluations concern themselves with estimates of the costs and benefits of regional policy and perhaps the most thoroughgoing analysis has been that of the economics of incentives undertaken by Marquand (1980). In discussing costs, she recognises those to the exchequer *vis-à-vis* the opportunity costs normally associated with any economic initiative. Direct exchequer expenditure consists of loans, grants and so on, less repayment of loans, of interest and of capital arising directly from these outgoings. New exchequer expenditure is an estimate of the effect of expenditure on regional incentives on the exchequer accounts after allowing for flowbacks in the form of an increased tax revenue and reduced government spending as a result of the impact of regional policy (see also Moore and Rhodes, 1977: 38-42; Pinder 1983: 94). A major problem is, of course, that costs are incurred in the short-run whereas the benefits arise over a period of decades. Using different assumptions, Marquand (1980a: 98) offers both direct and net cost per job estimates in 1978-79 prices and directs some attention to the cost effectiveness of regional versus other macroeconomic policy in terms of employment creation. Despite a sophisticated analysis, she concludes that there is no unequivocal answer as to what the opportunity costs of incentive investment may be. Overall, she finds it highly probable that positive regional policies have had a positive effect over the period 1970-80. Moreover, one could not conclude that the diversionary effects of policy have led in general to any inefficient use of real resources. So much accords largely with the work of Moore and Rhodes (1977) over the earlier policy-on period of 1963-70 that programmes were of net national benefit in as much as they then increased the overall utilisation of labour. Real disposable income was enhanced because real output rose and general taxation could be lower than would have been the case in the absence of regional policy.

Broadly, therefore, the British studies appear somewhat more positive as to the effects of regional policy than their continental counterparts. While they are certainly the more comprehensive, they remain less than totally conclusive because of the substantial methodological difficulties of seeking to measure unalloyed policy effects. The expenditures and potential welfare impacts involved underscore the importance of such research. In the future it is likely to attract more interest as a result of the concern with policy efficiency expressed in Chapter II. As will also be shown, the milieu of intervention is likely to become more difficult, demanding use of the most refined instruments available.

CONCLUSIONS

Notwithstanding the cause, imbalance in regional systems is a fact of life in OECD countries and discussion here has dealt with the measures available to policymakers to pursue either substantive aggregative or distributional aims. Evaluation studies, however, suggest difficulties often associated with fulfilling the operational aim (outcome for effort). This raises questions of the ability of either centralised or decentralised regional policy to withstand or modify the extra-national forces impinging on economies as detailed in Chapters I and II.

The next two chapters present alternative but not mutually-exclusive foci for future regional policy. The first (Chapter IV) develops a model of the policy environment and details some private and public sector responses leading to endogenous development. Chapter V concerns technological initiatives which, possessed of significant qualifications and risks, will suit only certain nations and regions.

NOTES

Guide to Table 3.3

1. Incentive-type abbreviations:
   CG = capital grant
   IRS = interest-related subsidy
   TC = tax concessions
   DA = depreciation allowance
   LRS = labour-related subsidy

2. The PAT scheme is administered generally in an automatic manner, but with some discretion in respect of both larger investment projects and projects in the service and research sectors, both of which are administered centrally.

3. For projects with up to Fl 18 million of eligible investment, there is virtually no administrative discretion in the investment premium scheme. Rates of award are fixed and conditions of award are overt. In contrast, for projects with more than Fl 18 million eligible investment only the award relating to the first Fl 18 million of eligible investment is automatic. Any further award is wholly discretionary. Moreover, in no case would more than the standard fixed rate award for the area in question be paid in respect of total eligible investment.

4. These schemes are administered in an automatic manner except for very large projects (involving investment of more than 1 000 million escudos) and projects involving activities deemed to be at a "reorganisation stage".

5. Rates of award are determined by location. The award decision is automatic for firms expanding their employment by ten or less and discretionary for firms expanding their employment by more than this.

Chapter IV

STRATEGIES FOR REGIONAL DEVELOPMENT

FRAMEWORK AND POLICY MODEL

Across Europe and probably elsewhere in the OECD there is no certainty that regional policy has in recent years achieved its three major aims (Bartels and van Duijn, 1982: 97). Now, as the OECD (1983e: 5) has commented, "the solution of what are deep-seated and persistent regional structural problems has not been rendered any easier by the course of economic events". The broad dimensions of the regional problem have already been outlined but it is also appropriate to view it as one part of the crisis of the welfare state which emerged in the 1970s. At an OECD conference on social policies for the 1980s, a Yugoslavian academic, Sefer (1981: 121-22), put the view that:

> In reality, the 1960s and early 1970s were not as idyllic as could be concluded from the available and presented data on economic trends and the results achieved in social development. In actual fact, this period was not one only of progress. While the scope and form of state interventionism as a positive element contributing to the stability of economic development in the 1960s and early 1970s have evidently been exhausted, the contradictions emerging from such intervention have also been accumulating ... the problems that resulted from the ever increasing role of the state in the regulation of economic process (particularly in the distribution of income) accumulated gradually, and the effect of positive influences of state intervention lessened, while the negative ones gained in strength. Thus, we see a gradual weakening of the positive results of such a policy, and the strengthening of the negative ones.

Comparisons with the social welfare and manpower policy fields suggest that regional development has not been alone in its problematic performance of late. The 1980s have produced persuasive critiques on government activity from both right and left. The former case could be loosely summarised as one against increasing state intervention or at least, an insistence that public funds are spent effectively and efficiently (cf. the operational aims of regional policy). On the other hand some leftist writers have disputed the socioeconomic system that created the problems in the first place (cf. Ross *et al.*, 1984). Given these varied political perspectives, the state might expect little quarter in any efforts it makes in regional development in the 1980s. The emergence of depressed industrial areas and the shake-out in manufacturing is probably the greatest postwar challenge to be faced by regional policymakers. Their lot may have been easier before 1980 when the fundamental international and structural causes of decline were only dimly perceived. In the absence of better information, it may have been possible to retain a loose industrial policy involving subsidisation up to society's capacity to pay, with regional programmes used to support affected firms. All that has changed. Most political commentators would dismiss such a response as naïve and simply prolonging an ailing form of organisation. OECD nations have tried either rightist or leftist approaches to the recent economic crisis, or they have gone from one to the other. To date, none has chosen to adopt a position at either extreme of the political spectrum and for this reason the corresponding prescriptions need not be rehearsed here. This chapter and the next are about what has happened or is happening in the regional policy field rather than what might happen or what some party *hopes* will happen. Yet even this modest focus requires a theoretical context.

Assuming a state role in fostering regional development, the question is not with the operational objective which can be taken as given but with investment which can, of course, come from two sources, those external and internal to the region. As Table 4.1 shows, in the case of some European countries the degree of exogenous (i.e. extra-regional) control varies but, generally, in peripheral regions, it has incorporated over half the total activity. In Northern England, Scotland and over all Ireland, ratios are particularly high. To Wettmann and Ciciotti (1981: 70), what may be of key importance in such a situation is the organisational structure of the inward investment, the nature of technology used, the degree of integration of exogenous and domestic firms and, in the case of takeovers, the resultant structures created.

Table 4.1. **Extent of exogenous ownership of manufacturing enterprise by region, selected countries, Europe, 1973-78**

Country or Part	Region	Exogenous Control Measurement Parameter	Percentage	Year
England	North	Employment	79	1973
Scotland	Total	Employment	59	1973
Northern Ireland	Designated assisted areas	New plants (set up under the IDA's New Industry Programme 1960-73)	62	1978
	Designated non-assisted areas		46	1978
Ireland (Eire)	South	Employment	55	1977
France	All France less Paris region	Employment	44	1973
Germany	Peripheral regions	All new firms established in peripheral regions	50	1978

Source: Wettmann and Ciciotti (1981 : 70).

The techniques for attracting exogenous investment, set out in some detail in Chapter III, have been very fully practised by policymakers over the past 20 years. In the halcyon days of the 1960s and early 1970s, regional development could apparently be achieved simply by slotting another branch plant into its appointed place. In economies in which exogenous investment was an important determinant of development, much relating to the welfare of inhabitants may have depended on where that investment was located. Now, however, there is growing evidence in OECD countries that in the long-run the supply of exogenous "mobile" industry will become severely limited as developed markets are filled, economies of scale improve and new investment opportunities open in other nations and compete for capital (cf. Oakey, 1983: 61). Societies lacking growth (i.e. with few other options) will be scarcely predisposed to reject investment proposals even if they are regionally inequitable. Unless populations are prepared to shift to participate in what development is available, the net result will be continued inequality.

Countries with restricted growth prospects may thus become the "price takers" of future regional development, forced to attend mainly to its aggregative as opposed to distributional aims. More discretion to engage in spatial reallocations may lie with a few "price making" nations whose growth is relatively assured. Yet it could be suggested that for both groups, endogenous rather than exogenous sources of growth could now be the more significant. To this dimension, one could adduce also an orientation to levels of technology as an important likely future determinant of progress. A spinoff of technological superiority may be an ability to engage in the distributional as opposed to solely aggregative aims of regional policy based on the growth emanating from innovations and products developed. A notional schema which ranks control/technology possibilities from one to four suggests that the one effected may be significant in establishing the resultant regional policy. In the absence of firm statements in the literature as to whether these ends are mutually exclusive or in some way compatible, a graded tradeoff is proposed of distributional and aggregative aims. The above ideas are integrated in Figure 4.1.

This diagram is a matrix of control/technology positions associated with the potential for strategy in regional development. Present reasoning would favour endogenous, higher technologies (particularly of new products rather than processes) as providing growth in employment and other factors which could serve the distributional aims of nations with an interventionist outlook (Cell 1). Conversely, one can be fairly sure that exogenous, low technology development (Cell 4) might offer only an aggregative outcome. Some doubt exists on the other two broad possibilities, which is why they have been equally ranked. For instance, Oakey (1983: 63) has written that "the employment potential inherent in imported technology is poor because of the 'second hand' nature of much of the technology involved".

Figure 4.1.   A POLICY MODEL OF REGIONAL DEVELOPMENT

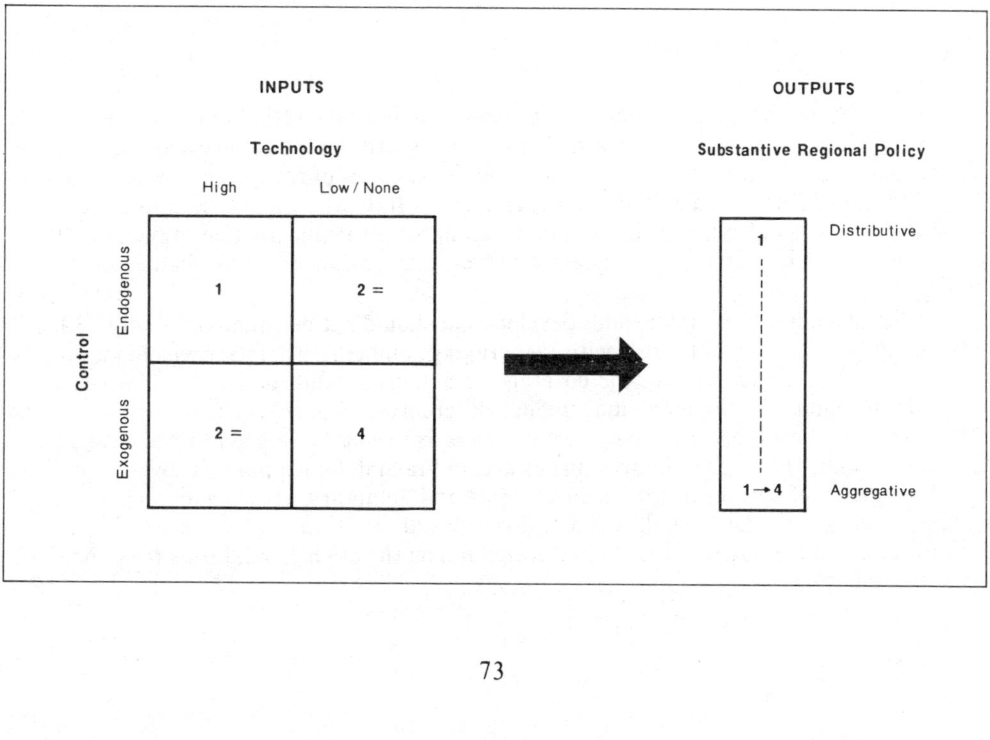

This recognises that nations tend to keep leading-edge innovations close to the home "core" area. On the other hand, the cell of endogenous, low technology is also problematic because of the strong competition exercised in low technology areas from non-OECD sources. Enterprise may generate some endogenous growth but its prospects for stable regional development seem clouded.

Given this model, it is possible to examine issues relating to control and technology. In the next chapter, technology's role in spatial development is the focus. Here we begin by examining strategies which rely on existing technology or organisation. The approach is first to explore progress in tapping endogenous potential and then to look at such strategies as the fostering of small and medium enterprise, enterprise zones, direct public intervention, and service industries.

ENDOGENOUS DEVELOPMENT

Endogenous potential in the widest sense includes factors which regions can supply in the development process such as physical and environmental resources, transport and communications infrastructure, urban structure, and accumulated physical and human capital (the last referring to the skills, education, entrepreneurial abilities and ingenuity of the populace). Development involves co-ordinating these factors towards productive ends. Wettmann and Ciciotti (1981: 4*) talk of regional innovation potential as being a bottleneck factor in the process. It is defined as the network of those economic activities and functions of individual firms and their environment which determine the speed and scope of technical and organisational modernisation and the ability to compensate for the loss of old markets by opening new ones. These concepts are largely European-inspired and have existed for scarcely more than five years. Discussion therefore remains exploratory and the present aim is to consider general issues and problems which have been presented to the OECD Working Party over the last eighteen months.

Basic Issues

As the idea of endogenous development gains strength, the OECD Working Party has made several important distinctions. First it is necessary to differentiate between spontaneous development and that stimulated by public authorities. Cases of the former are rare and the exemplar is found in the northeast and central regions of Italy where a diffuse industrialisation has occurred which makes use of reserve labour available within local, essentially agricultural communities (cf. Chapter VI). This model, however, may be difficult to replicate elsewhere in the OECD.

A second point is that endogenous development should not be equated directly with self reliance (cf. Segal, 1979) but rather with encouraging competition in international markets in products new to a region. Third, the coverage of activities is not limited to the secondary sector. Endogenous development may reflect different approaches in various parts of an economy. If this view is accepted the question arises as to whether the concept should extend beyond economics into social welfare and culture. In Finland, for example, it covers new ideas for the provision of social services in rural areas and voluntary activities of various kinds. Experience in Austria has been that at first it is necessary to stimulate cultural activities as a basis for economic initiatives. The United Kingdom, on the other hand, limits the concept to the economic arena.

74

Necessary Steps

An approach to endogenous development is via an audit of regional strengths and weaknesses. Among the latter, which could restrict the ability of an area to participate in processes of innovation and structural change, are functional deficiencies in the collection and processing of information, planning and decision-making, technical development and product design, market search and organisation and management and financing. These deficiencies relate more to the quality and characteristics of individual firms rather than the presence or absence of individual industries.

Perhaps environmental conditions form a block to the effective performance of headquarters or decision-making functions or to the ability to generate and diffuse innovations. Of key importance in the audit would be analysis of the degree of labour market diversification and availability of professional skills, the capacity of social systems to absorb technological and structural change (e.g. training systems and labour-management relations), and the density and diversity of information and communications infrastructure. The last point is taken to include the availability of venture finance, commercial services, and linkages between the business and science complex. Also significant could be the extent and quality of management (not science) education in developing a pool of entrepreneurial talent appropriate to small or larger enterprises. Further, the performance and attitudes of regional development authorities themselves are a significant point (Manners, 1981: 287)

Part of the purpose of the regional audit could be to establish innovation potential as one means of development. Empirical research points to spatial concentrations in innovation and considerable time lags in diffusion of new ideas. Frequently this works against smaller firms in peripheral regions which cannot rely regularly on complex internal information and labour sources, but instead require easy access to contact systems and contract personnel when any major product or organisational change is contemplated. Indeed, the need to make regional information networks richer is critical in any attempt to move simultaneously towards endogenous and more technological development, the potential desirability of which was indicated in Figure 4.1. Enhancement of regional systems may no more than offset the spatial thrusts of national technology policies which, as will be seen, favour places with substantial initial advantage.

Wettmann and Ciciotti (1981: 13*-22*), working among the European Community nations, show how auditing could lead to the establishment of a typology of regions organised according to their endogenous potential. First come traditional, highly urbanised and effectively "stranded" regions which enjoy high centrality and good agglomeration economies and well as much industrial and technological experience. The main barrier to structural change is a "petrification" of social and industrial structure due to a dominance of large organisations and the lack of a favourable environment for small and innovative firms. Both development and redevelopment is required and such measures may require a greater effort than ordinary, externally-directed regional policy might propose.

A second set of externally controlled peripheral regions suffer primarily from their location (e.g. Scotland, and Italy's Mezzogiorno), the lack of density and diversity of labour markets and information systems and, most importantly, lack of local entrepreneurship due to the existing management structure. This contrasts with the situation of a third set of regions such as around Toulouse in France or Upper Franconia in Germany which possess at least a locally-based sector of autonomous small firms which could provide the entrepreneurial potential necessary for adopting new production technologies, developing new products and markets, and responding to government stimuli. Yet these regions, just as the second group, may never become centres of innovation. The task is to speed up the adoption and diffusion of new technologies, to modernise the product mix and to compensate for the loss of old markets by developing new market potential.

A final set, agricultural regions without an industrial base, poses a different problem. Apart from intensified agricultural production, there are but two routes for endogenous development: tourism or a food industry based on local products. Both require scarce entrepreneurial talent. Moreover the creation of a food industry is a major step in social, technological and managerial organisation.

According to the authors, different policy prescriptions should be applied to the four sets of regions. The stranded areas, first, should undergo stimulation of their small firm sector both in original innovation and in the early adoption of new procedures. Policy in all other (peripheral) regions would focus on small and medium firms because of their entrepreneurial potential, market adaptability and modest scale of operations. Since most firms, because of inadequate entrepreneurship and technological capacity, will not be potential innovators, emphasis should be on diffusion, modernisation, and development of the product mix rather than original strategies.

In general, endogenous development should focus on the enhancement and augmentation of human capital in problem regions by way of subsidies for management or research and development activity, vocational training in new technologies and trainee programmes for senior school and technical college students. Another thrust is the creation of a modern institutional infrastructure which would help offset a lack of services and venture capital. This would assist the uptake of technology in problem regions as opposed to those with initial agglomeration advantages. Additionally, the co-operation of sub-university, higher educational institutions could assist endogenous regional development: these organisations may be locally staffed, and occupied with applied problems as opposed to universities which operate often on an international circuit of more basic scientific research (Wettmann and Ciciotti, 1981: 20*). Further insights can now be obtained by turning to related themes which can support endogenous development. First among these is the stimulation of small and medium enterprise.

SMALL AND MEDIUM ENTERPRISE (SME)

The 1970s have brought a reversal of the postwar trend of small firm decline which has been observed in many advanced countries. In part, this stems from events described in Chapter I. First, the energy crisis tended to reduce optimal plant sizes particularly in capital intensive industries. A rise in transport costs raised interest in siting plants close to their primary inputs or markets and, in some cases, this may have required smaller facilities. Moreover, the shake-out of labour from large enterprises left a pool of unemployed who may have considered entrepreneurship as a new way of make a living. Simultaneously, smallness became socially acceptable (if not "beautiful") after the growth consciousness of earlier eras. Perhaps, also, increased incomes paved the way for small firm growth in instigating a demand for batch or customised products both of a high and low technology nature (Storey, 1983: 5-6). Many service activities belong in the latter category.

Small business assistance policies have been pursued in advanced industrial countries for largely social and political reasons – support for individualism and entrepreneurship, resistance to the growing concentration of the modern economy, aid for an important political constituency. Recently, as advanced countries have experienced rapidly rising unemployment, recession, and major structural economic changes including the decline of large older manufacturing firms and the absence of mobile industry to buttress distressed areas, there has been increasing interest and activity with regard to small business as an instrument of national, regional and local economic development. Small business development is seen by some as a component of the strategy of endogenous economic development.

The classification of firms to SMEs is generally based on size (e.g. number of persons employed, annual turnover), qualitative considerations (e.g. relative size or market power of firms within industry sectors) or a combination of both. Yet there is no common definition of SMEs in OECD countries. Even if one agreed that SMEs could be defined simply by the number of persons employed, problems arise in that countries use different employee benchmarks. Table 4.2 below shows the size bands used to describe SMEs in different countries. The OECD is working towards improving the comparability or at least to understand the differences of country statistics. Attempts are also being made to collect data on industrial establishments' employment size groupings.

Table 4.2. **Definitions of small and medium-sized firms in industrial sector, OECD countries, 1981**

Country	Numbers of Employees
Australia	1-99
Belgium	1-50
Canada	1-99
Denmark	1-50
France	1-500
Germany	1-499
Ireland	1-50
Italy	1-500
Japan	1-299
Netherlands	1-200
Sweden	1-200
United Kingdom	1-200
United States	1-500

Source: van Heesch (1984 : 6).

According to a major OECD (1982*b*, 1982*c*) study, SMEs account for 45 to 70 per cent of industrial employment in Member countries. The lowest percentages are found in medium-sized countries whose industrial history goes back furthest – the United Kingdom, Germany and France. The highest occur in the smallest countries or those that began their industrialisation process much later – Benelux, Scandinavia, Ireland and Australia. Japan and the United States, with large domestic markets and for particular historical reasons in each case, come between the two. SMEs also account for a substantial share of value added, turnover and investment, although the actual figures are less than their share of total employment. They enjoy a dominant position in several industrial sectors. This is the case, for example, in metal manufactures, plastics finishing, food and allied products, textiles and clothing and various product sectors. While the place of SMEs in the different sectors varies little from country to country, their relations with large firms, especially through subcontracting, may vary appreciably.

With this background it is possible to turn to aspects of SMEs which are most relevant from the viewpoints of endogenous development and regional welfare. Apart from their prodigious numbers, features common in describing the importance of SMEs are their contribution to employment and job creation, their assumed flexibility and capacity for innovation.

Employment Potential

In light of world economic trends and the behaviour of large companies, there has been considerable speculation that any significant job creation in OECD countries will take place among SMEs, particularly those operating in new areas of technology. In France, for example, there has been a redistribution of employment towards SMEs. In 1974, 26 per cent of wage earners worked in small establishments (of less than 20 employees). By 1980 this figure had increased to 30 per cent. On the other hand there was a reduction in the share of wage earners employed in large establishments (with more than 200 employees); in 1974, 36 per cent of wage earners worked in such establishments, whilst in 1980 this figure had dropped to 31 per cent.

In the Japanese economy the place held by large firms is falling visibly. The proportion of gross domestic product accounted for by the 1 320 largest firms was nearly 21 per cent in the mid 1960s, 18 per cent in 1970 and around 16 per cent in the early 1980s (Van Heesch, 1984: 9). In the period 1972 to 1981, the workforce of small enterprises rose faster than that of medium and large scale business partly because of the growth in the number of small firms [Japan (Ministry of International Trade and Industry), 1983: 93].

These results, however, must be viewed with an eye to experience elsewhere. In the late 1970s in the United States, it was also believed that small business was the major source of new job creation (cf. Birch, 1979: 8-9). Subsequent research has qualified its role with the finding that the majority of positions created were in the service sector and were in general, jobs of poorer quality which were less likely to survive. In the United Kingdom it appears that large firms still contribute most to net employment creation and that the contribution of small firms is likely to be significant only over a long term. Moreover, employment growth may be offered by no more than a minority of quite successful companies.

Success is, of course, an element which cannot be unquestioningly attached to small business performance. Van Heesch (1984: 11) posits that in the first four or five years of existence, some 60 per cent of newly created small enterprises disappear. While this entry and exit certainly precludes ossification in advanced economies, it may be disruptive, wasteful of resources and certainly does little for job stability or durability. Employment creation, although probably in sum a steady and growing amount, has a dynamic and fast changing pattern in which jobs may be lost quickly to appear somewhere else in a newly established enterprise. Job security will therefore only represent a minor aspect of the job creation process. On the other hand, the opportunity to enter a business for a limited period may be useful to some people. Obvious beneficiaries might be casual or part time workers. More broadly, small business can: help the transition of the unemployed into the workforce; begin a spinoff process of new entrepreneurs; offer on-the-job training; and provide jobs to the less skilled. Besides the actual number of jobs created and their longevity, aspects such as the above may be important in regional development.

Innovativeness

According to surveys made in the 1960s, individual inventors and small firms have accounted for many important innovations since the turn of the century. Modern industrial societies grew out of small firms and many large enterprises began as small innovative ventures. Technology has, however, increased in complexity, raising the importance of industrial research as a source of major innovations. More than half of the industrial research and development in the world is undertaken by 40 large firms and SMEs are only a modest force in national industrial research (OECD, 1982c: 12). This is because they are often service-oriented, may lack adequate research and development facilities and may not concentrate in growth or export sectors of the economy. Large firms bring forth the majority of innovations in most industries, particularly those which are capital intensive or in which there are high development costs.

By the end of the 1970s, firms with less than 1 000 employees contributed around five per cent to (measured) national expenditure on industrial research and development in the United States, and ten per cent in Germany. Firms with less than 500 employees accounted for about five per cent in the United Kingdom and ten per cent in France. Nevertheless, small firms, at least in some countries, continue to be very active sources of innovation: those employing less than 1 000 people contributed nearly half the "major" innovations in the United States in the early 1970s (OECD, 1982c: 16).

Although it is estimated that only about ten to 20 per cent deliberately undertake innovative activities (ranging from in-house research and development to searching for new products), SMEs play an important role in speeding up the development of products with industrial applications from discoveries or new concepts coming from large industrial, governmental or university laboratories. Most of the innovative activities consist of propagating the technologies that are currently being transferred from advanced sectors, in particular those like microelectronics and new materials, which underlie present structural change. SMEs have an important role in inventing a wide variety of applications for these technologies and in doing so diffuse technology through the entire industrial system.

Small firms have been found to be particularly effective in the application of specific discoveries or developments to the production of high performance goods for new and emerging markets and also for older and fragmented markets. Examples can be found in health care and medical equipment (lasers), telecommunications, security and analytical/detection equipment (software). SMEs also have expertise in many specialised industrial processes such as in surface treatment of metals. In these areas the problem is often one of continual adaptation of non-standard products (or of products which lack technical perfection) in close co-operation with consumers/users.

The number of SMEs operating in the new high technology areas and the formation of new technology-based SMEs is still rather modest in most OECD countries (new formations are estimated in dozens a year); consequently new technology-based firms have generated only a small proportion of the new jobs created. Although the population of such high technology SMEs is relatively small, their potential to develop technologies and "radical" innovations is generally regarded as promising. Many small firms have been the first to launch into the applications of genetic engineering. Moreover, in the 1970s it was a relatively small firm, Intel, which launched the first microprocessor. In this case the technology had apparently been perfected but IBM delayed or hesitated in putting it on the market. In this way SMEs have the potential to introduce a dynamic element in the economies of OECD countries.

From this evidence, which is admittedly partial, it appears unlikely that a rapid proliferation of new, highly innovative small firms will lead regions on the path of endogenous development. Success may be patchy, unpredictable and hard-won. These are, however, still early days in the relations of community and government with small business and perhaps much more could be achieved with appropriate development policies. Recent thinking on this issue is outlined below.

Structural Change and Sector Development

Discussion about the innovative role and responsibility of small firms should not lose sight of the part this sector plays in lubricating the wheels of a dynamic economy. In part, this is done by the introduction of (monopolistic) competition which allows structural change to proceed more atomistically than if just large enterprises were involved. Also, small firms support large ones through subcontracting and so facilitate a division of labour in the economy. In this capacity, radical authors would see the small firm providing a pool of reserve labour, the level of which will be regulated essentially by the product needs of the larger firm. Thus, small firms provide a first buffer to shocks in the economy which may permit greater employment stability among important large employers. The fact that SMEs, sometimes under difficult circumstances, show a remarkable flexibility in comparison with large firms is illustrated by the example of the steel industry. SMEs, the so-called "mini-mill" operators, entered the industry at the time when the giants were experiencing their greatest postwar crisis. The mini-mill operators to date have been successful because of their one common characteristic, flexibility. Using the technique of electric arc steelmaking and with scrap metal as the primary input, the mini-mills have steadily expanded production to the extent that in some product areas the large integrated steel mills have been excluded from the market.

Flexibility and a capacity for structural adaptation are qualities governments seek to foster in an economy. For this and other reasons, most OECD nations have initiated or expanded programmes to assist small business nationally or in particular regions. These initiatives have included: debt and equity financing, advisory services, entrepreneurship training, management assistance, government procurement, incentives for investors in small firms, tax incentives, technological and other information, factory space, regulatory reform and export promotion. The business community has often been drawn into these efforts in order to provide expert advice, investment capital, facilities, information and training. Attention has also been directed at the establishment of co-operatives, community enterprises, worker-owned enterprises and other new ventures which can provide jobs for the hard-to-employ. Universities have also been involved in efforts to provide advice, training, information, commercially useful ideas, and even new entrepreneurs.

Much attention in several countries has been accorded the financial needs of small firms. The approach has been mainly through micro as opposed to macroeconomic measures (cf. Chapter III). Programmes have been initiated for providing longer-term debt and equity financing, tax incentives to investors, unsecured credit, financing for technological innovation and modernisation of equipment. Young, independent, growing firms which are commercially viable can be prevented from becoming profitable and growing further by the absence of capital. Traditional private sector financial institutions may be unwilling to provide the necessary financing because of the higher risks involved in such investments, the need for longer-term horizons, and their lack of expertise in working with small firms and assessing small business investments.

There are also important questions about what are the most cost effective ways of providing financial assistance. Forms of aid such as loans, loan guarantees, interest subsidies, grants and equity financing have different value for small firms in different financial situations or stages of development, and are more or less costly to government. And, finally, it is important to consider the benefits to small firms of other public-assistance programmes such as business tax credits, procurement, and support for research and development. This latter question is an instance of the concern for the inadvertent consequences of government programmes on particular economic objectives, and more co-ordinated approaches to business development.

Small firms also have other needs, and governments have responded to them with various programmes. Demands have been identified for management training and assistance, technical advice and information, technological improvements, marketing, better premises, infrastructure and other environmental improvements, and regulatory relief. There are less obvious ways in which governments can sustain and upgrade small businesses. In employment or public works proposals, the choice of scheme will be crucial in determining the degree of small business involvement. A house rehabilitation scheme will involve scores of small companies: a civil engineering scheme such as road building which costs the same amount may not. An energy conservation scheme for existing buildings will need the help of lots of little companies; a railway electrification scheme may not.

Governments at the national, regional and local levels, together with the business community and universities, have established various organisations to deliver assistance to small firms. New development finance organisations have been established based on the recognition that special skills, experience and attitudes are required to reach out to small businesses, to assess its people and projects, package financing, work with small business people, and provide management advice and assistance. In some cases, commercial banks have been used to deliver government subsidised financial assistance to small firms. They have also collaborated to establish special institutions for small business financing in which risk is shared. In other cases, organisations have been established which recruit private sector financing, technical and management expertise. In the United Kingdom private firms have established numerous local enterprise agencies which are staffed by business people and provide advisory and other assistance to small competitors. The Dutch have formed regional development companies employing businesspeople to stimulate the growth of firms.

In some countries, small business federations are effectively the tecnhnology transfer system, the major source of training, and the centre for research and development. The South Korean small business federation, for example, provides low interest loans and selects around 1 000 small firms each year for special attention and encouragement. The Japanese have 191 technical and research institutes to help and advise firms belonging to Japan's small business federation and to test their products. The federation of boutiques de gestion in France, and Business in the Community in the United Kingdom, are creating networks offering help and advice to small firms: traditional networks are still strong among Chambers of Commerce, and the trade associations, several of which support a research institute. The main interests of the associations, however, tend to be in the retail trade and local services rather than in manufacturing, so they are not particularly appropriate as a technology network.

Regional economic development is not interested in all small firms, but mostly in those that can make a contribution to the adjustment and growth of distressed economies and to employment creation. Different types of firms will have different needs. For example, capital intensive small businesses need larger amounts of capital to finance fixed investment; retail and service sector firms need working capital; and new firms need equity financing. Firms at different stages in their life cycle will also have different requirements. Policymakers must be concerned with the survival and expansion of existing small businesses as well as aiding the establishment of new firms.

As shown above, numerous instruments and agencies exist but more work is required to establish their ease of application at the regional level. If small firms are in future to be seen as a vehicle of endogenous development and local-area progress, it may be necessary either to focus regional policy tools towards this sector or, alternatively, to instigate greater spatial selectivity in the delivery systems of existing small business agencies. Co-ordination of small business and regional authorities is necessary to avoid policy overlaps. This will be all the more important as regional policy takes account of such constructs as the enterprise zone and as it develops increasing interest in the service sector as a means of economic development.

ENTERPRISE ZONES

Enterprise zones, a phenomenon of the 1980s, represent a highly specialised blending of measures for endogenous development and small business which is presently a facet of urban rather than regional policy[1]. As the OECD (1983*g*: 73) has pointed out, the distinction of urban and regional problems and policies is not always clear because the spatial entities involved are highly interdependent. What is clear and also more important is that almost throughout the entire postwar period but particularly in the last decade, many cities in OECD countries in Europe and North America have experienced decay and dereliction involving emigration from inner areas, rundown of housing and commercial building stock, the shutdown and suburbanisation of industry and some offices, erosion of the tax base, emergence of social problems and poverty, financial plight and a host of other ills. These factors add up to an "inner city problem" which in many cases has persisted despite what are now seen as radical planning efforts of the 1950s and 1960s to erase socioeconomic blight simply by tearing down and rebuilding city neighbourhoods. This, of course, is the subject of another debate altogether, one poorly served by peremptory excerpts here. It must suffice to say with Butler (1982: 76) that:

> Mass unemployment is rarely cured by putting the unemployed in new houses, and a failure to generate jobs in a community will lead to a deterioration of rebuilt areas – no matter how many design prizes they receive.

The enterprise zone concept arose in recognition of the fact that inner cities were once centres of a vital small business economy which, it was argued, was gradually etched away over the years by the requirements of ever increasing government regulations and restrictions. Small business was adjudged particularly appropriate as a counter to inner city problems. As it grew, it would require individual entrepreneurs to devote more time to managerial roles, so allowing low-skilled labour (in abundant supply in inner cities) to be employed in the day to day running of the business. Direct aid for this type of job generation would possibly be more effective than defensive aid to hold jobs of workers in ailing industries; more, also, than initiatives which were intended to create jobs but which sometimes acted simply to redistribute existing ones (a view that some people would hold of certain regional policy). It was never suggested that the problem areas lacked indigenous initiative – an underground cash economy was thought to flourish. The problem for policymakers of the late 1970s was to elevate indigenous activity to allow greater local employment and prospects of legitimate business expansion. Key inhibitors, however, were the barriers to entry imposed by public reporting, planning and requirements: to avoid them, many potential operators simply stayed small and illegitimate.

Onset and Outcome

In a speech to the Royal Town Planning Institute of the United Kingdom on 15th June 1977, Professor Peter Hall of Reading University unveiled the idea of a "freeport" to attack structural decline in traditional industrial economies. He argued that residents of many inner city neighbourhoods (and, equally, of stranded regions) have been bypassed in the rapid evolution of the post-industrial economy. They lack the skills to adapt to high technology production even if the necessary industries could be induced to locate in the affected areas. A freeport solution would simultaneously:

a) Be outside British foreign exchange and customs control so as to attract overseas investors;

b) Be based on unrestrained free enterprise with a minimum of personal and corporate taxation, government intervention or public services;

c) Allow union activity but prohibit closed shops; and

d) Foster residence based on free choice, with inhabitants accepting the lower public costs and benefits in the same way as firms (Butler, 1982: 97).

The notion of recreating Hong Kong of the 1950s and 1960s amidst a British city was borne of desperation at the failure of a range of policies from outright physical renovation to soft social engineering. Suitable areas would be those with little to lose by trying out a radical new scheme. What Hall had called "an essay in non-plan" could further become a mechanism for continuous, unplanned experimentation and adaptation in tightly defined inner city areas. The aim would be to see what an unfettered market could achieve (Hall, 1982: 417).

The political launching of the idea came in mid-1978 by Sir Geoffrey Howe, then Conservative Opposition spokesman on economics. He proposed a watered down version of "freeport" which would nevertheless allow people of viewpoints incongruent with a welfare economy to test their hand. His enterprise zones would thus have six main features:

i) Detailed planning controls would be dropped leaving only the most basic anti-pollution, health and safety restrictions;

ii) All public land in a designated zone would be auctioned within a specified time;

iii) All new development would be free of rent control;

iv) Enterprises establishing in the zone would be exempt from capital gains tax resulting from development;

v) Businesses would be guaranteed that tax laws would not change over a stated period and that wage and price controls or certain other employment provisions would not apply;

vi) No government grants or subsidies would be offered in the zones.

The chance to act came in early 1980 when the Conservatives took power. Rather than setting up special legislation, the Government amended two existing Acts, measures for enterprise zones coming into effect that November. As constituted, the provisions deal with the designation and administration of the zones, tax changes, planning and zoning modification and special regulations.

Briefly, the key points are as follows. Local authorities are invited to submit proposals for enterprise zones: they cannot be imposed on an area by central government. Fiscal concessions are exchanged for a relaxation of local development controls, agreements lasting usually ten years. Development value realised from the disposal of land in the zone in this period is exempt from the normal 60 per cent capital gains tax. Industrial, commercial and retail (but not residential) premises are exempt from property tax and the local authority is reimbursed for lost revenue by the national exchequer. Plant and machinery is depreciated 100 per cent for tax purposes in the year of purchase: construction, extension or improvement of all commercial buildings is similarly handled. Simplified and streamlined procedures are applied by the local authority to any development proposal. Government statistics reporting requirements are slashed and the red tape in customs handling is reduced. Finally, normal regional assistance on subsidies applying in the general area are retained as additional benefits (Botham and Lloyd, 1983: 27).

Quite clearly, it is of more use to trace the evolution than propose set definitions of enterprise zones. Their purpose can vary in different countries or contexts. The aim in the United Kingdom is to encourage industrial and commercial redevelopment of derelict or cleared areas of heartland cities, a partial policy, as it were, for some stranded regions. The programme has focused on new construction of various types of enterprises rather than small business *per se*. In fact, conditions appear more to suit branch establishment by medium or large corporations or chains, and retailers and service sector businesses may find depreciation provisions and the avoidance of capital gains tax to their liking. This is by and large a programme to attack blight in a fairly gross way: few incentives have been provided for residents, so their potential contribution to a differentiated environment may fail to materialise. Provisions for the sale of public land have also been excluded so that government will still have considerable scope to regulate activity.

What else has been dropped? The Government stopped short of tackling aspects of employment legislation apparently considered restrictive within the business community. The United Kingdom's membership of the European Economic Community was advanced as a reason why the zones could not enjoy free trade status[2]. There was no commitment to the idea of a social laboratory for economic strategy and, indeed, the sorts of firms to be attracted are hardly likely to want to be "guinea pigs". Finally, the entrepreneur seems all but overlooked. "The provisions seem suited exclusively to the businessman with plenty of capital and a heavy tax bill, who is in a position to hire a bulldozer and put his money into property" (Butler, 1982: 109). Is this a criticism? Possibly not, since some investment may be better than none at all, particularly in the areas to be redeveloped. It all depends on social preferences and priorities. What emerged was only one of a number of strategy options.

Unleashed onto the "market" of local authorities, the enterprise zone plan received a satisfying response and the number of applications had to be pared down to seven for initial development. By early 1981, eleven sites were under consideration ranging in size from 90 to around 525 hectares (roughly the size range of traditional industrial parks). Most were derelict, or supported vacant buildings in areas practically unpopulated. Information provided in November 1984 by the British Department of the Environment indicates that there are 17 zones in England, three each in Wales and Scotland, and two in Northern Ireland.

The British experience, examined in detail here, reveals possible options inherent in enterprise zones and the way a policy prescription, as it develops, will range among them. Further variations can be noted briefly in the experience of another major proponent of the concept, the United States[3]. Its Urban Jobs and Enterprise Zone Act of 1980 sought also to improve inner-city areas for business development by reducing tax burdens on firms locating in depressed neighbourhoods. Subsequent legislation and a direct presidential endorsement have firmly implanted the idea in the American psyche. Writing before March 1984, Weiner (1984: 3, 9) reports that 21 states have passed enterprise zone legislation and nine have programmes in place[4]. Moreover, under the Enterprise Zone Employment and Development Act of 1983, the federal secretary of Housing and Urban Development would designate up to 75 areas as enterprise zones over a three year period. Overall, the American aim is far more socially oriented. To qualify, a potential zone must have a population of at least 4 000 people who suffer unemployment and poverty well above the national average. Its size could vary from that of a small census tract to around 300 hectares. Once declared, a non-refundable general payroll tax credit becomes applicable for employers increasing net employment in the zone, investment tax credits apply, capital gains tax concessions are offered investors, companies engaging specific types of local labour receive special tax credits, and employees working in the zone also receive non-refundable tax credits (Butler, 1982: 132; Weiner, 1984: 10). Resultant growth in economic activity is intended to change the characteristics of zone residents, for one thing, overcoming their underclass mentality which is self-defeating. The desire to open up the underground economy is important too.

This résumé highlights substantial differences in intent and application in the British and American formulae. The former appears far more as an industrial or commercial renovation programme for non-residential areas, whereas the latter is apparently a more discriminating and finely-tuned urban and social rehabilitation scheme. It provides explicit employment incentives in addition to certain capital or development provisions. Another notable difference is that it does not call for a federally financed elimination of local property taxes. The enterprise zone concept thus demonstrates significant versatility but there are problems whichever strategy is tried.

Assessing the Zones

In proposing enterprise zones in cities, governments have to learn to "back off" the private sector and recent commentaries suggest that this is achieved only with difficulty. Of British experience, Botham and Lloyd (1983: 27-28) focus on important ideological issues. What has been created is not what was originally proposed: the emphasis has shifted from deregulation to concessions or assistance, and "non-plan" seems to have become planning in a different form. To the extent that government fails to withdraw, the zones become just a type of regional mini-policy. This outcome is obviously a result of compromises negotiated in bringing a seminal idea to reality but it does not alter the fact that what is to be assessed is what is now being implemented. The original idea is essentially irrelevant. Moreover, it is difficult in the British case to attribute development solely to private initiative since the public packages constitute a major incentive. Among the public provisions, it will be hard to differentiate the role of special zone measures from those broader areal measures which remain effective anyway.

Against this backdrop, a burgeoning literature now attends the assessment of enterprise zones on both sides of the Atlantic. Overall, its conclusions are problematic but some reports, considered here at the outset, are more optimistic than others. In Britain, the administering Department of the Environment has retained Roger Tym and Partners for its official evaluations. The consultants' latest (1984: 141-51) report defines the primary objective of the zones as to promote the development and productive use by private interests of the designated sites and thereby create wider benefits such as *a)* securing a net increase in economic activity in areas larger than the zones themselves; and *b)* contributing to town planning or other objectives. In 1981-83 these aims were underwritten with £132.9 million of public expenditure[5] and the result was the attraction (in 15 zones) of 725 firms offering 8 065 jobs. Just under half the companies and positions were in manufacturing. Wholly new firms accounted for some 60 per cent of the entrants in 1981-82 and 1982-83 and, in the latter timespan, their employment rose to half the total. Yet these are gross effects: in net terms, probably 85 per cent of incoming firms would be operating in the same region had there been no enterprise zones. Between four and twelve per cent of completely new firms might not have started but for the zones. Perhaps ten per cent of firms achieved greater output than they would have done in the absence of the zones. The consultants concluded that the zones offer potential economic benefit but that various steps are required to ensure a successful outcome.

Formal assessment of this kind in the United States is complicated by the variation in national and state provisions and the number of zones potentially involved. Nonetheless some appeal from the federal formula is drawn in respect of employment creation by Weiner (1984: 15). He foresees that many types of structural unemployment could be reduced. The most significant assault on the problem could be the circumvention of minimum wage laws made possible by employment tax credits. Such wage subsidisation could encourage on-the-job training which would in turn reduce present and future unemployment due to mismatches of skills. A healthier local economy would lower job search and commuting costs to inner city residents and possibly reduce joblessness occasioned by locational factors. Unemployment resulting from public transfer payment disincentives and inefficient job information networks might also decline. On the other hand, the tax credits proposed are non refundable and strong capital provisions are lacking in the American package. Little may thereby be achieved in spawning new business. Further, some tax benefits could be capitalised in rent and land prices, so tempering the expansionary incentive.

To these guardedly positive evaluations can be adduced many others which are more querulous. For instance, an ever-present risk in enterprise zone development is that of providing windfall gains to business that would have developed of its own accord (Taylor, 1981: 434). This is especially so in the British "renovating" strategy in which larger-scale operations are attracted. It applies far less as one moves to the idea of trying to generate small business from within a designated area. In any case in which firms move into a zone, the possibility is raised that the development is simply pinching investment from other areas (Norcliffe and Hoare, 1982: 271). In the broad context no net growth is being created though the public sector is foregoing considerable pecuniary or non-pecuniary revenue in the process – a "deadweight" subsidy. On the other hand, there may be social value in removing blighted precincts of inner cities as opposed to developing greenfield sites and, arguably, this may not be attainable without extra social outlay.

Butler (1982: 162) has pointed out that "the net cost of an enterprise zone depends on the difference between the revenue that flows into the treasury from new companies, and the reduction in tax revenue from firms already in the zone or firms that relocate there, together with the net tax savings obtained by investors in the zone". The cost is further reduced if account is properly taken of savings in welfare costs if new work is provided to otherwise unemployed people. All this reasoning suggests that zones function better when they generate rather than redistribute business. If zones can operate by tax breaks rather than grants or incentives, a treasury "pays" only when development actually occurs. The more traditional stimuli involve a heavy "up front" commitment of public money at high risk in the hope that development will be forthcoming. Hence there are significant differences in financing implications as one moves from one conception of the enterprise zone to another. Ideally, using tax breaks, the more depressed an area is, the lower will be the cost of a programme since loss of revenue on present activity will be very small. In this way, the economics of public expenditure on enterprise zones which fulfil the intended function of generating business could be "practically the reverse of normal urban programmes" (Butler, 1982: 163).

Notwithstanding the retreat from a "pure" experiment, the emergent zones have raised significant concern in leftist circles in the United Kingdom and elsewhere. The move toward an unregulated market economy is seen as a gain for capital. Non-wage labour benefits are often reduced and a threat is perceived to the social wage itself (Harrison, 1982: 424-26). The substance of these claims depends to a certain extent on the particular enterprise zone formula in question and, given likely evolutions in implementation, may have to be judged retrospectively over a period of years. In the short-run, they leave one reflecting on the relation of the social wage and international competitiveness in an era of hypermobile capital. From another angle, Goldsmith (1982: 439) simply questions whether there will be sufficient aggregate growth to support all the intended zones.

The demarcation of zone boundaries is a specific problem but one as sensitive as that of regional delimitation (cf. Chapter III). Excluded businesses may often feel discriminated against and see themselves as bearing the cost of others' successes (cf. Massey, 1982: 431; Norcliffe and Hoare, 1982: 271). Alternatively, such firms may in due course benefit from any success not only in bordering a more vital neighbourhood but from spread effects which could enhance their property values, trading prospects or borrowing capacities.

Yet this does not exhaust objections which focus on the micro level. Jones and Manson (1982) saw significant problems in the United States' proposals which stipulated that some percentage of the employees of assisted businesses be of local (i.e. zone) origin. These and other conditions would make any zone legislation less than liberal and would misguidedly seek to recreate a nineteenth century milieu in the midst of modern cities. As well-intentioned as the new ideas may be, they are impractical in the face of empirical evidence compiled over several decades on dispersing workforce patterns.

Inducing economic activities to locate in propinquity to populations suffering high unemployment and poverty will not necessarily solve those problems. Requiring that the activities employ those populations and, what is implicit, that those populations accept those jobs addresses those problems but creates others. Making it necessary for those requirements to persist over some extended time period in the face of high rates of residential mobility, job mobility, and turnover adds difficulties an order of magnitude greater (Jones and Manson, 1982: 341).

A residential requirement issue, largely avoided in the United Kingdom, is thus a thorny one. Untoward situations can be envisaged in which zone workers might have to be fired if they chose to move to residences outside the zone. There are, however, some counter arguments. First, the problem is minimised if locally oriented small business, as opposed to other types, is generated. Second, perhaps if a primary concern is really with local employment, incoming business should be screened according to its potential to need local people. Corporations have managed to site facilities to utilise local labour at the global scale: why should it therefore be impossible for private enterprise to match labour demand and supply at the scale of several blocks in a highly familiar domestic city?

The above represent no more than a sample of views aired in the assessment of enterprise zones. Patently, the issue must be approached on a case-by-case basis since the implications of relatively subtle changes in enabling legislation can be quite marked. While it is probably true that the zone concept has had some teething troubles, few would deny that there are teeth in the original proposals and some authorities or even small states must wonder at the potential of free port status if such were wholly and readily attainable under multilateral agreements. While this linking of micro economies and the world trade scene only underlines points made earlier about the "globalisation" of competition, it should not distract attention from the lower level practicalities in integrating zones into existing policy structures and making them function as intended. Over the next few years careful monitoring of international experience would be the most sensible course to follow.

OTHER STRATEGIES

Even if enterprise zones were to become part of a fully-fledged regional strategy, they might not be deemed desirable in all OECD countries or, for that matter, other nations in the world. The establishment of economic and regional priorities is a matter for individual governments as is the focus and choice of measures adopted. Two other chief strategy possibilities are raised here: direct public intervention for regional development; and expansion of the traditional sectoral focus of regional policy (i.e. manufacturing) to include the service industries.

Direct Public Intervention

Direct public intervention in regional development has been studied by the OECD Working Party for some eighteen months, and details on European experience have now been assembled. By "direct intervention" the reference is mainly to public investment enterprises. They have developed since the first oil crisis in response to acute problems in highly disadvantaged areas. The lack of exogenous investment made it necessary in some way to stimulate endogenous potential and the investment company was one of the authorities' responses to the situation. Traditional incentives proved inadequate to attract new investment but the public sector could no longer simply remain passive.

The policy is founded on twin goals. One is to attract new investment through the creation, extension and restructuring of private companies; the other is to stimulate economic public initiative, with the state itself starting new projects and setting up or extending companies. In these activities the focus may be on specialisation in advanced products and systems with a higher value added content, promotion of technology and its industrial applications, product renewal and increases in the international exposure of firms, industrial synergy among regional enterprise and the promotion of research into new products and alternative technologies. Notwithstanding their operating environment, regional companies do not take more risks than private firms: they are not speculative operations and most have strict criteria for assisting applicants.

In Belgium, regional investment companies have three functions. They are firstly development banks, the purpose of which is to stimulate the creation, restructuring and extension of private firms; next they encourage public support and proceed to set up companies; and, finally, they carry out the industrial policy of the state and regions. Belgium now has a National Investment Corporation (SNI: Société Nationale d'Investissement) which assists small and medium firms, increases the capital of domestic or foreign joint-stock companies, sets up commercial firms in areas of importance to the economy, takes shares in firms in difficulties and establishes specialised subsidiaries for designated purposes. There are also two Regional Investment Corporations (SRI: Sociétés Régionales d'Investissement) which undertake parallel roles in individual regions. The Walloon Corporation, for example, has since 1979 purchased shares in private firms in the form of joint stock or approved co-operative arrangements, taken up convertible or ordinary bonds and engaged in loan activity for cases of restructuring. Finally, there exist Regional Development Corporations (SDR: Sociétés de Développement Régional), the function of which is to manage regional data banks, maintain sectoral interests and participate in the management of firms in difficulties.

More restricted detail is presently available for other European OECD members. In Spain, public initiative rests with a national holding which participates in heavy industry, and with regional investment companies which usually take minority positions in small or medium enterprises. In the Netherlands the main objective of regional development companies is to contribute to the strengthening of regional economic structure and the creation of employment. They stimulate the development of the regions' own potential and create a link between regional and national industry. To this end they help existing firms, especially small and medium-sized ones, to maintain their position. They provide assistance for the development of products and for innovation, and they promote as much as possible the settlement of new firms. To achieve this objective they can take participations, which may always be repurchased by the firm. Besides providing finance, development companies have the general task of promoting as much as possible the social and economic development of their region.

In Italy investment companies take temporary participations in the capital of firms which are faced with difficulties of adaptation, financing or management. The national holding IRI (Institute per la Ricostruzione Industriale), a management body with several financial subsidiaries and several hundred operating companies, takes permanent positions mainly in heavy industry, aeronautics and telecommunications as well as through oil and electricity holdings (Kreile, 1983: 199). Of interest are pointers from a senior official of IRI concerning the role in regional development of public investment (Wade, 1977: 189-90).

i) Parity between public and private companies must be preserved. The objective of management must be profit maximisation within given constraints. The private sector must understand that public companies will not be subsidised and that the overall aim is to augment, not reduce, private investment;

ii) Holdings must be multisectoral with both up and downstream industries to encourage spinoff or satellite developments;

iii) Public companies should not be limited in advance as to which sectors they can enter;

iv) Public industry is unlikely to be successful with small-scale enterprise;

v) Public industry alone cannot be relied upon to solve regional problems.

Due to its operations, the public sector controls 30 per cent of overall investments in Italy. It is to be remarked that public holdings are legally obliged to direct their major new initiatives to the south of the country.

In Sweden the purpose of regional companies is to promote the industrial growth of development regions. They were created mainly because traditional aid proved insufficient to tackle the regionally concentrated structural problems (steel and shipbuilding) and because more active methods were needed to create new industrial jobs. In the form of participations the necessary financial means for reconversion to new products are awarded to troubled firms and capital is granted to small and medium-sized companies. Sweden also has companies dealing with product development and others which grant assistance to firm managers. In the last year or so, Swedish policy has increasingly been that public companies should be run along similar lines to private sector firms.

In France, many direct aid bodies have been created for the promotion of investments. Their aims are both broad and diverse. Subordinated loans (prêts participatifs) are non-guaranteed loans assimilated to company equity to finance programmes for efficient small and medium-sized enterprises. They can be used in France or abroad. As another example, regional development corporations (SDR: Sociétés de Développement Régional) aim to strengthen the equity of expanding enterprises, offer medium term credit and long-term loans and to engage in property leasing. In general, the major French priorities lie with small and medium enterprise and with industrial reconversion.

This account of the role of public investment companies thus reveals an overwhelming concern among policymakers with regionally concentrated problems. Direct intervention has sometimes been the only feasible initial strategy with which to deal with the loss of a region's sole industry. Once the acute situations have been addressed, the companies were able to take a positive role in fostering endogenous development with the major focus on small or medium enterprise. It should be stressed that public investment companies wish to carry out their projects in full co-operation with and not against the private sector. Generally they prefer to take minority participations and to transfer them to the private sector if the latter wishes to acquire them.

As with enterprise zones, these companies represent an adjunct to traditional (i.e. "departmental") regional policy. Perhaps some current instruments or measures will eventually have to be dropped to make way for them. Whether the companies are integrated into the existing policy framework or supplant part of it will be a matter of note for several OECD countries. Of equal concern in the staffing of such companies will be to ensure that financiers (the acknowledged experts on a case-by-case basis) are matched with economists or other social scientists who will promote broad goals and undertake the necessary performance evaluations. Otherwise there is some danger of not seeing the forest for the trees.

Service Industry

Goods are material, permanent, made by people using machines and are sold or otherwise distributed to people who may use them at their will. Services, by contrast, are immaterial, impermanent, made by people for people and consumable only at the instant of production (Gershuny, 1978: 56). They fall into two classes: producer services are used within the commercial sector by firms, whereas consumer services are final ones provided directly to consumers.

In every country of the OECD, the share of civilian employment in services has risen since 1960 (Table 4.3). For the Organisation as a whole, the percentage rose from 43 to 58 in 1982. As Gershuny and Miles (1983: 1) have observed, employment in services is a critical issue for industrial countries in the 1980s. Until quite recently, it was assumed that, even if jobs were increasingly lost in manufacturing and other traditional sectors, the expansion of services would easily maintain employment levels (Daniels, 1983: 301). Now, growing doubt attends the idea of a smooth transition to a "service economy" or "post-industrial society". This is in part because services, like manufacturing, are rapidly automating. Collier (1983) provides ample evidence of trends in branches of services which were erstwhile strongly labour intensive. A Boeing 747, for example, is not simply an aeroplane, but actually a highly productive fixed-sequence robot which has revolutionised transportation. More particularly, new information technology is likely to enhance productivity in many other parts of the service economy (OECD, 1980c: 88).

It is reasonable to say that for much of the postwar period the relationship of regional policy and the service industries has been tentative or even cautious. Marquand (1980b: 14) has listed the main regional policies in four groups. They include those which:

a) Relate only to (all or some) tertiary activity;
b) Include the tertiary sector on broadly the same basis as the secondary sector (although often with special qualifications or restrictions);
c) Explicitly exclude tertiary activities and thereby constitute a bias against them; and
d) Are really national policies but have a significant bearing on the regional distribution of services.

Her analysis among European Community countries found that in Belgium, Denmark, Germany, Italy and the Netherlands, regional policies for service industries differed only in minor respects from those applying to manufacturing [type (b)]. In France, Luxembourg, Ireland and the United Kingdom there are some specially designed schemes [type (a)], though the last also had some exclusionary [type (c)] measures. The most important national policies with regional repercussions for service activities included tourism planning and

90

initiatives for public sector decentralisation. Many countries have planning and licensing policies, while controls have also existed in the United Kingdom, France and the Netherlands. The location of office activity has been a matter of central importance.

The same enquiry uncovered a quantitative and usually a qualitative bias in favour of manufacturing in terms of aids granted. A rough distinction could be drawn between countries with a broad approach to the issue of the tertiary sector in regional policy, viewing it in terms of the overall development and well-being of less favoured regions, and those with a narrower perspective which saw manufacturing as the chief means to enhance regional employment and income. Marquand (1980*b*: 15) concluded that the United Kingdom, France, the Netherlands, Luxembourg and Italy had demonstrated the more active or wide-ranging approach (see also OECD, 1978*a*: 37-39).

A number of arguments have been advanced as to why aids to services should be more restricted than those to manufacturing (cf. Daniels, 1983: 304-05). It is contended, for example, that they provide welfare gains of very limited duration; that their productivity is lower; that they may not be export-promoting or import-substituting, but oriented only to the domestic needs of a local population; hence, that the support of new entry to the sector might simply jeopardise existing businesses; and, finally, that services are not as worthy of assistance as genuinely footloose industries. Without going into detail, one can note that such arguments are effectively dismissed in the report to the Commission of the European Communities. It holds that there is no case for withholding aids from service activities in areas where manufacturing is eligible except in the case of some consumer services in markets which are already adequately supplied (Marquand, 1980*b*: 19). On the other hand, some discrimination among types of services is recommended to regional policymakers. Producer services (and office occupations) tend to concentrate in certain regions and parts of regions and especially in larger cities with rich infrastructural and contact networks. Consumer services instead serve mainly local populations. Generally, the best prospects for effective regional policy in the tertiary arena lie with the producer services, notably higher-level ones. Some evidence from the United Kingdom and Denmark has indicated their potential willingness to choose assisted area locations, and sufficiently strong and well-designed programmes may be able to offset their tendency otherwise to cluster in core areas (Marquand, 1980*b*: 13). The European Economic Community regional fund regulation stipulates that assistance can only be forwarded to tourism and those services which have a choice of location. This clearly includes many of the higher level producer services: but the point of the rule in actually prohibiting aid to other types of business which are most likely market-oriented is sensible as an anti-protectionist device.

Possibly the issue of regional and service industry policy has been explored more fully in Europe than in other parts of the OECD (cf. OECD, 1978*a*: 37-40). There can be little doubt, however, that as opportunities for achieving spatial development through manufacturing become more restricted, the services will attract increasing attention as an agent of potential growth. Could they, indeed, become the only truly prospective focus of regional initiatives, most manufacturing-oriented policy constituting essentially a holding operation? This question raises much broader arguments as to the future of services and, through them, the prospects for employment growth. A number of angles are worth reviewing.

In 1978, Gershuny put forward the view that, at least for the United Kingdom, the consumption of services as a proportion of total consumption had actually fallen in the foregoing 20 years. He identified a process of substitution: services previously provided from outside households were increasingly replaced by production *within* households using the capital goods of manufacturing industry. Technological development had enabled provision on a much more capital intensive basis in which not only household but also business

91

Table 4.3. **Employment in services as percentage of civilian employment, OECD countries, 1960-82**

	1960	1970	1975	1980	1981	1982	60-67	68-73	74-79	80-82	60-82
United States	56.2	61.1	65.4	65.9	66.4	68.0	57.9	61.5	65.0	66.8	61.9
Japan	41.3	46.9	51.5	54.2	54.7	55.4	42.9	47.5	52.3	54.8	48.1
Germany	39.1	42.9	47.6	50.3	51.0	51.8	40.4	43.6	48.4	51.0	44.7
France	38.5	46.4	51.1	55.3	56.2	57.2	40.8	46.8	52.5	56.2	47.4
United Kingdom	47.6	52.0	56.7	59.6	61.5	62.6	49.1	52.8	57.2	61.2	53.8
Italy	33.5	40.3	44.2	47.9	49.1	50.6	35.9	40.4	45.4	49.2	41.3
Canada	54.1	61.4	64.6	66.0	66.3	68.2	56.1	61.5	64.8	66.9	61.2
Total of above countries	45.9	51.8	56.5	58.9	59.7	60.9	47.8	52.3	57.0	59.8	53.0
Austria	35.7	43.2	47.9	50.8	51.7	52.8	38.4	43.8	48.8	51.8	44.3
Belgium	46.4	52.0	56.5	62.3	63.6	64.7	47.8	52.7	58.2	63.5	53.9
Denmark	44.8	50.7	58.8	62.4	63.3	64.0	46.9	..	..	63.3	..
Finland	26.3	38.6	46.3	51.8	51.9	53.0	30.7	39.9	48.8	52.2	40.6
Greece	25.5	34.2	36.8	39.5	40.3	41.9	28.2	34.3	37.5	40.6	33.9
Iceland	42.4	44.0	47.5	49.8	51.7	52.0	42.1	44.8	48.3	51.2	45.6
Ireland	39.0	43.1	45.8	49.1	50.6	51.5	39.8	43.0	46.7	50.4	43.8
Luxembourg	38.4	46.8	50.3	56.7	57.4	58.5	40.3	..	52.6	57.5	..
Netherlands	49.7	54.9	59.4	63.6	65.2	66.3	51.0	55.6	60.7	65.0	56.6
Norway	42.9	48.8	56.4	61.8	61.7	62.5	45.0	..	58.1	62.0	..
Portugal	24.4	37.1	32.2	35.5	36.8	37.0	28.2	36.6	33.0	36.4	..
Spain	31.0	37.4	39.7	45.1	46.6	47.8	33.9	37.7	41.6	46.5	38.5
Sweden	44.0	53.5	57.1	62.2	63.1	64.1	46.1	53.4	59.0	63.1	53.6
Switzerland	38.9	45.5	50.8	53.3	53.7	54.5	40.3	45.9	51.6	53.8	46.5
Turkey	13.4	19.2	21.3	23.1	23.5	23.9	16.0	19.2	22.2	23.5	19.5
Smaller European	31.2	38.4	41.2	45.0	45.8	46.6	33.7	38.7	42.4	45.8	38.9
Australia	50.1	55.0	59.4	62.4	62.8	63.7	52.0	55.5	60.5	63.0	56.5
New Zealand	46.8	48.6	53.5	55.4	56.0	55.7	47.6	50.7	53.9	55.7	51.1
Total Smaller	32.7	39.9	43.1	46.8	47.6	48.4	35.3	40.3	44.2	47.6	40.5
Total EEC	40.2	46.0	50.5	53.9	55.0	56.1	42.1	46.5	51.5	55.0	47.4
Total OECD-Europe	36.6	42.8	46.6	50.1	51.1	52.0	38.8	43.2	47.6	51.1	43.8
Total OECD less US	38.5	44.8	48.9	52.2	53.1	54.0	40.6	45.3	49.9	53.1	45.9
Total OECD	43.0	49.2	53.6	56.4	57.2	58.3	45.0	49.7	54.3	57.3	50.3

Source: OECD (1984a: 37)

consumers could serve themselves. Growth in service employment had emerged from medicine and education but that could contract as such services were automated. The other source was expansion in services dealing with the ownership of material goods (distribution, banking, finance and insurance), and in occupations which improved the efficiency of material production (managers, technologists and so on). Though growth in these particular fields was likely to continue, progress toward a self-service economy inevitably entailed critical problems of unemployment such that a small and highly productive elite could more than serve the bulk of society in privatised, nucleated households.

A later book by Gershuny and Miles (1983) takes fuller account of the recent revolution in communications and computing. Whereas privatising had been argued as influential in the future demand for services, information technology was seen as important in establishing an infrastructure through which a new range of social innovations could be transmitted. Prospects for economic growth may lie with such innovations as final service functions. The overall employment implications of the introduction of new technologies remain uncertain until a clearer view can be obtained of the types of innovations which could be forthcoming.

These are essentially market-led prescriptions on the future of services which give considerable latitude to economic forces. They imply, however, that assistance by regional authorities to service industries should be well-researched lest counterintuitive and potentially counterproductive outcomes prevail. For instance, could officials find themselves aiding the establishment of 100 jobs in a firm, the products of which will displace 500 other workers in the region within a decade? This might well obtain in some producer service industries. On the other hand, as an aid to employment, should efforts be made to arrest any trend of privatisation into households of service delivery? If so, can "real" services and jobs be provided or does the economy end up as one of touts and tinkers, as can presently be seen in various parts of the world featuring disguised unemployment[6]? These issues (relevant also to small business development) are not readily resolvable and now, for different reasons than before, the cautious attitude to the service sector among regional policymakers might be more easily defensible.

Notwithstanding these caveats, the importance of understanding the potential of services in spatial development emerges from an United States analysis by Noyelle (1983). It argues that, left to market forces, advanced services will continue to concentrate most vigorously in the core of the urban system. Centralisation has been the general pattern among such producer services as banking and finance, transport, advertising and consulting. Though some ambivalence has characterised the location of national headquarters and divisional offices of large firms, levels of concentration remained essentially intact in the period 1960-80. Yet there were also certain examples of decentralising tendencies, in data processing, warehousing and trucking for example. The policy implications of these trends call for planners to examine the economic base of their city or region in an attempt to encourage types of service (and other) activity which will enable adjustment to cyclical or structural change in the future. Daniels' (1983: 306-07) agenda of necessary research topics is only the starting point.

CONCLUSIONS

Simultaneously, the task of regional policy has become more complex and it is under closer political scrutiny than before. For the 1980s, the assignment is more than one of siting an apparently endless supply of factories. Forthcoming regional development may have an aggregative or distributional focus depending on a country's position with regard to two key variables – the endogenous or exogenous control of its economic enterprise and its level of and capacity for technology. The examination of control possibilities in this chapter suggested that new investment is likely to be hard-won and greater reliance is indicated on endogenous development. Endogenous development, however, may impose new demands on regional policymakers and will require the creative use of instruments described in Chapter III. Growing interrelationships are foreseen among regional and a variety of other policy arenas, the cases of small and medium business and enterprise zones being illustrative. Some success towards the substantive goals of regional development could be equally forthcoming from direct public intervention or a focus on service industries, though the latter may be problematic as a result of technological factors. These are, of course, the other element in the suggested model of regional development. They are explored in detail in the next chapter.

NOTES

1. This point should be clearly understood. Enterprise zones are spatially tiny. They are only one facet of urban policy and their administration is usually handled by urban affairs departments. They are discussed in this chapter because of the underlying interest of the idea for regional policy and to clarify various misconceptions which appear to have arisen surrounding them.

2. The "freeport" idea was revived in the 1983 Budget (Botham and Lloyd, 1983: 26) and several separate freeports now exist in the United Kingdom.

3. In Belgium employment zones known as T zones have been established in Flanders and Wallonia and a number of enterprises have already located in them. The T zones, each of which covers an area of 150 hectares, are situated in development areas and are aimed at creating a favourable climate for investment in advanced, employment-creating sectors by means of fiscal advantages.

4. Kansas, Missouri, Illinois, Louisiana, Kentucky, Ohio, Florida, Maryland and Connecticut. The various programmes cover 180 zones (Weiner, 1984: 10, 15).

5. According to Norcliffe and Hoare (1982: 270-72), the total cost over a decade of the British programme may be £1.4 billion. Accordingly, the authors imply that its relationship to urban, regional or employment policy could stand closer definition.

6. The present account does not attempt to extend this argument into a consideration of the underground economy which may be highly significant in some countries. For an introduction, see Gershuny (1979) and OECD (1982*d*).

Chapter V

TECHNOLOGY AND REGIONAL POLICY

In a world recoiling from a decade of recession, "technology" has emerged as a factor important for many sectoral aims and potentially capable of restoring growth and prosperity. In the United States, a recent Department of Commerce (1983: iii) report recognised significant gains to the economy from high technology industry: its low growth of prices combined with great increases in productivity which enhance living standards; its output growth twice that of national manufacturing; its contribution to trade and competitiveness; and its importance for defence and security.

These aggregate achievements are widely endorsed – perhaps the only major question concerns the impact of technology on employment. Study of spatial repercussions has occupied the OECD Working Party since the Stockholm Ministerial Meeting of April 1982 and has fostered continued optimism in the applicability of regional policy. By late 1983 the group was ready to comment that:

> Innovations and new technologies have advanced rapidly in recent years but their effect has been most beneficial in terms of employment and industrial expansion in the countries and regions most able to develop or apply them. These are not necessarily the weaker regions. However, a positive implication is that their location factors may permit their establishment in weaker regions, and in some countries a new feature of regional policies has been to link technological progress with planned regional development.

Clearly, the task of accommodating technological development and wedding it to regional objectives will not be easy – perhaps no easier than dealing with the contractionary problems of 1974-83 raised in foregoing chapters. Yet the necessity was underscored by the remark of a delegate to the OECD Workshop on Research, Technology and Regional Policy in Paris in October 1983:

> We have squarely to face the fact that, with or without government intervention, new technologies will shortly become established in our production systems. In ten or at the most 15 years' time, they will become commonplace and it will be too late to turn around and deplore the fact that they are unequally distributed throughout our countries. This consideration is the driving force in land-use planning.

The extent to which aims will be achieved in Member countries is presently an open question. The Workshop did not produce a doctrine but rather a method for approaching, examining and solving some of the problems raised by balanced development of regions during a period of crisis and technological change. Having established workable definitions of terms and reviewed the genesis of technological change, this chapter goes further to explore key factors which will determine future impacts. Pointers and options are drawn from study of several existing high technology complexes but futures other than the highest technology ones are also validated for regional development. Finally, certain of the more problematic issues in regional technological development are raised with respect to advanced educational institutions, firms and government.

PARAMETERS OF TECHNOLOGICAL CHANGE

"Technology is simply the way things are done" (Macdonald, 1983: 331). This definition cuts through a lot of the woolliness which has surrounded the concept in economics. There, technology has been regarded as shifting production possibility curves rather than inducing movement along them. The difficulty is that, whereas conventional inputs can be regarded as contributing directly at any given time, technology influences production over a longer period. Excluded as a short-run factor, it thus becomes an exogenous variable in most production functions. Generally, economists have seen technology as embodied in capital stock, introduced when the discounted stream of future benefits exceeds costs (including normal profits) by an amount greater than foregone net benefits using old equipment (Clark, 1971: 309). While it is correct to conduct any evaluations in net present value terms, it should be remembered that technology refers not just to development in capital (hardware) but also to organisation (Cappellin, 1983: 464-65). This has been made clear in a venerable definition which asserts that:

> Technological change is the advance of technology, such advance often taking the form of new methods of producing existing products, new designs which enable the production of products with important new characteristics, and new techniques of organisation, marketing and management (Mansfield, 1968: 10-11).

Though there are other definitions of technology or technological change, most stress variation in factor inputs per unit of output, the revision of techniques or technical possibilities, and matters related to the body of information, skills and experience required for the production and consumption of goods and services. Technological change must be held apart from the diffusion of existing information. A piece of knowledge is considered a technological change when first discovered but not when passed between parties. Even so, its effect on the recipient may parallel that of discovery on the donor (Australian Science and Technology Council, 1983: 26). This is but one issue in the genesis of technological change which must be appreciated by regional policymakers. Further aid is derived from two models, that of the product cycle and Kondratieff waves. They offer a grounding for a consideration of levels of technology currently exhibited in productive enterprise.

The Product Cycle

A useful approach to the theory of product cycles is the distinction between process and product technological change (cf. Thwaites, 1983: 36). The former refers to modifications in operations to: improve the quality of a good or service; remove hazards; simplify processes; and reduce price to facilitate market penetration, competitiveness and profitability. Process innovations are used within the industry concerned and characterise the manufacture of food products, iron and steel, vehicles, textiles and clothing, and leather and footwear (Pavitt, 1983: 5). As such they often involve labour-displacing capital alteration. Alternatively, in certain cases, the process development can increase labour requirements if the growth in product demand exceeds that of labour productivity.

96

Product technological change usually applies outside its sector of origin. It will regularly raise employment levels in an enterprise by requiring the production of new or modified goods and services. The only catch is that to the extent that the new product substitutes for or replaces an existing good, employment (and other resources) could be freed in competing enterprises. In practice it is often difficult to distinguish process from product innovation since the former can also modify product form. There is a constant interplay in technological change between labour-increasing and displacing forces though in recessions the latter may dominate. Ultimately desirable are completely novel product innovations but they are rather rare since change is incremental and evolutionary rather than revolutionary in character (cf. Australian Science and Technology Council, 1983: 29).

The relation between product and process development can be conceptualised, first, in the innovation cycle (Malecki, 1981a: 294-96). In the history of a new product, the initial concerns are with its functional performance which could be sub-optimal due to inadequate production machinery, organisation and so on. The second phase is concerned with production variation to exploit opportunities created by expanding internal capability. Individual products now become high-volume, allowing process innovation to improve manufacturing techniques. The third phase emphasizes cost reduction through incremental variations to both products (now essentially standardised) and processes.

This innovation model complements a product cycle model developed from work on trade theory at the Harvard Business School. It argues likewise that products undergo three distinct stages in their life cycle: an innovation stage during which a new good or service is introduced in a home region and diffused into new markets via exports; a growth stage in which interregional and international demand expand sufficiently to allow foreign investment and the transfer of process technology; and a standardisation phase in which production can be shifted to low cost locations. As Rees (1979: 48) indicates, firms have to expand internationally if they are to prolong the standardization phase of the cycle and they must also innovate to create new cycles. Each stage thus has different spatial manifestations. The innovation phase which demands continuing research and development, product adaptation, testing and standardization is usually carried out in a technology-rich area, often near a firm's home base (Oakey, 1984a: 157). Standardized activities, by contrast, favour low-cost peripheral areas, one possibility being that, with sufficient agglomeration of production and local demand, they could themselves evolve as a focus of innovations. In the event, a common outcome of this structural differentiation is a spatial division of labour which separates high-skill, well-paid innovative and administrative jobs to settings quite apart from those of low-skill, low-wage jobs involved in standardized operations. Malecki (1981a: 292; 1983: 100-01) provides extensive documentation of such tendencies for the United States and France and additionally points out that a region is specialised if it has only standardized manufacturing, notwithstanding its diversification among several industries.

Recently, observers have considered that specialisation at the innovation end of the product cycle is a strategically sound posture. The ability to innovate is seen to underwrite the generation of new firms and the urban growth of an area. Schumpeter (1942: 81-86) saw capitalist innovation as a process of "creative destruction" producing new economic structures in new locations which by-pass existing facilities which become obsolete. This has certainly been the experience of economies such as the United Kingdom and United States and corresponds with the dismantling of much traditional industry in advanced countries which has occupied this book to date. Technology may thus provide a dialectic of aggregative and disaggregative forces in regional development, introducing the possibility of waves of activity at sub-national levels (Rees, 1979: 52).

Waves of Change

Toffler's (1980) popular idea of waves of change is endorsed in conventional analyses proceeding from the seminal work of Kondratieff in the 1920s. From examinations of a number of economic indicators, Kondratieff (1935) postulated the existence of long-term trends of activity based on eras of fifty or sixty years and suggested that when one of these "waves" of expansion got underway, innovations that had remained dormant would find commercial application. In 1939, Schumpeter specified the case by suggesting technological change as the stimulus to the waves. He argued not only that innovations concentrated in groups but also that the diffusion process was continuous: it was possible to associate a major innovation with an economic cycle. Thus, steam power dominated the first Kondratieff wave (1818-42), railways the second (1843-97) and electricity and automobiles the third (1898-1949). Later writers have regarded the postwar years as a fourth cycle based on the development, accelerated by the Second World War, of technological possibilities apparent since the 1920s (cf. Rothwell, 1982: 364). The 1950s saw the flowering of "new" industries such as electronics, synthetics, solid-state devices, agro- and petrochemicals and pharmaceuticals. In a dynamic growth phase till the mid-1960s many new manufacturing jobs were created in advanced societies. As has been shown, industrial maturity and stagnation emerged in the 1970s and process rather than product innovation prevailed in the now highly concentrated new fields of production. Few commentators are prepared to guarantee that the 1980s will bring a lift from the trough of the fourth Kondratieff wave (cf. Jones, 1982: 15), despite the incipient revival in the United States and some other economies[1]. On the other hand, the foundations may have been laid in the mid-1970s in impressive breakthroughs in microelectronics which promise to revolutionise many products and aspects of human living. Apart from these innovations, work is proceeding in a number of fields now regarded as "high technology".

Levels of Technological Activity

The foregoing theories view the industrial or service economy as characterised at any time by sectors surging ahead in technology while others may be making little progress. Within any sector, there will be "leading-edge" and "follower" firms to say nothing of marginal enterprises with truly outmoded product or process technology which would be eliminated by any fall in prices received (Taylor, 1983: 106-07). In addition, the technological capacities of a firm extend over several functions: research and development, production, administration, marketing and so on. Given this matrix of possibilities it is understandably hard to define levels of technology in a broad sense. Much private and public sector interest now attends "high technology" but analysis has so far been hampered for want of accurate delineations. The term does not equate with research and development since basic or low technology products can be researched. It is doubtful whether high technology production facilities correspond in location with the general pattern of "research and development" establishments (cf. Buswell, 1983: 15-17). Indeed, the spirit rather than the letter of high technology has proved easier to define. The former is explained by Macdonald (1983: 331):

High technology is high ... because of the relatively high risk involved, the possibility of high return, its high pace of change and its high information intensity. Those are the characteristics ... against which national comparative advantage should be assessed.

Addressing the same question, the United States Department of Commerce (1983: 3) argued that high technology industries are characterised by the simultaneous presence of two characteristics: *a)* an above-average level of scientific and engineering skills and capabilities compared to other industries; and *b)* a rapid rate of technological development. Research and development inputs relative to sales are usually high and, in most cases, industries feature a relatively large number of small firms (Malecki, 1981*a*: 291).

Concerted attempts to nominate actual examples of "high technology" in the last two years have inevitably devolved on product characteristics. The OECD considered the question in 1983 for purposes of trade analysis. It resorted eventually to the United States Department of Commerce (1983: 35-36) list of high technology products, the so-called DOC-2 list. It consists of eleven categories: aircraft and parts; computers and office equipment; electrical equipment and components; optical and medical instruments; drugs and medicines; plastic and synthetic materials; engines and turbines; agricultural chemicals; professional and scientific instruments; industrial chemicals; and radio and television receiving equipment. The United States department, however, warned that, even at the most disaggregated level, product data frequently contain technology-intensive and non-intensive goods. Moreover, high technology industries are by definition dynamic. Thus a product or industry list must be expected to change.

Australia took a somewhat different approach, forging its high technology policy around 16 "sunrise" industries seen as offering the foundations for future development (Jones, 1983: 44). They include biotechnology, personal computers, computer software, custom-made computer chips, scientific instrumentation, medical technologies, lasers, communication technology, industrial ceramics, solar technology, shape memory alloys, fusion, robots, intermediate technology products, hydrogen generation and storage, and biomass. While this list is congruent with Macdonald's definition, it covers both products and technologies (e.g. lasers) which is perhaps less "pure" than the United States' approach. It also combines manufacturing and service activities. Notwithstanding these points, it is usefully considered as adding to our idea of high technology. Both approaches, American and Australian, underscore the need for regional analysts carefully to define their terms in an area of discussion as vague as it is vogue.

HIGH TECHNOLOGY COMPLEXES

Throughout the world, a number of areas have become the meccas of high technology, as witnessed by the regular pilgrimages they receive from industrialists, civil servants and politicians. It is worthwhile to consider some of them here to see what lessons they offer from the viewpoint of regional policy. In this respect, a classification is relevant. Steed and DeGenova (1983: 264-65) have proposed four types: *a)* centres produced principally from the growth of indigenous firms and their spinoffs; *b)* research-oriented centres usually oriented to a park site; *c)* centres developed by attracting manufacturing facilities of high technology companies; and d) ones resulting from large expenditures of public funding. These groupings are not mutually exclusive and each source of growth may contribute to the development of a complex. The examples reviewed come from Canada, the United States, the United Kingdom and France.

Canada: Agglomeration in Ottawa

Canada, like other OECD nations, has been affected deleteriously by the post-1974 recession. Yet this period has seen the rise of a technology-oriented complex in the federal capital region of Ottawa-Carleton-Hull, one which before knew no major manufacturing activity. Unusual interest therefore attaches to the development which by 1980 employed over 15 000 people with projections of up to 100 000 by 1990 (Steed and DeGenova, 1983: 265).

The region's advantages are characterised broadly as accessibility to the federal government; the existence of some public corporations; a well-developed science and technology research infrastructure; opportunities for government sales; and an attractive sociocultural and recreational environment of appeal to the necessary workforce of scientists and technical personnel. The major activities concern electronics, telecommunications equipment, avionics, scientific equipment and medical instruments. They have a high value to weight ratio and so are unimpeded by transport costs. They sell on performance before price, often to industrial, government or institutional markets.

According to Steed and DeGenova (1983: 266) from whom the present account is taken, the complex began as early as 1920 as a fledgling research milieu [Type (b)], the driving force being the Canadian National Research Council. Government funding for the sake of indigenous research and development capability during the Second World War was characteristic of Type (d) development. After 1960 manufacturing facilities [Type (c)] began to show interest in the area, spawning various offshoots throughout the 1970s [Type (a)]. By 1982, nine high technology firms near Ottawa had individually over 300 employees, the largest pair engaging nearly 2 000 each.

Speed and DeGenova (1983) provide one of the few empirical accounts of a high technology complex based on a survey of 45 firms in the Ottawa complex. They were principally very young (60 per cent less than ten years old) and in aggregate had doubled their employment since 1976. The vast majority were domestically owned, though nearly a third of employment was provided in foreign subsidiaries. Key location factors were the federal presence, the original residence of company founders, or the existence of other high technology firms. In spite of this last factor, companies generally purchase and sell less than a

Table 5.1. **Executives' ratings of ability of eleven cities to satisfy their firms' locational requirements, Ottawa Technology Complex, Canada, 1981**

Alternative city	Total number of responses	Very satisfactory 1		Satisfactory 2		Acceptable 3		Unsatisfactory 4		Very unsatisfactory 5		Less than acceptable (columns 4 and 5)
		No.	%	No.	%	No.	%	No.	%	No.	%	%
Halifax	38	0	0.0	3	7.9	5	13.2	8	21.1	22	57.9	79.0
Montreal	39	5	12.8	7	17.9	8	20.5	11	28.2	8	20.5	48.7
Ottawa	44	28	63.6	12	27.3	3	6.8	1	2.3	0	0.0	2.3
Toronto	40	15	37.5	16	40.0	6	15.0	2	5.0	1	2.5	7.5
Hamilton	37	3	8.1	5	13.5	10	27.0	11	29.7	8	21.6	51.3
Kitchener-Waterloo	37	4	10.8	7	18.9	11	29.7	9	24.3	6	16.2	40.5
London	38	1	2.6	7	18.4	10	26.3	10	26.3	10	26.3	52.6
Winnipeg	38	1	2.6	5	13.2	7	18.4	13	34.2	12	31.6	65.8
Edmonton	38	2	5.3	6	15.8	7	18.4	12	31.6	11	28.9	60.5
Calgary	38	3	7.9	11	28.9	8	21.1	6	15.8	10	26.3	42.1
Vancouver	36	4	11.1	7	19.4	11	30.6	8	22.2	6	16.7	38.9

Source: Steed and DeGenova (1983: 275).

quarter of their inputs or outputs around Ottawa: all export internationally up to 40 per cent of their volume.

Finally, an interesting aspect of the Steed/DeGenova survey was an exploration of potential "footlooseness" among companies. Accepting the usual cautions about subjective and hypothetical questions, the authors gauged the acceptability or otherwise of major Canadian cities to subject companies. Results are shown in Table 5.1. Ottawa and Toronto were clearly preferred high technology sites among this sample of Canadian entrepreneurs. By contrast, rather peripheral locations such as Halifax or Winnipeg were rejected by a majority of respondents. The authors (1983: 276) conclude: "(the) figures ... reveal a disjunctive spatial surface, with substantial differences among Canadian cities in their acceptability as locations for high-technology firms with the sorts of requirements apparently considered important by the innovative denizens of Ottawa's sunrise strip".

This detailed Canadian study, then, shows several factors of note to the regional analyst: a) the ability of technology centres to attract firm creation and employment growth in spite of a depressed macro environment; b) the importance of a governmental nucleus; c) the contributions to growth from different sources as a centre develops; and d) the "bounded footlooseness" of occupants. Overall, Steed and DeGenova (1983: 267) rate Ottawa as a "second-rank" concentration of high-technology activity, more akin to the United States' North Carolina Research Triangle than to Boston's Route 128 or California's Silicon Valley. It is to these complexes that discussion now turns.

United States: The Archetypes

More than the Canadian example, the three United States technology complexes to be reviewed here[2] trace their origins to facilities in higher education. Research Triangle Park in North Carolina was jointly developed by the three major universities which lie at its apexes in the small towns of Durham (100 000 people), Raleigh (150 000) and Chapel Hill (50 000). The park, which claims to be the largest planned research park in the world [United States (Congress), 1982: 46], opened in 1959 on a largely unoccupied site of 5 800 hectares which was formerly infertile farming land supporting pine woods. Occupancy is limited to organisations engaged in research, development and scientifically-oriented production though some flexibility was exercised in 1965 to allow IBM to enter the area and engage in aspects of computer manufacture (Hamley, 1982: 61). Early land sales by the managing agency, the non-profit Research Triangle Foundation, were slow but in 1970 Burroughs Welcome, the pharmaceutical corporation, was attracted by the specialised biological and medical research capabilities for which Duke University and the University of North Carolina were noted. By the early 1980s over 40 tenants had established including Data General and Northern Telecom (electronics), Becton Dickinson (life sciences), the United States Environmental Protection Agency, the National Centre for Health Statistics and several State research agencies (Walker, 1983: 47). Recently, General Electric announced plans to build a $US 50 million microelectronic research and development plant there.

The Park has strict covenants including large lot sizes and low plot ratios to protect its wooded environment and a sizeable portion of land is still to be developed. The locale offers a "sunbelt" climate, favourable business tax structure, low unionisation, low land costs, lack of pollution and the prospect of profitable partnerships with the universities or other firms. Currently, around 20 000 people are employed, this figure again representing the summation of sustained growth despite the era of recession. The region's lifestyle has become one of the Park's strongest selling points (Cruze, 1983: 9). According to Walker (1983: 42), it blends two trends in urban growth in the United States: information-based industry and small city living. The regional planner might add that the "critical mass" of three co-operating universities, together with active local and state government support, was instrumental in what has been achieved.

Boston's Route 128 agglomeration is probably the oldest high technology complex in the United States [cf. United States (Congress), 1982: 43-44]. The State of Massachusetts has long supported a large machinery industry to serve textile and other mills. During the Second World War, the emphasis shifted to supplying defence and, later, space contractors, all of which led development increasingly towards electronics industries. By 1961, the Boston ring-road, Route 128, was a 130 kilometre semicircle with over 300 offices and factories (Mazur, 1984: 67). The figure was soon to double as local developers began to provide industrial park settings. Now firms are moving to greener pastures like Route 495, still only half an hour from Boston but with less expensive land. Such diffusion causes authors like Dorfman (1983) to discuss as the high technology economy the State of Massachusetts rather than Route 128 or Boston itself.

By some measures, this State leads the other 49 in its share of high technology employment in manufacturing, though California, New York and Illinois have absolutely more workers. The development in Massachusetts has been largely indigenous [Steed and DeGenova Type (a)], depending on local starts and spinoffs but, as Malecki (1981b: 76) has pointed out, Boston has also benefitted substantially from federal defence (but not space) contracts so elements of Steed and DeGenova's Type (d) centre growth must also be admitted. The same pattern is characteristic of California's Silicon Valley.

The two complexes, however, have different foci. Massachusetts is principally concerned with the research, development and production of mini-computers, being the headquarters of such firms as the Digital Equipment Corporation (DEC), Data General, and Wang. These and other companies also manufacture accessories and peripherals (including word processors) but attention concentrates on the producer capital market. Massachusetts' growth has been based on product innovation and many industries, including important new ventures in biotechnology (Mazur, 1984: 64-65), aim at relatively specialised markets. The interrelations within the complex are apparent in the character of leading industries by employment: electronic components and accessories, office computing and accounting machines, communications equipment, measuring and controlling instruments, photographic equipment and supplies, and guided missiles and space vehicles (Dorfman, 1983: 302).

Briefly, what accounts for Massachusetts' ascendancy? Several factors seem critical. The state has a tertiary education infrastructure which some consider the finest in the world. Institutions such as the Massachusetts Institute of Technology and Harvard University excel in high technology fields and are strongly integrated with the business community. The cultural and natural attractions of the region ensure that graduates choose to remain around Boston, providing the necessary skilled labour supply for industry and, potentially, a pool of entrepreneurs to commence new businesses. The technological infrastructure provided by small and large firms is extensive, covering both hard and software. The external and agglomerative economies manifest themselves in a capacity for rapid delivery of materials and services which is critical for high technology operations. The complex is sufficiently prominent to have built up a venture capital market – 40 firms in Boston alone (Mazur, 1984: 66). Finally, the area had a significant headstart on many other parts of North America.

In spite of all these advantages, the Route 128 case shows that no region is invulnerable to market forces and economic change. Mazur's (1984) article is largely concerned with setbacks suffered after the late 1960s. Defence contracts dwindled in the post-Vietnam era and Massachusetts lost its competitive grasp of the semiconductor industry which is now the hallmark of Silicon Valley. In part, this is attributed to a general and property tax policy which by the late 1970s left Massachusetts as nearly the highest taxed state in the nation. Further, energy costs became a pronounced disincentive to new industrial location. Since 1979, industry and government have partnered to try to overcome these drawbacks: the powerful business lobby called the Massachusetts High Technology Council, with 140 members, bargained to provide 60 000 new jobs in return for tax cuts. Both these aims have been achieved leaving the state in a better position to compete with California and other established high technology centres.

Silicon Valley is held as the high technology exemplar of the United States and the world (Figure 5.1). In fact, its employment in around 3 000 firms accounts for less than half the high technology workers in California: roughly 200 000 in Santa Clara County which covers the Valley south of San Francisco, as opposed to 250 000 in Los Angeles (Rohwer, 1984: 7). While semiconductors are the complex's *raison d'être*, it is also strongly identified with microcomputers ("personal" computers) and micro applications such as games. As Bostonians have stressed, these consumer products have become "commodities" and face tough competition from producers in East Asia (Mazur, 1984: 65). The move in the early 1980s of Atari's production from the Valley to Taiwan and the downturn during 1985 in Valley

Figure 5.1. **SILICON VALLEY, SAN FRANCISCO, UNITED STATES, 1984**

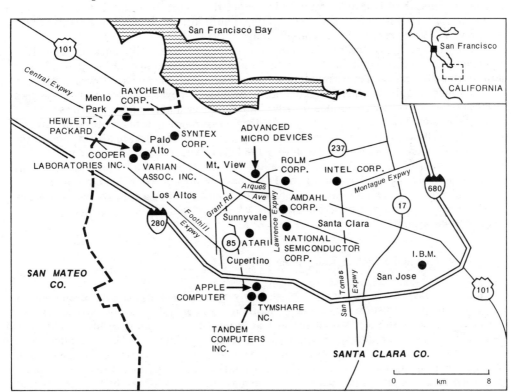

Source: International Herald Tribune, 27th April 1984.

industries may corroborate these points. On the other hand, the region is strong in electronics for the defence and aerospace industries, together with the necessary software. No relocation scenario is envisaged for such production. Moreover, the breaking up of the American Telegraph and Telephone corporation is helping to create swift expansion in the market for computer-related communications equipment.

The story of the recent growth of the Valley is as well known as to need no elaboration here. More relevant is to note the support afforded the complex from the 1940s onwards by government defence contracts to the electronics industry [United States (Congress), 1982: 43]. There is also the role of Stanford University in the decade after the Second World War in developing an industrial precinct and fostering close links with electronics firms (Henkin, 1983: 46-47; Hambrecht, 1984: 75). The move of William Shockley, one of the inventors of the transistor, to his home town Palo Alto in 1955 was a milestone for later development (Macdonald, 1983: 337-38). The Shockley Transistor company's spinoff in 1958 of Fairchild Semiconductor was the key event, since replicated many times, which has produced the present indigenous self-generating development [Steed and DeGenova (type a)].

It is true that, with Stanford and the University of California at Berkeley, Silicon Valley enjoys an excellent academic infrastructure but this may no longer be critical to its progress. Macdonald (1983: 341-42) suggests that the information flow largely proceeds from industry to campus. "Silicon Valley is conducive to the activities of the semiconductor industry precisely because there is so much semiconductor activity there". In part, this can be taken as a reference to over 80 venture capital firms apparently located in the San Francisco area (Hambrecht, 1984: Oakey, 1984a: 158-59 Rohwer, 1984: 7).

Other advantages of the region lie in its charisma, lifestyle, willingness to take risks, opportunity of inter-firm mobility for personnel, and access to a supply of low skilled labour derived from Hispanic and other immigrants to the State. This may have allowed production activity which would not otherwise have been possible. However, the prospects for such a workforce have recently deteriorated in view of great rises in land and housing prices not only in Santa Clara but in California as a whole. Further, a slowdown in infrastructural investment in the late 1970s has manifested itself in highway jams, while doubts are also evident in the quality of Californian education (Rohwer, 1984: 21). These negative externalities raise longer-term questions about the next boom industry in the State and whether regions such as Silicon Valley are not already saturated. There have been signs of a shake-out at least in personal computers and even in venture capital; the degree to which any retraction is offset by developments in very large scale integration (VLSI) and other microelectronic advances remains to be seen.

Europe: The United Kingdom and France

Recession hit the United Kingdom particularly hard and one response has been to foster initiatives aimed at arresting the decline in manufacturing or restructuring local economies. One of the success stories has occurred at Cambridge in East Anglia in high technology development focused around the famous university there. Marsh (1984: 6) mentions that since 1978 some 200 firms have sprung up in the city, covering computer hardware and software, instrumentation, biotechnology and general engineering. Start-ups are now said to be proceeding at the rate of two per week. *Time* magazine of 18th March 1985 reports that local high technology now employs 13 700 people or around 20 per cent of the regional workforce.

For present purposes, the interest in this milieu lies with the Cambridge Science Park, situated northeast of the university. England's oldest science park, it was conceived in the late 1960s and opened in 1973 to firms of several classes:

a) Ones with strong research and design functions which related to the work of the University;

b) Ones in which initial components are so closely integrated as to require control by the same executive personnel; and

c) Ones which did not involve bulk or mass production but which would employ a high proportion of scientists, technologists, technicians and craftsmen (Moore and Spires, 1983: 5).

Owned by Trinity College, the Science Park falls fairly clearly into Steed and DeGenova's Type (b). In their comprehensive survey, Moore and Spires (1983) report that growth has been quite slow, with 25 firms and 27 300 m^2 of floorspace in operation in 1983. Chemicals, instrument and electrical engineering are the functions of 18 companies, most others supplying business or professional services. Mean employment size is 40, the range ten to 250, and the aggregate workforce 495 people. Of all firms, 22 are considered to deal in high technology and, again of the total, 16 are in research and development. Companies include Bethseda Research Laboratories involved in genetic engineering, Cambridge Mass Spectrometry in electromagnetic radition test instruments, Scan Laboratories in laser deflection technology and Optronics in fibre-optic communication systems.

These and most of the other firms on the park are lessees, taking a 25 year lease and paying rent to Trinity College. According to a report in the British *Financial Times* of 21st January 1983, the College had spent some £3 million and was examining the option of selling sites to finance further development. The project is costly in part because of low plot ratios and the need to provide central amenities and open space to ensure a high quality environment.

How valuable has this science park been in terms of academic-industry links and in generating jobs? Moore and Spires (1983) are fairly sanguine on these issues. Only about a quarter of park firms have links with the university, perhaps corroborating Macdonald's (1983: 335-36) observations; the desire to establish such links influenced original location in only 28 per cent of cases. The authors put the lack of interaction down to the divergence between the basic research interests of many university departments compared with the applied concerns of management. Thus, location in the science park relies on more mundane factors, ones not dissimilar to those found in a company survey of an ordinary industrial estate by Wadley (1984).

Concerning employment, the Cambridge park clearly employs more white collar staff than local industry but recruits fewer personnel locally. Moore and Spires (1983: 24) argue that, given the similar nature of firms on and off the science park, the availability of land elsewhere and the rationale for location in the region, it is likely that any potential new development could have been accommodated but most likely in a piecemeal fashion. A similar rate of job creation would probably have been secured anyway. In this light, the park could be held simply to formalise the locational advantages already extant in the region. The case seems to show that, as in industrial location in general, any micro level incentives (such as a park) are unable by themselves to outweigh the macro context of the environment. But what remains unknown is the extent to which the park "advertised" the region and was perhaps an initial bait for some of the other high technology firms which ultimately chose to locate elsewhere around Cambridge.

The final case to be examined is the French initiative at Sophia Antipolis, midway between Nice and Cannes on the Riviera coast. The name is that of an association founded in 1969 of scientific leaders and regional planners in the Alpes-Maritimes Département to promote what would now be called a "technopolis", embodying wisdom, science and technology. The core area of about 150 hectares was planned by a non-profit organisation and consists of park offices, facilities and cultural amenities. Around it are situated roughly 2 400 hectares of wooded hilly land which forms the site for over 60 large and small public and private enterprises engaging in scientific and technological activities. They include: Air France's computing operations; the Centre International de Récherches Dermatologiques; the Ecole Nationale Supérieure des Mines de Paris; the Centre de Récherches Archéologiques de CNRS; CERAM (Centre d'Enseignement et de Récherche Appliqués au Management); the Digital Equipment Corporation's (DEC) European technical headquarters; prototype research workshops and underwater acoustics of Thompson CSF; headquarters of Dow Chemical France; and many others.

This park, probably combining Steed and DeGenova's (b), (c) and (d) elements, is dedicated to laboratories, service activities in science or computing, and research (both physical and social science). Foci have developed in information processing, fine chemistry and pharmacology, solar energy, water research and higher education. Much of the current interest in the project centres on its attempt to develop a cultural community in much the same way as would obtain on a university campus. On-site and nearby housing has been constructed to integrate with the development so that, in all, it amounts to significantly more than just a research park. Indeed, it is projected as a centre of pan-European science activity. This bears consideration in light of the fact that the nearest university (Nice) is at least 25 kilometres from the site. This point, incidentally, has recently aroused comment from the Israelis in planning a science complex called "Region 2 000" in the relatively underdeveloped Western Galilee (Meyers, 1984: 7). However, it is difficult to dispute the apparent success of Sophia Antipolis. Its congruence with French decentralisation objectives, attractive local environment and situation in France's sunbelt playground should help in future to offset many of the disadvantages of its pioneering location. In the expansiveness of its objectives, it is likely to generate further international interest as an example of a concentrated technopolis.

TECHNOLOGY-BASED REGIONAL DEVELOPMENT

The exemplars of high technology have been paraded – but could analysts even 15 years ago have predicted their ascendancy? What do these complexes have? Are they intrinsically significant? These questions are the concern of this section. It first draws some general principles from the cases visited. Then it seeks to place high technology in the context of the manufacturing and service sectors.

Success in High Technology

High technology is probably as capricious as the world of pop music. For six "star" centres reviewed, there are hundred of science or technology parks in OECD nations struggling to "make it". Many can be expected to renounce their original objective and turn into hybrid industrial developments as holding costs dictate that other functions must be admitted (cf. Wadley, 1984: 272-75). Some will fail entirely.

These examples show that success in technology-oriented development is neither assured, quick, nor easy. Various generalities emerge. The first factors common to all centres reviewed are longevity and initial advantage. None began much later than 1970, and two could count on around 40 years' growth. Yet science parks and technological development were rather a dead issue till the late 1970s. Can the rush of late-starting developments hope to equal the external and agglomerative economies built up to the advantage of established centres?

A second advantage of the majority of the complexes is the assistance afforded over often many years by government. More than a decade ago, Clark (1971: 298-300) pointed out that in both East and West basic scientific and research and development activity tended to cluster around techno-industrial complexes. In the period 1961 to 1965, California alone received nearly 40 per cent of all federal United States research and development funding. What this suggests is a process of cumulative causation in which established growth poles of research activity with initial advantage and appropriate infrastructure are able to derive the lion's share of public allocations to the detriment of peripheral regions. A paper by Schnee (1978) not only underscores this fact but, by reference to the United States defence and space programmes, demonstrates the critical role of governmental and, in particular, military patronage in establishing technological expertise among firms. It spawned the early semiconductor industry, for example. Malecki (1981b: 74-75) pursues the analysis, demonstrating that aerospace and electronics production in 1977 received nearly 80 per cent of United States federal research funding. The bulk of the money followed these industries to three Californian standard metropolitan areas and a few sunbelt cities. Regional impacts thus flow from sectoral and apparently aspatial procurement policies and much depends obviously on the size of the expenditures involved vis-à-vis other, perhaps more spatially-oriented, programmes. The role of government in rewarding and perpetuating initial advantage in research and technological development cannot be discounted and it may be very difficult for initiatives within peripheral regions to change the course of events.

A third factor relates to local private or public initiative. An ideal is perhaps the self-perpetuating growth caused by company splitting and spinoffs [Steed and DeGenova's Type (a)] which seems to characterise at least Ottawa, Silicon Valley, and Cambridge (city). This meiosis may presuppose no particular regional development effort. To set up the process, however, most areas will have to make a considerable effort, either in terms of regional or local government, nearby education institutions or other agencies. The evidence here suggests that the local response is particularly important in the smaller, planned developments and may be essential to a self-generating takeoff in which a complex begins to enjoy significant scale economies. Active participation and partnership will thus likely be involved in new ventures which now must overcome the initial advantages of the cases cited and many other centres as well (cf. Rosenberg, 1985: 34).

A fourth point bears on the desirability of a satisfying working environment for employees in technology complexes. It is an extension of the so-called "golf course effect" noted since the early 1960s in enquiries into factory location. It connotes more than a pleasant plant: executive residential areas should feature an acceptable climate, agreeable scenery and so on (Malecki, 1981c: 316). These factors are noted in every case study. Whether they will weigh against the efforts to attract new enterprises of authorities in stranded regions of outmoded industry remains to be seen. One suspects so. Further, environmental issues now clearly favour sunbelt locations. As one regional development director remarked to the author: "Why should an executive have to shovel out his drive in order to get to work or see his factory roof collapse under the weight of snow?" Some exaggeration may apply but such considerations, translated into energy or lifestyle terms, are obviously to be taken seriously.

These four major issues seem central in the high technology cases studied. They are, however, broadly-conceived and need to be interrelated with factors influencing high technology plant location which will underwrite the growth of a complex. Guidance on this point can be drawn from a United States (Congress) (1982) study which surveyed 691 high technology firms in California, Massachusetts and other States. Interregional locational determinants found "very significant" or "significant" by these firms were: labour skills and availability (89.3 per cent of firms), labour costs (72.2 per cent), tax climate (67.2 per cent), academic institutions (58.7 per cent), cost of living (58.5 per cent) and transportation (58.4 per cent). Other desiderata included access to markets, regulatory practices, energy costs, cultural amenities, climate, and access to new materials. As far as intraregional location was concerned, the availability of all types of labour except unskilled was clearly the most important factor ("very significant" or "significant" accounting for between 87 and 96 per cent of companies depending on class of labour). The tax structure (85.5 per cent), community attitudes to business (81.9 per cent), cost of property and construction (78.8 per cent) and good transportation for employees (76.1 per cent) were also significant [United States (Congress), 1982: 22-28].

Maybe the factors cited, or their ranking, would vary in different countries (cf. Japanese case study in Chapter VI). Different considerations might apply in the growth of planned or unplanned complexes. Local excellence on one particular factor might outweigh other aspects of location. Success may be achievable with something less than locational "perfection". For instance, not all of the six complexes reviewed in the present chapter had immediate access to an (international) airport or (high-level) university, though these are facilities held important in some of the literature. The need for a skilled workforce cannot be dismissed, but perhaps one can be attracted without too much difficulty if other conditions are right, as at Sophia Antipolis. Specific shortcomings are likewise at least temporarily admissable as with traffic and congestion in larger cities, high land and housing costs in Silicon Valley and the tax problems of Massachusetts. In broader perspective it is a case of each region taking stock of its strengths and weaknesses and knowing, based on national economic factors, where it can "pitch" within a technology hierarchy to attract enterprises and jobs.

Classifying the Options

In industrial development the general task is to match technology to the region (or *vice versa*) with the ultimate aim of ensuring company profitability to underwrite employment generation and the tax base. Based on a resource audit, some regions should therefore be asking whether they are really in the market for higher technologies or whether their pursuit would be simply a waste of scarce resources. Despite the popular mood today, there are other development options as shown in due course.

Say, however, a region opts for a high technology strategy: which type of complex is likely to deliver the best results? Steed and DeGenova's (1983: 264-65) classification can now be used prospectively. Type (a), the indigenous spinoff complex, is a private sector option and probably the most desirable. Yet it assumes a high rate of product innovation, entrepreneurial verve and the scent of profit – all commodities which are less than universal. Type (b), the research-oriented complex may alone be a weak development tool (Malecki, 1981c: 320); require a fair public sector input with possibly poor tax implications; have limited employment potential (Braun, 1984: 155); and be slow to consummate (as in the Cambridge case). Faster results may be obtainable with Type (c), the foreign subsidiary development, but there are significant drawbacks to be discussed presently. Type (d), government intervention, is the pure public sector course which may be essential as an initial stimulus but which, overly pursued, could run into diminishing returns.

Apart from questions of the ideal type of complex, regional authorities must consider the sort of industries to be allocated or attracted. Given the definitional deficiencies mentioned and the rapid advances being made in some fields, this will require continued research with the objective of establishing local comparative advantage. It seems fairly clear that few regions will acquire a full range of high technologies or industries (Pavitt, 1983: 11). Thus some targetting seems more efficacious than a "shotgun" approach in which an area aims to solicit any form of production and achieves as a result a para-economic, unintegrated complex. A case in point has occurred in the resource-rich state of Queensland, Australia, where immediate comparative advantage in higher technologies appears to lie in solar energy, biomass and large scale chemical engineering. One paper has recommended attention to them in preference to technologies such as microelectronics or genetics. Other Australian states are likely to perform better in these fields because of initial advantage and, in part, because they have to: unlike Queensland they have lost a significant portion of their manufacturing workforce because of contraction in traditional industries (Wadley, 1986). This example, and reasoning, would certainly be relevant to other countries and areas.

And, Failing High Technology

The account to date has dealt mainly with the case of product-innovative high technology. Because of its visibility, competitive potential and allegedly positive employment prospects, this is now the "flagship" case and in many ways the easiest to discuss. In fact, there may be a hierarchy of possibilities for regional development as listed in Table 5.2. By this depiction, technology can be high or low, endogenous or exogenous (diffused), and oriented to product or process innovation. Enterprise can be export or domestically oriented. The interaction of these parameters has strong implications for resultant employment levels as a major element of "desirability".

First, higher technologies are to be preferred since lower forms (often associated with bulkier commodities) are susceptible to labour-saving process innovations. For its part, process innovation in a region can be endogenous or imported (diffused) but, in terms of competitiveness, even process innovation may be better than none at all. Domestic production is bounded in scope by the size of national demand whereas the limit on exporting is the extent of the world market itself. Perhaps production which is very strongly export-oriented could also afford to be of low technology and subject to process innovation: overall market growth might offset productivity gains to keep employment stable. If Table 5.2 is viewed as an extension of the (Chapter IV) model in which the output is labour demand, various trade-offs can be imagined. Yet, the general rule and advice to regions is as follows. "For the sake of competitiveness, some innovation is better than none. For the sake of employment, jump as high up the scales of this table as comparative advantage allows".

What of life with some, but not the highest technology? Based on postwar experience of several now highly successful OECD economies, this seems quite possible (Malecki, 1983: 111). Heaton and Hollomon (1984: 5) have criticised a lack of attention in the

Table 5.2. **Dimensions of technology**

Technology	Source	Innovation type	Market	Apparent desirability
High	Endogenous	Product process	Export	Greater
Low	Exogenous	None	Domestic	Lesser

United States (and surely elsewhere) to diffusion policy. Its aim would centre around various process innovations which may be necessary to maintain productivity and competitiveness. At the same time, to offset any employment losses, a region could undertake some lower-order product innovation, perhaps by combining or adapting tried and proven technologies. The microprocessor revolution alone offers numerous opportunities. For instance, the application of electronic control systems in households still resides more in science-fiction than reality. Most of the housing stock in OECD countries was built for a prior era in which technologies, energy costs and lifestyles were vastly different from today. Thus, infrastructural improvements to dwelling and other building stock offer significant possibilities for secondary and service producers and this is but one field in which microelectronic adaptations could be marketed.

Another case for attention to industries other than high technology ones is raised by Rasmussen and Ledebur (1983: 756). They argue that there is a danger in following the efforts of other nations (or regions). Simultaneous stimulation of high technology fields may raise the level of competition so that no nation's (region's) industry earns the anticipated rate of return. Excessive competition may predispose failure. Further, economic balance may require a pooling of expected risks and rates of return across a spread of industries rather than just a few in order to avoid possibly erratic or highly variable market outcomes. This proposition is well understood in the capital-asset pricing model within the theory of finance and is only one of a number of important issues to be considered in regional technological development.

DEVELOPMENT ISSUES

In the OECD's October 1983 workshop on "Research, Technology and Regional Policy", over 100 delegates from Member countries heard papers on three principal themes: *a)* technological change and the location of industry; *b)* policies to encourage regional research and development and technology-based activities; and *c)* the place of the university in regional development. The meeting recognised first that a strong technological component will be indispensable for regional policy. Yet, notwithstanding the various definitional problems, the view emerged that high technology, *per se*, was an insufficient condition for ensuring viable development. Though such industries represent a major area of comparative advantage for the OECD and figure prominently in many Members' exports, they may actually account for only five to 10 per cent of all manufacturing. For this reason, the risks of heavy investment proportionate to the spatial development outcomes should be clearly appreciated and alternative approaches, as outlined above, should be actively pursued. Ultimately, regional technological development will proceed through three parties: higher educational institutes, firms and government. The effectiveness of each hinges on development issues of the following types.

Academia: Mobilising Resources

Higher education institutes (for convenience, "universities") are crucial in socioeconomic and cultural development to provide and attract qualified personnel or induce them to remain in a region. Their educational and ancillary services can be a great resource, especially if they are actively allied with regional development aims (Rosenberg, 1985: 36). The 1960s and 1970s were periods of major tertiary education expansion in OECD nations, but that has now ended there will no longer be "new" and "old" universities, but only old ones. Their adaptation to novel conditions is a prime concern for academics, government and the community in general. The basic expectation is that institutions will contribute to the creation of jobs and flexibility of the workforce, in part by extending their scientific and technological expertise to all types of companies.

Certainly, this has been done in some of the leading high technology complexes reviewed above; the OECD Workshop similarly contains papers describing several excellent examples of university-industry contact. But not all technology centres appear to require proximity to a university and, more generally, debate is unfolding as to whether such institutions are well organised to interrelate with firms at all. For example, the OECD Working Party contains delegates who argue that technological invention depends on higher science and technology institutes, while another group considers that technological invention is essentially the doing of industrial laboratories attached to firms.

Resolution of these viewpoints requires the recognition that high technology is different from high or pure science in that technology exists and is developed for commercial applications. Some would confuse strength in high science with that in high technology. There are linkages but they are complex. An area can be competitive in a high technology industry yet make few if any contributions to the underlying scientific base [United States (Department of Commerce), 1983: 3]. The reverse is equally true.

All this really means is that universities may foster high science but not necessarily high technology. Macdonald (1983: 335-36) sides with the second group of OECD observers mentioned above by urging that the major participants in innovations are accountants, managers and salesmen, not high-status scientists and engineers. High technology is not about basic but, rather, applied research. To Macdonald, it is non-scientific, "even anti-science in its desperation to avoid problems and undirected enquiry; it seeks the quickest and easiest route possible through what is so expressively termed 'black box technology'". Oakey (1984b: 243) corroborates this view, at least for the United Kingdom scientific instruments industry, by writing that links between firms and universities are infrequent and of a low technology supportive nature.

In a world of developing technologies, universities are thus in no position to wait for industry to beg their favours. If they do not prove capable of making systematic contributions to regional development, other bodies will assuredly take their place. According to the workshop rapporteur, "an internal revolution" may be needed in some institutions. Four elements could be involved.

First is the need to mobilise skills and experience to attack complex social and environmental problems. This is particularly important in smaller nations such as Finland where universities are considered to have played a big part in transforming an erstwhile agrarian economy (Antikainen, 1981: 447). In the United Kingdom, the Science and Engineering Research Council (SERC) has many programmes aimed at achieving "relevance" of research, relevance defined as a contribution to technological innovation and industrial performance. Braun (1984: 151) discusses "innovation bonding" and "instrument bonding". The former would bridge the gap between pure science and applied technology by having university staff as special advisers to industry; the latter envisages particularly strong links between scientists and instrument manufacturers in an innovation centre setting. Overall, though, Braun argues that "there is no prescription on how to increase the chances of pure research proving beneficial to innovation, except perhaps the need for close personal contacts in an information network consisting of both academic and industrial researchers".

This should not be taken as an argument in support of doing nothing. In various institutions in advanced countries, "academic freedom" is jealously guarded, producing what to the outside observer might appear a haphazard programme of research. Moreover, local projects may be eschewed for ones with an international focus, the latter appearing better on *curricula vitae* and carrying more weight in staff promotion. There is a need to question the directions and management of some campuses: they may lack even the most rudimentary performance review procedures. A primary step will be to make them efficient in what they do: the next is to make them more effective towards social aims and needs. The Working Party considers that universities should be encouraged to launch multi-disciplinary operations in co-operation with government authorities and, to this end, their ability to manage large scientific and technological research teams should be strengthened (for example, by provision of administrative staff).

The second element concerns university-industry links. These are important principally in assuring the supply of skilled personnel [though unless universities remain close to the technological frontier, it is hard to see how their graduates can be readily slotted into firms (cf. Braun, 1984: 150)]. In maintaining closeness, research-based co-operation is recommended. To illustrate, Australia now has nearly 30 tertiary consulting companies, the largest of which take in up to $A2 million worth of contract work a year (Kavanagh, 1984: 51). Moreover, a draft national science and technology policy proposed the abolition of all financial restrictions on academics' consulting activities. Both these initiatives could direct scholars towards industry and have the ultimate effect of enticing them to join or start up firms. The turnover of staff so created would generally benefit universities in a "no-growth" funding situation.

The third possibility is a commercial midwife role for universities in their region. Sometimes scientists may have a viable product but no ability to develop and market it. Universities could offer schemes such as incubator factories, as has been done at the Rensselaer Polytechnic Institute of New York in the United States (Phalon, 1984). This may involve the provision of production facilities or auxiliary management for newly-created companies. An alternative is to help small but growing industries which can benefit from technological advice, and assistance in management and marketing. Unless university business schools are especially well equipped, this course could involve intermediary institutions ("brokers"). One example is the semi-government authority ANVAR in France.

Such thinking has produced innovation centres which go beyond mere university-industry links and may play any or all of the following roles (Braun, 1984: 152):

a) The screening of ideas emerging from private inventors or research institutions and help with developing, patenting, market research, venture capital, public funding, selling licences or starting up production of new products;

b) Keeping in touch with data banks of new products and helping small or new firms to start the manufacture of such products;

c) Help with obtaining licences, funding, market research and further development;

d) Port of first call for manufacturers who do not know where advice might be available on new processes or equipment which may help them improve their manufacturing efficiency;

e) Extension of above ideas to the service sector for the provision of new or improved services; and

f) Provision of suitable premises for starting up high technology firms, including the sharing of some facilities.

In the United States, the National Science Foundation in the mid-1970s established three innovation centres at the Massachusetts Institute of Technology, Carnegie-Mellon University in Pittsburgh and at the University of Oregon in Portland. Their role is to assist students and others evaluate technology and research and development results, develop new products, establish new business ventures and provide assistance to inventors. Many more, specialising in particular fields, have subsequently been developed elsewhere in the United States. Some are technology centres allied with universities while others are independent incubators supported entirely by the State (Brody, 1985: 18-19). Ireland has a publicly-funded centre at Limerick near the National Institute for Higher Education. It offers data banks, workshop facilities and incubator factories. The German Federal Ministry for Research and Technology (BMFT) Centre in Berlin concentrates on the dissemination of technological and market information, aiming to unite potential suppliers and users of technology (Braun, 1984: 152-53).

The Workshop suggested two other possible forms of midwifery for universities. They could encourage large science-based firms with which they have good links to develop more systematic university-oriented strategies among their subsidiaries. The other possibility is for institutions to attempt to assist in cases of industrial restructuring, most likely by advocating ideas or spinning off projects which could be developed in the region. As the Working Party noted, however, any of these interventions would depend on the availability within academia of leaders capable of taking initiatives and maintaining a spirit of enterprise in the project teams concerned.

The fourth element relates to incentives. It is unrealistic to expect universities, especially the traditional ones, to adjust spontaneously to new requirements. The university response will inevitably be determined by the career prospects of staff and the way in which research is organised. Measures are thus demanded which ensure that individual performance reviews take account of the emerging situation, particularly in the case of activities that are not "research" in a strict sense but which aim to turn research findings to account and to the benefit of a region's industry. Of equal value are joint educational programmes for academics and industrialists, both of a formal nature (e.g. management problems) and by way of colloquia or seminars on issues of social or scientific interest. The OECD further supports an adjustment of restrictions on academics which limit their involvement with outside clients. This may consist of improving academics' ability to take out individual patents or engage in paid consulting.

The Workshop thus envisaged fairly fundamental changes for universities and other institutes, numbers of which may have done little in the way of internal restructuring despite great changes in the milieu over the last decade. Though this sector well illustrates the magnitude of the task in technological regional development, issues relating to firms may be more significant and again require supra regional action if they are to be resolved.

Firms: Controlling Technology

Managerial control has become a key theme in recent analyses of corporate investment behaviour at all scales. In a perceptive paper Dunsford (1983: 295) argues that a firm's motivation for investing in process innovations is likely to be efficiency – but not in the strictly technical sense. Efficiency cannot be divorced from questions of reliability, predictability and control. Thus the incentive for management in introducing numerically controlled machine tools or robots may have as much to do with centralised control as productivity. Such investment may contribute to a deskilling of a workforce since its tasks are made routine while decision-making power resides in management which finds its role in this process of "cybernation" in overseeing the necessary programming (Robson, 1979: 59). On this basis, Levin and Rumberger (1983) present the paradox of the "low skill future of high technology" while Reich (1984: 27) foresees that high-volume standardised production will be to a great extent replaced by flexible-system production in which integrated teams of workers identify and solve problems. These "workers" are presumably an amalgam of white collar and skilled personnel, a small group who direct what may be an even smaller group of low-skilled operatives.

Parallels exist between these micro level corporate investment responses and those macro ones to do with plant location. One of the implications of the internal division of labour described before is truncation with respect to the decision-making and innovative role of standardized production units (i.e. branch plants) (cf. Hayter, 1982). To Oakey (1979: 342), the industrial conglomerate is a closed system working towards company objectives. Agreement of these objectives and a country's regional development policy is purely incidental. Thus, a firm is unlikely to decentralise anything to branches that requires day-to-day supervision from head-office: the distant operations enjoying (probably labour) cost advantages handle only the routine. As Thwaites (1978: 456) has remarked:

> The firm can decide, to a large degree independently, at which thresholds in the product or technological cycle it will devolve production to the region, if it will renew it and when it will withdraw. The region may not experience the full product cycle, only those portions corporations in aggregate decide it shall receive ... while the technology introduced may be new to the region it may not be in the vanguard of advance which can lead to further advance.

Research activity offers scale economies in central locations (Malecki, 1981b: 317). Except in one or two industries, branch units tend to employ few research staff. This limits the range of occupations open to a regional populace and further reduces the possibility of innovative ideas or entrepreneurial spinoff. From United Kingdom evidence, Thwaites (1978: 458) concludes that because branch plants do not have the facilities or the need to plug into regional information systems they demand and diffuse little knowledge. Nor do they import knowledge from exogenous sources for the potential benefit of the region. Self-sustained growth based on this type of enterprise was arguably "a long way off". So much is also clear from a recent analysis by Cooke *et al.* (1984) which reduces much of the United Kingdom's semiconductor industry to an internationally-owned enterprise concerned not with innovation but with adaptation and mass production for European markets. For all these reasons, technological and regional development via the Steed and DeGenova type (c) (subsidiary) complex may appear less than optimal.

In absolute terms, the bulk of industrial research is carried out by large firms for reasons of its barriers to entry, the scale of projects required, risk, ability to use results and corporate domination of key sectors (Thwaites, 1978: 447). Regardless of the productivity or outputs of this research, big companies thus at least determine the locus of *inputs*. A study of location trends in research and development in 330 large United States corporations over the years 1965-77 by Edward Malecki (1979) revealed that, although the function was evolving away from a dependence on some large city regions, it remained markedly metropolitan in character. The comparative advantages of city size in attracting corporate headquarters location, manufacturing, and university and government research also showed little sign of reversal. Later, from an extensive international literature review, Malecki (1983: 102-03) reported that research and development and corporate headquarters, in contrast to manufacturing, are located overwhelmingly in metropolitan areas and disproportionately in many larger areas. Moreover, the locations of investment by multinationals within most countries are much more concentrated than those of domestic firms, with core areas preferred. This does not auger well for peripheral regions searching now not simply for investment but investment in innovatory activities with horizontal or vertical spinoffs.

Government: Sovereignty and Technology Policy

The situation described above is likely in future to ensure that governments' technology and regional policies become more closely linked: it is useless to have them at cross-purposes. Braun (1984: 124) defines technology policy as "the totality of measures taken by government and its agents which directly control the creation, application and use of technology". Though such measures may be very extensive, not all governments may choose to apply them (Table 5.3). Joseph (1984: 95-97) records two opposing approaches, based on divergent views of the cause of poor innovative and technological performance.

The non-interventionist stance stresses market forces as the most powerful influence on resource allocation for the advancement of technology. Government action should aim at creating a neutral economic environment for innovation in which firms make balanced judgements of the appropriate level of investment activity. Few circumstances justify direct intervention since, generally, the market is regarded as a more efficient agent. Under this approach, the allocation of scarce resources to key technologies or industries is not favoured. Public strategies to overcome uncertainties of innovation will similarly be downplayed. Problems such as imperfect information flows, restrictive practices by multinationals and heavy reliance on imported technology are considered insufficient to require government attention. Indeed, its action is probably restricted to the provision of scientific and technological infrastructure (such as laboratories), all direct financing and promotional activity being left to the market.

The alternative interventionist approach understands poor manufacturing performance in terms of the structural conditions outlined in Chapter I. It argues that these fundamental changes require policies very different from traditional ones in order to offset structural weaknesses such as low technological capacity, reliance on mature or low technology sectors, insufficient technical expertise in management and poor trade in high technology products. Greater intervention is fostered in all stages of innovation and more emphasis is placed on policy planning and integration. Attention is focused on the development and exploitation of national comparative advantage in terms of key technologies and industries. Finally, there is a preference for creating a strong indigenous technological capacity. Foreign subsidiaries of multinationals are seen as contributing to industrial weakness through their heavy reliance on overseas technology, low innovative drive and frequent disinterest in exporting.

The corporate trends and potentials described in the foregoing section now predispose a number of OECD countries towards an interventionist and sometimes nationalist view. In future it seems probable that regional authorities in general and, otherwise, the smaller or semi-peripheral OECD nations will be much concerned with "technological sovereignty", the capacity and the freedom to select, to generate or acquire and to apply, build upon and exploit commercially technology needed for industrial innovation (Grant, 1983: 240). Capability implies at least sufficient indigenous technical competence to brief consultants, negotiate the purchase of and operate new machines. It is different from self-sufficiency – the competence to generate a process or machine *ab initio*. Freedom, by comparison, refers to the absence of contractual obligations and management directives that restrict the licensee's utilisation of acquired technology.

Table 5.3. **Examples and targets of technology policy**

Type of measure	Examples	Target			
		Ambience	Industry	General innovation	Specific innovation
Financial	Grants, loans, subsidies, financial sharing arrangements, loans and gifts of equipment, provision of free services, provision of building	Ease and cost of credit	Investment in regional factory building	Making venture capital readily available	Supporting specific research and development programmes
Taxation	Company, personal, indirect and payroll taxation; tax allowances, tax deductible expenditure	Supporting entrepreneurial spirit	Making investment allowances	Allowances for innovative investments and research and development expenditure	
Legal and Regulatory	Patents, environmental regulations, health regulations, inspectorates, protection of designs, arbitration services, monopoly regulations, planning permissions for buildings and enterprises	Patent laws; monopoly regulations	Factory legislation	Health and safety regulations	
Educational	General education, universities, technical education, apprenticeship schemes, continuing and further education	General educational provision; support for higher education	Technical training schemes		Training schemes in specific new areas
Procurement	Defence purchases, central government purchases and contracts, local government purchases, research and development contracts, prototype purchases	Level and type of public expenditure	"Buy at home" policies	Procurement specifications	Research and development contracts and orders for specific new equipment
Information	Information networks and centres, libraries radio and television, freedom of information advisory services, statistical services, governmental publications, data bases, museums, exhibitions, liaison services	Libraries, broadcasting, government statistics	Liaison services	Information programmes on specific new technologies	

Table 5.3. **Examples and targets of technology policy** (*continued*)

Type of measure	Examples	Ambience			
		Industry	Target	General innovation	Specific innovation
Public Enterprises	Innovation by publicly owned industries, setting up of new industries, pioneering use of new techniques by public corporations correction of imbalances by public enterprise, participation in private enterprise, investment by public corporations	Strength of public sector	Active regional policies	Participation in new ventures, innovative policy in state industry	Public enterprise in new technology; specific innovations in public enterprises
Public services	Investment and innovation in health services public building, civil engineering and construction, transport, telecommunications, consumer protection	Transport and communications			Development and use of specific innovations
Political	"Atmosphere", honours system, intervention versus non-intervention, regional policies, labour policies	Access to information; public opinion			
Scientific and Technological	Technical standards, government research laboratories, testing stations, support for research associations, learned societies, professional associations, research grants	Technical standards		Research and development availability from public sources	Specific research development support
Commercial	Trade agreements, tariffs, currency regulations		Tariffs, trade missions		International co-operation in new ventures

Source: Braun (1984: 126, 128-129).

The potential of corporations in limiting regional or national capability is clear. Likewise, technological freedom can be restricted by depriving licensees of sovereignty while allowing the benefits of transferred technology. This is done: *a)* by imposing contractual restrictions on markets, the conduct of research and development, the retention of improvements and the ability of the licensee to use the know-how after the license has terminated; *b)* by making it difficult for the licensee to acquire capability (e.g. supply provisos, contractual restrictions); and *c)* by securing direct corporate control over the licensee. Of the three techniques, direct control is the most effective and perhaps the most common, and readily lends itself to other anti-competitive practices such as restrictions on exports.

Attitudes to processes of truncation and technological sovereignty will vary among regions or nations. Resource-rich areas which merely require technology to exploit their natural advantages and create manufacturing employment by import replacement may be little concerned. Freedom will greatly bear on small industrialised nations trying to retain their place in world markets for manufactured products (i.e. much of the OECD membership). Grant (1983: 252) critically contrasts the technologically aware civil services of Scandinavia, some other European nations and the newly-industrialising countries with the "regulation-oriented" administrations of British-origin countries "untroubled by the problem of technological sovereignty and unable to harness effectively national scientific and technological resources to the tasks of national development". Among the latter group, India has demonstrated increasing awareness of technological issues while Canada, greatly penetrated by multinationals, has emphasised the importance of recovering technological sovereignty and halting the process of de-industrialisation. There, under the former administration, evidence of a national consensus was apparently emerging: the foreign investment review process was strengthened and domestic participation in energy projects was to be increased (Grant, 1983: 260). Yet the textbook on sovereignty is unlikely to be written in Canada: Japan has already seen to that, on the way acquiring Korea, Taiwan and Malaysia as students.

Given that governments can be expected to pursue the more active (nationalist) technology policies, an integration with regional initiatives will be required. Study of the interface is presently not well developed. Technology policies, however, are fairly easily defined as in Table 5.3. Here it will be seen that many are directly congruent with the "regional" measures discussed in Chapter III. Thus it is fairly straightforward to introduce spatial graduation into technology policy concerning financing, tax and commercial affairs. The regional implications of procurement policies were noted earlier and reference has likewise been made to the contribution to infrastructure in different areas which can be made in the placement of public enterprise and services. Given the demographics of advanced countries, it is unlikely that education policies will bear as heavily on regional development as in the past; the other elements of Table 5.3 may also exercise only indirect or minor spatial impacts.

The reconciliation of technology and regional policies thus seems attainable: the targets of each fit together. Co-ordination was a key concern of the recent OECD Workshop which saw several steps in developing a "regional technology policy". First, it would probably be useful to specify priorities (e.g. will the emphasis be on the development of a region, a technology or an entire industry?; if a differentiated policy is proposed, how are the claims for resources of individual regions, technologies or industries to be ranked?). As far as the regions are concerned, there will need to be an inventory of opportunities, potentials and local resources available. Systematic cataloguing should focus in particular on the role and methods of any university present. Fieldwork should underpin the design and planning of measures to enhance local technological environments. It would utilise the capacities of training establishments, research centres and chambers of commerce to create indigenous initiative.

Other elements of a regional technology policy concern the selection of agencies most adapted to tasks at hand. Two types have so far proved their effectiveness: *a)* lightweight structures with a small incentive-type budget such as in the Rhône-Alpes region in France; *b)* bigger organisations with considerable financial and personnel resources capable of running a wide range of actions (e.g. the Scottish Development Authority in the United Kingdom). In both cases, flexibility and independence have been vital to success. Such agencies become the vehicles of technological as well as regional policy by selecting projects or firms for assistance, attempting to mobilise capital markets and advising on the placement of public works and contracts. Large-scale structural projects, especially those in telecommunications or transport, may be especially significant in enhancing the regional technological base.

A further element is deregulation. Stress should be laid on the need to make more flexible or even abolish all kinds of regulations that inhibit initiative. The case of university personnel has already been cited. In administering public schemes of industry support, it is also necessary to keep procedures transparent and reduce delays in decision-making. This applies particularly to dealings with small and medium enterprises which may lack the working capital to sustain protracted uncertainty in the outcome of grant applications for research and development or other technological initiatives.

CONCLUSIONS

Technology is capricious, "wayward", and its parameters are not easily defined. These qualities add further imponderables to the difficulties normally associated with any type of social enginnering. The current onslaught of "high" technologies, visible and fashionable as they may be, hold substantial risks for those who would foster them with public funds. Some technologies have been built up into regional industrial complexes, but not without difficulty. Only so much can be drawn from examples of leading centres which developed in recent years because technology is constantly evolving and there is no guarantee that future processes will have similar spatial manifestations. Still, high technology is not everything and viable options exist for regions to adopt other levels and styles of production. In one form or another, technology will need to be adopted to underwrite the continued competitiveness of regional economies. Its pursuit, however, raises a great number of questions as to the role of higher educational institutes, firms (particularly multinational corporations) and governments.

To varying extents, the regional policy of OECD countries has come to grips with these issues. Such policy, however, cannot and does not change overnight and thus its capacity to address leading edge questions is tempered by traditional concerns such as those with peripheral or stranded areas. It is instructive now to examine selected nations' programmes to appreciate the outlooks they reflect and the divergent measures being tried. Such case studies will also give some indication of the applicability of the development model constructed in Chapter IV.

NOTES

1. Nor should it be assumed that Kondratieff waves are the only way of interpreting technological innovation.
2. See an alternative account in United States (Congress) (1982: 42-47).

Chapter VI

REGIONAL POLICY: SELECTED STUDIES

As outlined in the Preface, a series of OECD publications during the late 1970s and early 1980s provided accounts of regional policy in various Member nations. As governments have changed, many of these statements may require updating. Such a situation is recognised by the University of Strathclyde which has found it necessary to outline regional policy incentives in Europe on an annual basis (Yuill and Allen, 1980-1984). In the present overview, the aim can be no more than to put some flesh on the bones of the discussion to date: it is impossible to review the regional situation in 24 countries since such an exposé would form another report in its own right.

In the absence of a full survey, it is not possible to nominate "representative" examples of countries' regional policies, even if this were deemed useful. More suggestive is the range of policies seen in the light of viewpoints presented in this work: first, that the scope for a country's regional policy is increasingly determined by structural change in the international economic environment which allows policymakers greater or lesser latitude; and, second, that the levels of endogenous control and technological advancement in an economy are likely arbiters of success towards the more complex aims of regional policy.

In accord with these arguments, and the practical limitations, aspects of policy in two nations are studied in this chapter. One features an unitary governmental system while the other is a federation. Japan is first considered as a leading core industrial country espousing policies of positive adjustment. Economic and technological progress over the last two decades has allowed an enterprising approach to regional policy, exemplified in the new "technopolis" plan. The prospective use of high technology industries towards the distributive aims of regional development is the focus of interest.

The second example, Australia, has been described as a "semi-peripheral" nation, remote from the traditional core of Europe but well placed to participate in developing Pacific basin markets. The small size and vast distances characterising this economy pose various impediments to regional policy as foreseen in Chapter IV and V: in addition, the case highlights considerations common to federal environments in which states may actively compete for development (cf. Dubnick, 1984). Herein, and in respect of the scales involved, the Australian study provides a contrast to that of Japan which involves different applications of the policy model advanced earlier.

JAPAN: POSITIVE ADJUSTMENT AND TECHNOPOLES

Japan is an archipellago of four major and around 3 900 smaller islands, covering in total 377 700 quare kilometers (Figure 6.1). The population in 1983 was estimated at 119.5 million, second in the OECD and seventh in the world. Of the land area, 72 per cent is mountainous and thus population densities on the remainder are as high as 2 000 persons per square kilometre [Japan (Prime Minister's Office), 1984: 10, 15-16]. Extensive conurbation has developed in a 350 kilometre arc along the Pacific coast of the main island, Honshu: the foci are the metropolises of Tokyo, Osaka and Nagoya. Urbanisation is associated with the rapid postwar shift to an advanced manufacturing and service economy. Japan is poorly endowed with basic industrial or energy resources and has had to rely on purchasing what it needed for processing into manufactured exports. Concentration has increasingly developed around low bulk, high value products which have a high value added and can stand transportation costs. Some smaller OECD European nations adopt the same strategy but Japan is held to have been conspicuously successful in fostering a climate for technological innovation and securing its adoption.

The twin themes of landuse problems and the technological thrust provide the backdrop for this case study. It follows an OECD Working Party tour to Japan in May 1984 in which attention was not on all aspects of regional development as usually pertains in an OECD country visit but on just the most recent and noteworthy one. The present paper, having outlined aspects of Japanese industrial policy and regional development, likewise devotes itself to an account of the "technopolis" concept which is now of considerable interest to OECD Members and other countries in the world.

Industrial Policy

A profile of post-1960 economic development in Japan is obtained in Tables 1.1 to 1.4. The first shows the country's phenomenal 10.5 per cent annual average growth rate from 1960-68, followed by an average 8.8 per cent per annum from 1968 to 1973. The first oil crisis might have ended the "miracle" of growth but, since 1973, Japan has still registered annual performances well above the OECD average. Inflation is low but not as low as unemployment (Tables 1.2 and 1.3). Though the share of manufacturing workers in total employment has marginally declined (Table 1.4), absolute numbers remain about the same as in 1970. On the other hand, output in constant price terms has more than doubled, another manifestation of "jobless growth".

Japanese industrial policy currently has several aims (Konaga, 1983: 19):

a) Improving the standard of living and welfare of the population;
b) Promoting the international division of labour through the transfer of certain industries to developing nations (cf. Chapter I);
c) Ensuring economic security for Japan through a stable, long-term supply of natural resources and energy; and
d) Harmonising industrial activity and social needs such as environmental protection, as befits a small, densely-populated country.

Founded in a mixed market philosophy, these aims presuppose two major tasks for present national industrial policy (Sawada, 1983: 101-04). First is the promotion of high technology development as a means of expanding economic frontiers and revitalising world development. Research and development in Japan is primarily a private enterprise function and government involvement accounts for less than one-third of the non-defence effort. It is directed at the fundamental stage of technological development in areas of pressing social need. Some government work is to do with very large scale or risky projects; other initiatives concern the laying down of technologies for use in the next one or two decades (e.g. new materials, biotechnology, future electron devices). Indeed, Japan's Ministry of International Trade and Industry (1980: 42-44) lists its technology priorities as: a) increased utilisation of alternative

Figure 6.1. **TECHNOPOLIS SITES AND SELECTED URBAN CENTRES, JAPAN, 1984**

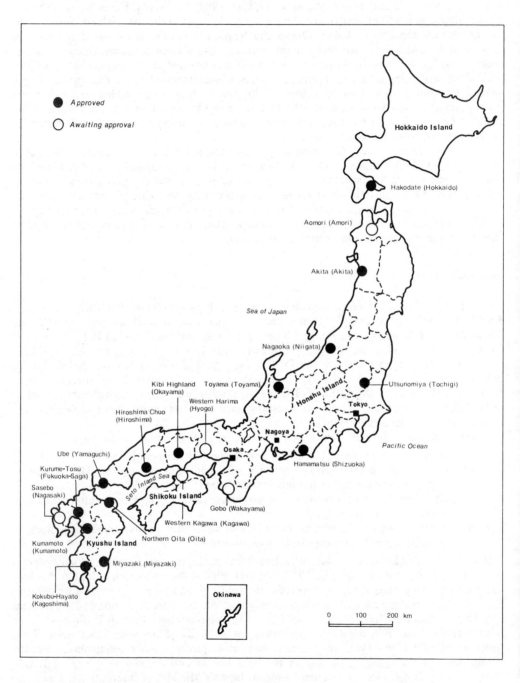

Source: Japan (Ministry of International Trade and Industry), unpublished internal documents.

energy and energy saving to overcome constraints; *b)* qualitative improvement in the standard of living and community facilities; and *c)* increasing the overall knowledge-intensiveness of the industrial structure.

The second task is that of promoting structural adjustment in a number of industries deleteriously affected by the second oil price shock. They include aluminium smelting and petrochemicals. A similar need may exist for other reasons in a different group of industries such as textiles, clothing and shipbuilding. What is required is to foster adjustment without resort to protectionism. This involves the reduction of excess production capacity, and company or plant amalgamations or joint ventures. Such thinking is very much in line with that of the OECD in its 1983 promulgation of positive adjustment. Japan now claims an average tariff level lower than that of either the United States or the European Economic Community. The market is being opened to direct investment by foreign firms though since 1980 Japan has become one of the world's largest net exporters of long-term capital (OECD, 1984*e*: 10).

Japanese industrial policy is indicative, consisting of indirect guidelines to development. It is dominated by the Ministry of International Trade and Industry (MITI). The tools of policy consist, first, of MITI's "visions" which can cover aggregate or structural elements. A vision seeks to analyse changes in the economic environment, clarify emerging trends and outline policy tasks for the establishment of a facilitating industrial structure.

A second tool is central government financing, especially in projects involving high risk or long lead times. Funds may be provided through the Japan Development Bank for not only industrial development but also energy, environmental or urban projects (these last three being now by far the more significant). As in various European countries and the United States, the medium of assistance is loans.

Tax incentives and budgetary appropriations form the other major tools. Both are kept to a minimum. From 1976-82, for instance, around 90 per cent of tax privileges were either rationalised or abolished (Konaga, 1983: 21). What budgetary assistance is available is directed principally to small business and energy development.

Regional Development

Japan's technological progress, free enterprise focus and push for positive adjustment offer only one explanation for MITI's advocacy after 1980 of a technopolis plan. The other basis is rooted in the country's regional development since the 1950s which has now produced a strong desire among prefectural governments for economic revitalisation. Here, the starting point is to consider the strong rural to urban immigration which accounts in part for the growth of the major conurbations and which was not arrested until the mid-1970s. Job availability and wage levels may have promoted this movement of people who failed to find the opportunities they sought in their regions of origin. The more peripheral areas lost young people and those well-qualified, thus making the task of development in future all the more difficult. Such trends are now a matter of serious concern in view of Japan's ageing demographic structure, since care of the elderly has long been a family responsibility. These is a desire among the young to remain in their home area: to help them stay there is a key objective of policymakers.

Japan's regional problems were last reviewed by the OECD in 1976. Then as now they consisted of:

a) The existence of backward areas such as Hokkaido;
b) Over-concentration in the three major metropolises; and

123

c) Under-concentration in and potential emigration from intermediate regions (i.e. those falling between the backward and the metropolitan areas).

The history and current status of regional development policy is depicted in Figure 6.2. Following the immediate postwar recovery (1945-55), Japan entered the first of its high growth periods characterised by the problematic concentration of industrial and other economic activity in major metropolises. The first moves to arrest this trend occurred in the 1960 National Income Doubling Plan. Its title became an aim of the First Comprehensive National Development Plan of 1962 (Zenso) which sought balanced regional development in the establishment of 15 new industrial cities under a key point development concept. In addition, the consolidation of six industrial development areas in the Pacific belt was proposed. This was the era of Japan's rise as a nation of heavy engineering and chemical industries (Furuki, 1983: 182), many of which were energy-intensive. Yet such was the expansion of the 1960s that the Zenso plan became outmoded and it was replaced in 1969 with the New Comprehensive National Development Plan (Shinzenso).

This plan was pitched until 1985 and fully accepted that Japan was a high growth economy. Its development formula consisted of *a)* attaining greater efficiency in development through urban links provided by new transport and communications networks; *b)* planning large development programmes in selected sectors; and *c)* promoting extensive environmental conservation projects. By 1972 a system for regional development was in force but the problems of over- and under-concentration were becoming more complicated. The emphasis on industrial progress in the new cities proceeded to the detriment of social infrastructure. Air and water pollution became major concerns and anti-development lobbies emerged at local levels.

In November 1977, therefore, the Third Comprehensive National Development Plan (Sanzenso) was laid down, again targetted to 1985. After the shocks of the early 1970s, stable growth was a keynote in an attempt to actualise limited natural and energy resources. The plan sought to change people's consciousness and improve the overall living environment. Between 200 and 300 "integrated residential areas" were proposed as the vehicle through which the new ideas could be put into practice. Pending the release in 1986 of the fourth national plan (Yonzenso), the three schemes described provide the spatial planning framework for the technopolis initiative after 1980.

The Technopolis Plan: Prospects and Problems

"Technopolis" is a word coined to fuse the idea of technology with the "polis" of the ancient Greek city state, thus proposing an amalgam of scientific, industrial and urban development. The technopolis plan, first put forward in 1980, is a new strategy for the development of the intermediate or backward regions, aiming at the creation of attractive towns in which industry, research and development, academic activity and residential living are all closely integrated.

MITI, the proponent of the plan, observed that increasing numbers of Japanese would prefer to settle in non-metropolitan regions but, for this to be possible, it was necessary to provide suitable opportunites for creative work. The Ministry also considered that regional economies within Japan's 47 prefectures were approaching a point at which they could be independent of public investment and take charge of their own development. High technology enterprises, it was felt, should now respond to these issues by dispersing their research and development and production among the various regions. MITI would cement the relationships and underwrite its plan by providing certain fiscal and financial benefits to areas selected for development.

Figure 6.2. **HISTORY AND CURRENT STATUS OF REGIONAL DEVELOPMENT POLICY, JAPAN, 1945-1984**

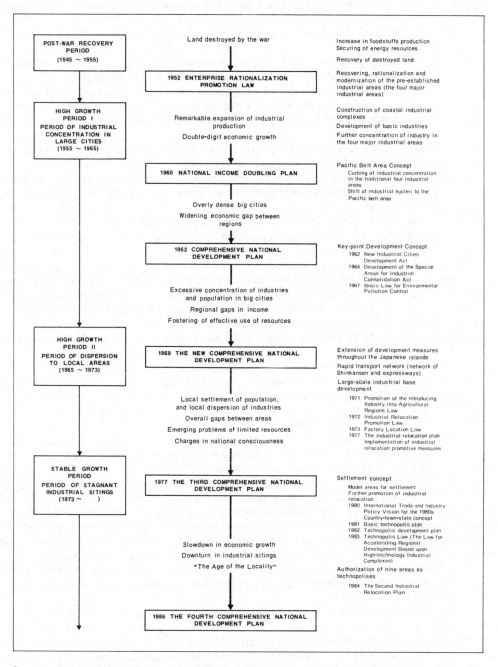

Source : Japan (Ministry of International Trade and Industry), unpublished internal documents.

Such was the interest among prefectures in the plan that 40 expressed a willingness to entertain these high technology developments. Having originally thought of two or three test projects, MITI found it necessary to draw up a list of selection criteria (cf. Maruyama, 1985: 80):

- i) Areas selected should not be ones where industry was already heavily concentrated;
- ii) They should be areas which offered favourable physical, economic and social conditions for the development of industry based on high technology;
- iii) They should be areas already with a considerable number of enterprises which are either engaged in high technology activities or have the potential for doing so;
- iv) Land for industry and for housing should be available, as should prospective water supplies;
- v) Nearby should be a city with a population of 150 000 or more which would play the role of parent providing certain urban facilities;
- vi) There should be easy access to a university or other institute of advanced technology where courses and research facilities of a high technology nature would be available;
- vii) There should be easy access to an airport, expressway or other means of rapid transport so that round trips could be made between the technopolis and Tokyo, Osaka or Nagoya in a day.

Another selection test was that prefectures had to be willing to provide the local initiative to develop a technopolis by 1990, in line with planning guidelines. A prefectural plan was thus sought, allocating land appropriately to industrial, academic and residential purposes and necessary public and private infrastructure. In some cases in which greenfield development was proposed, this would involve a rural resettlement programme.

The outcome of the situation is described by the Japan External Trade Organisation (1983: 2):

After great difficulty in turning down half the suitors, in 1982 MITI finally altered its initial plan and chose 19 areas involving 20 prefectures as prospective technopolises. (After) fiscal 1983, each year some of the 19 nominees, as their plans are finalised, will get the go-ahead from MITI to build their supermodern, technology-oriented communities with a variety of government assistance.

The *Japan Economic Journal* of 17th May 1983 next reported that foreign investment would be invited in the technpoles. MITI was to despatch delegations to the United States and Europe, stage a series of symposiums and work out packages for prospective entrants. By early 1984, it appeared that 14 regions involving 15 prefectures would be the first to proceed (Figure 6.1; Table 6.1). In mid-July, Anderson (1984: 5) indicated that the selection of the 14 was finalised and that MITI was ready to begin financing the plan. Programmes adopted typically relate to areas of a thousand or so square kilometres, the range being from 220 to 2 422. The proportions of individual prefectures designated as technopoles vary from 1.2 to 31 per cent but normally about one-seventh is involved. Existing populations range from 100 000 to 1 150 000 and average half a million. Within prefectures, between six and 60 per cent of the populaces are presently in a designated technopolis site, the average being 22 per cent (OECD, 1986 : 16).

These variations reflect the heterogeneity created by local participation which in Chapters IV and V was posited as a critical ingredient in regional technological development. Most sites have several universities or technical colleges (Table 6.1). Transport connections are usually very good either by air, road or rail. Internal integration is also under consideration since a technopolis need not be nucleated as at Sophia Antipolis: the components can be some

126

distance apart in the designated area. Physical development is thus proceeding with quite large tracts currently being laid out and serviced with roads and utilities. According to the OECD (1986 : 17) study group, "there is evidence of considerable confidence in the materialisation of individual technological and industrial developments".

Is this justified? By mid-1984 the concept of technopolis was sufficiently well-known to allow commentators to pose some questions. The OECD (1986) report leaves little doubt that members of the study tour were impressed with MITI's blending of technology and regional policy and in undertaking a bold new distributional initiative at a time when many other economies were simply trying to "make ends meet". It was not entirely clear, however, which high technology industries would be admissable in a technopolis. After some analysis, the report (OECD, 1986 : 22) concludes that up to 58 individual industries have been proposed but that 39 are contained within four groups: electronics, mechatronics, biotechnology and new materials. While this demonstrates a high degree of common interest, there is unlikely to be in the new plans any significant specialisation of technopolises or localisation of industry. On the other hand, the proposed industries share the characteristics of high value and value added, low weight and easy transportability. They should also enjoy a high income elasticity of demand which will allow output increases beyond the end of the century.

Further doubts have been expressed on the location of the 14 technopolises and whether it will be possible to attract good scientists and engineers (Anderson, 1984: 5). This is to question the very task that the Japanese have set themselves. Yet perhaps the enquiry misses the point insofar as it is claimed by MITI that the "scientists and engineers" are already in or would like to be in the targetted areas. Moreover, Western observers must be aware of elements of Japanese culture and character before forming hasty judgements. Have surveys actually been conducted of the living preferences of "scientists and engineers" or, following Macdonald (1983: 336), their supporting managers, marketers and accountants? Some years ago, maybe North Carolina also looked an unlikely settling-place for such personnel. And what of the similarities or differences of Western and Japanese high technology employees, the latter possibly with a lifetime employment offer and beset by increasingly severe problems of metropolitan living? Then there are the presumed disadvantages of the "remoteness" of southern Honshu and Kyushu. According to Nishioka (1983: 2), Kyushu has proportionally more airports than other parts of Japan. Apart from this, the Japanese National Railways Shinkansen (bullet train) reduces distances west from at least Osaka to only three or four hours' travel. The line presently extends to Hakata (Fukoaka) and the imperceptible "crossing" from Honshu to Kyushu by undersea tunnel scotches any idea of troublesome connections. The same applies to motor travel via freeways: there is a tunnel and a major bridge. Once on Kyushu, the technopolitans will find a climate and environment offering sunbelt conditions by Japanese standards [cf. Japan (Prime Minister's Office), 1984: 12]. Given that the place is already called "Silicon Island", these points should not be overlooked.

In the long run, distance may be less important than climate, environment and lifestyle. The technopolis scheme parallels others afoot in Japan. In the "teletopia" project of the Ministry of Posts and Communications, 99 communities are competing for the right to access fundamentals of the Information Network System. Each of the ten cities selected will build its own local system to serve its special needs and those of industry. Databases will be constructed and the systems will feature digital circuitry to make data quickly available. Videotext broadcasting and cable television will be provided as will inter-computer communications. In the long run, electronic shopping, home tutoring, medical diagnosis and video-conferencing will be added. Clearly, such developments should reduce feelings of remoteness: according to Anderson (1984: 5), the teletopians need not leave their videoscreens!

Table 6.1. Development plans, first 14 technopoles, Japan, 1984

Prefecture	Technopolis region		Target industrial sectors	Measures taken to strengthen research and development capacity
	Name of region	Principal university(ies)		
Hokkaido	Hakodate	Hokkaido University	Marine-related industries and those making use of natural resources (electronics, mechatronics, biotechnology, etc.)	Expansion of the Hakodate Industrial Research Institute; establishment of the Hokkaido Prefectural Centre of Industrial Technology
Akita	Akita	Akita University	Electronics, mechatronics, new materials, natural resources, energy, biotechnology	Expansion of the Akita Prefectural Institute of Industrial Technology
Niigata	Nagaoka	Nagaoka College of Science and Technology	Higher systems industries, urban industries (design, fashion), industries utilising local natural resources	Establishment of the Nagaoka Centre for the Promotion of Regional Technological Development and the Nagaoka Centre for Information Studies
Tochigi	Utsunomiya	Utsunomiya University	Electronics, mechatronics, fine chemicals, new materials, software	Establishment of the Utsunomiya Technopolis Information Centre
Shizuoka	Hamamatsu	Shizuoka University/ Hamamatsu College of	Optoelectronic industries, advanced mechatronics, home sound culture (electronic musical instruments) etc.	Establishment of the Institute for Research on Electronic Machine Technology and the Institute for Research on Medical Appliance Technology; expansion of the Shizuoka Prefectural Industrial Research Institute
Toyama	Toyama	Toyama University/ Toyama College of Medicine and Pharmacology/ Others	Mechatronics, new materials, biotechnology (medical, etc.), information industries	Relocation of the Toyama Prefectural Institute of Industrial Technology; establishment of the Centre for Research on Life Sciences and the Centre for Exchange in Advanced Technology
Okayama	Kibikogen	Okayama University/ Okayama College of Science	Biotechnology, electronics, mechatronics (medical and pharmaceutical industries) etc.	Reorganisation of the Okayama Prefectural Institute of Industrial Technology; establishment of the Centre for Research on Biotechnology
Hiroshima	Hiroshima	Hiroshima University	Electronics, mechatronics, new materials, biotechnology, etc.	Establishment of the Centre for Research on Frontier Technologies; expansion of the Hiroshima Prefectural Industrial Research Institute

Tableau 6.1. **Development plans, first 14 technopoles, Japan,** *(continued)*

Prefecture	Technopolis region		Target industrial sectors	Measures taken to strengthen research and development capacity
	Name of region	Principal university(ies)		
Yamaguchi	Ube	Yamaguchi University	Electronics, mechatronics, new materials, ocean development, biotechnology, etc.	Expansion of the Yamaguchi Prefectural Industrial Research Institute; establishment of the Yamaguchi Prefectural Institute of Industrial Technology and the Institute for Research on New Materials
Fukuoka Saga	Kurume Tosu	Kurume College of Engineering/ Kurume University	Mechatronics, fine chemicals, fashion, next generation (bio) industries, etc.	Creation of the Information Centre of the Centre for the Promotion of Local Industry
Oita	Kenhoku Kunizaki	Oita University/ Oita College of Medicine	Electronics, mechatronics, bioindustry, software	Establishment of the High Technology Research Institute and the Training Centre; expansion of Oita Prefectural Industrial Research Institute
Kumamoto	Kumamoto	Kumamoto University/ Kumamoto College of Engineering/ Others	Applied machinery industry, biotechnology, electronic equipment, information systems industry	Establishment of the Centre for Research on Applied Electronics Machinery Technology; expansion of the Kumamoto Prefectural Industrial Research Institute
Miyazaki	Miyazaki	Miyazaki University/ Miyazaki College of Medicine	Local-oriented (bio), introduction-oriented (electronics, etc.), and urban-oriented (urban systems) industries	Establishment of the Joint Research and Development Centre; expansion of the Miyazaki Prefectural Industrial Research Institute
Kagoshima	Kokubu-hayato	Kagoshima University/ Kyushu Gakuin University	Electronics, mechatronics, new materials, biotechnology, etc.	Establishment of the Centre for Research on the Development of Fine Ceramics Products and the Kagoshima Prefecture General Institute of Industrial Technology

Source: Japan Trade and Industry Publicity Inc. (1984: 55).

129

Projects like the technopoles and teletopias inevitably raise questions of costs. After Y 1 491 million in 1983, the government's 1984 budget for the technopolis plan was reckoned at Y 1 504 million or about $US6.25 million which had to cover: a) support for regional research and development; b) funding for industrial technology promotion organisations; c) financial assistance to smaller enterprises; and d) projects directly related to the plan. There will, in addition, be fiscal measures for designated high technology industries which locate in technopoles. They include a special depreciation allowance of 30 per cent for the first year for newly-constructed industrial machines installed in technopolis regions by corporations conducting business in specific advanced technology industries. Buildings and attached facilities will attract a 15 per cent allowance. Technopolis areas will be eligible for soft loans at 7.3 per cent interest: both high technology and certain infrastructural enterprises will be covered. The question, however, could be posed as to whether the differential of these over normal incentives will be sufficient to influence locational investment behaviour. This point may apply particularly to foreign firms. Large Japanese firms will have to weigh the alternatives of further domestic investment in technopolis sites as opposed to the country's simultaneous need to promote offshore investment for trade and balance of payments reasons.

Other doubts lie with the size of the government budget for projects related to the technopolis plan. For Anderson (1984: 5) the 1984 budget allowed "scarcely enough to buy the bulldozers". He points equally to the costs since 1966 of establishing Tsukuba Science City north of Tokyo and estimates that, on this basis, a complete technopolis could cost up to Y 250 000 million (roughly $US100 billion).

> With both central and regional governments already hopelessly in debt, there is little chance of sudden access to new funds. Intead, MITI is relying on industry and commerce to foot the bill (Anderson, 1984: 5).

Ignoring various important differences in concept and execution between Tsukuba and the technopoles, it is true that the scheme calls for private financing of much of the planned development including the Technopolis Development Corporations which will act as guarantors and training institutions. One must acknowledge, however, that the initiative is scheduled over 30 years so a focus on initial expenditures may not be especially appropriate. In this context, the OECD (1986 : 44) report is again prepared to speculate. Can authorities in Japan be any more certain than those elsewhere that the industry component of their plans will be fulfilled? It is impossible to be certain in any outright sense, but the Japanese economy has been highly successful over the last 30 or more years and there appears to be confidence that progress will continue at a sufficiently high level to justify the technopolis plans. On the other hand, despite 25 years of comprehensive national planning, acknowledged regional development aims appeared unsatisfied (cf. Furuki, 1983: 187-91) and the OECD (1986 : 44) party was left with the impression that some places were still trying to achieve their ambitions by presenting components of earlier plans in the new guise of technopolis.

Thus, the present consensus of (non-Japanese) observers appears to be that some technopoles will fall by the wayside. Others will assuredly succeed. The programme is founded in economic efficiency but could yield an appreciable amount of equity as a joint product. This will arise in part from cultural elements in Japan involving community participation, consensus decision-making and subsequent group alliegance. Some other countries may wish to adopt the successful elements of what is arguably the most enterprising regional development programme in the world today. Japan was once regarded as imitating others: now it is leading the way towards the risks and rewards of joint public-private enterprise. In sum, this case study corroborates the reasoning of the model presented in Chapter IV that a strong commitment to endogenous high technology development may allow pursuit of distributional as opposed to aggregative aims in regional development. So much is brought out in remarks attributed to Mr. Timothy Reid, former Chairman of the Working Party, by the Japanese newspaper *Asahi Shinbun* (24th May 1984) during the study tour:

> Some of the OECD Member countries have a view that, if their industry is to maintain an international competitiveness, they should exercise a centralised control and that they should not risk their industry to losing its competitiveness through decentralisation. However, Japan, like the United States, has a high international competitiveness in high technology and may therefore be able to afford to make use of its high-tech industry for regional development. I doubt if any other advanced nation is in the same advantageous position.

AUSTRALIA: DECENTRALISED DECISION-MAKING

Unlike the other nation under review, Australia has a long-distance economy and is relatively sparsely settled with just over 15 million inhabitants. Yet it is one of the most urbanised nations in the world with the latest (1981) census enumerating 75.5 per cent of the population in settlements of over 10 000 persons [Australia (Bureau of Industry Economics), 1985: 12]. By far the majority of urban dwellers live in six state metropolitan capitals which range in size from under 200 000 to over three million people (Figure 6.3). The country presents an urban hierarchy which is barren in the middle ranges (250 000 to 750 000) and, overall, there is a paradox of strong localisations of population separated by "wide open spaces". The regional framework has been compared with that of several other countries by Butler and Mandeville (1981: 32) based on their interpretation of OECD (1976a, 1976b) reports (Table 6.2). They portray Australia as a "region-less" nation and in a sense this is true: with exogenous settlement dating only from 1788 there may have been less time than in more established settings for diversity to emerge. Certainly from 1980-81 data assembled by the Australian Bureau of Industry Economics (1985: 85-90), regional disparities in unemployment by state in Australia were smaller than in the United Kingdom, Canada or the United States. Against an Australian average of 100 (equalling six per cent unemployment in 1981), indices for individual states ranged from 94 to 128. Simultaneously British regions ranged from 70 to 160 (base 100 equalling 11.2 per cent), Canadian provinces from 93 to 202 (base equals 8.3 per cent) and American states from 16 to 174 (base equals 5.8 per cent). Regional income differentials were also lower in Australia: a range of 87 to 104 about a national index of 100 (1981), compared with 81 to 112 in the United Kingdom (1976), 66 to 110 in Canada (1979) and 69 to 125 in the United States (1979). Notwithstanding this evidence regional problems definitely exist, possibly different from those of other countries and demanding of different policy responses [Australia (Bureau of Industry Economics), 1985: xv].

For much of the postwar period, the chief regional problem lay in a perceived need to decentralise population and economic activity away from the metropolises. Until relatively recently the bulk of the national spatial effort was directed to this end. In the 1960s and early 1970s there was apprehension that major urban areas were congested, leading to both economic inefficiency and inequities related to a lack of services. The population distribution was further seen as producing inequity in that many country centres lacked the range of services available in cities. Whether due to policy initiatives or equilibrating market forces (including natural resource development), the tide of urban concentration began to change after 1976. In the 1976-81 intercensal, the share of national population resident in settlements of over 100 000 persons fell from 64.4 to 62.9 per cent.

Simultaneously, the world economic situation led to the emergence of new, structurally-oriented, regional problems. In 1979 the Australian Study Group on Structural Adjustment (1979, 14.4-14.5) argued that location-specific interventions should be implemented within the framework of a long-term regional policy rather than as *ad hoc* responses to the problems of firms. Yet the Group (1979: 14.9) was unable to identify such a framework. This was seen to create difficulties in choosing an appropriate policy response to a particular regional problem.

Unlike Japan, Australia is a federation, consisting of six sovereign states and two now relatively autonomous territories (Northern and Australian Capital). The significance of the federal structure to Australian industry arises from the division of powers between the Commonwealth and state governments. The Australian constitution, dating from federation in 1901, specifies the powers of the former. Those not detailed, the residual powers, may be exercised by the states. They cover a wide range of functions which impinge on economic activity. While the Commonwealth maintains important fiscal functions such as acting as the prime raiser of revenue, states undertake much of the expenditure. Together, the residual legislative powers and consequent spending responsibilities enable states to exercise a significant influence through assistance to and regulation of industry [Australia (Industries Assistance Commission), 1981a: 37].

Section 99 of the constitution charges the Commonwealth not to prefer one state or any part thereof over another state or its component regions. Section 51^2 allows the Commonwealth to legislate concerning taxation but not so as to discriminate between states or part of states. Conditions of this type have historically restrained federal governments from highly directive action. States retain control of land and therefore land-use planning, as well as local government. Each state actively encourages economic development within its borders and provides a wide range of assistance measures to different sectors. Local authorities in both metropolitan and non-metropolitan centres also promote development, mainly by offering direct incentives such as the provision of industrial land and rate concessions for local government services.

Some of the states cover massive areas but there has not developed a recognised level of regional decision-making. Important policies have not varied significantly over the postwar era despite substantial changes to the national economy. According to the Australian Bureau of Industry Economics (1985: xiv), the relevance of available regional policy to today's milieu is an area of increasing concern. Some understanding of events during the 1970s underpins an exposé of the current situation at federal and state levels.

The Federal Role

After 23 years of conservative government, many Australians supported the Labor regime that came to power under E.G. Whitlam in December 1972. At that time the electorate was concerned about deteriorating metropolitan lifestyles, and the incoming prime minister had himself recognised that social inequality sprang more from where one lived in Australia than how much one earned. This and many other points are usefully brought out by Logan (1979) who traces the history of regional initiatives throughout the 1970s. On Whitlam's accession, there was relatively little regional policy at any level of government. A fledgling authority, NURDA (National Urban and Regional Development Authority), was in place to advise the federal government and to determine the extent, terms and conditions

132

under which funding for regional and urban development could be afforded the states. Under Labor it was renamed the Cities Commission and concentrated on physical planning – putatively on developments engineered by its partner organisation DURD (Department of Urban and Regional Development). DURD became the policy arm of the Commonwealth and for three years after 1973 was extensively funded to deal with regional and urban planning problems including assistance to and co-operation with state and local governments.

Tangible schemes of the Whitlam era were the 1974 SANMA (Special Assistance to Non-Metropolitan Areas) programme, a structural adjustment mechanism designed to dampen the disruptive (and rather localised) effects of the 25 per cent across-the-board tariff cuts of July 1973. Total payments in the three years to 30th June 1977 were $A66 million. Concurrently, the RED (Regional Employment Development) scheme was established to subsidise job opportunities in areas of high unemployment. These short-lived programmes were typical of those then applying in other OECD nations. More notable were the urban initiatives. Following the experience of state governments in the 1960s and the advice of

Figure 6.3. **AUSTRALIA STATES AND SELECTED URBAN CENTRES, 1985**

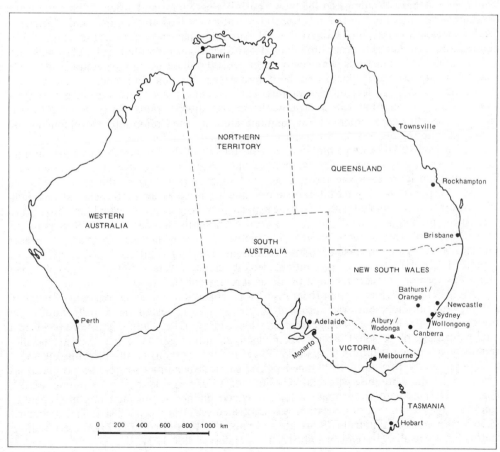

Table 6.2. **Comparison of spatial features,**
Australia and selected OECD nations

Nation	Similar features			Different features		
	Land mass	Existence of regional inequalities	Geographical population distribution	Land mass	Existence of regional inequalities	Geographical population distribution
United Kingdom				X	X	X
Finland			X	X	X	
Norway		X	X	X		
France				X	X	X
Canada	X		X		X	

Source: Butler and Mandeville (1981: 32).

consultants, both the Cities Commission and DURD proposed a selective approach to efforts to decentralise the population. Keynotes of the programme from 1973-75 were the regional growth centres which, after initial support, were intended to become self-sustaining. The leading one, Albury-Wodonga on the New South Wales/Victorian border, still maintains its development corporation but federal allocations to others at Bathurst/Orange and Macarthur (both New South Wales) and Monarto (South Australia) have now ceased (Figure 6.3)[1]. It is questionable whether this programme could have been consummated had Labor won the 1975 elections. The start-ups were costly (over $A100 million being allocated in both 1975 and 1976) and economic conditions both internationally and domestically deteriorated throughout the critical development phases. The incoming Fraser conservative government was unwilling to continue such large-scale spatial interventions. In 1976 DURD was incorporated into a Department of Environment, Housing and Community Development and from that time regionalism in Australia lost much of its prominence.

The period 1972-75 was a highly innovative one in regional policy in Australia though, perhaps in an expensive way, it fell far short of the strong interventions witnessed elsewhere. Over a decade later even the most committed supporters recognise flaws alongside the successes of the era. Among the latter must be counted: the elevation in the political agenda in a very short time of regional policy; and the rapid assembly of expertise which was brought to bear on the problems at hand. Yet, this expertise gradually dissipated after 1976 as teams were dismantled and budgets reduced or abolished. It was not simply that the Fraser government faced much worse economic conditions than had Whitlam in 1972 but, like its Liberal-National predecessors, its political ideology did not favour extensive spatial planning which was seen as an encroachment on the sovereignty of the states.

After 1975, therefore, a "new federalism" was proposed in which responsibility for urban and regional development was returned to the states. It rested on a restructuring of intergovernmental financial arrangements in which state and local administrations received a fixed percentage of personal income tax receipts as untied grants rather than as specific-purpose grants under Whitlam (Logan, 1979: 155). The Commonwealth's direct involvement was progressively run down in planned public service spending cuts. Some programmes remained, but their funding was relatively limited. An example is the 1977 Commonwealth Regional Development Programme which provided finance to selected non-metropolitan ventures. By the time its organisation was abolished on 30th April 1981 it had disbursed $A36.5 million in loan funds to 79 private and public sector projects in 39 non-metropolitan centres [cf. Australia (Bureau of Industry Economics), 1985: 127].

In March 1983 the Fraser government was replaced by a Labor administration under R. J. Hawke. Labor's 1984 policy platform commits the government to minimise the adverse regional impacts of changes in Australia's economic structure and to take full account of evolving demographic and regional development patterns. It further asserts that:

Regional adjustment and development issues ought to be handled by positive government regional policies in order to enable regions to develop their advantages in terms of both human and natural resources, to broaden their economic base and to provide increased trade, employment and educational opportunities within regions. These policies ought to be complemented by regional assistance measures to ease the problems of adjustment for those most directly affected by regional dislocation and structural economic change (Australian Labor Party, 1984: 219).

A framework for discussion of federal initiatives is provided by Filmer and Foster (1977). The constitution has determined that federal influence is exerted mainly through macro rather than microeconomic means (the latter being more associated with the states). Among the macro techniques, the two authors find little evidence of monetary policy applied to regional purposes, mainly because of difficulties inherent in its use which were outlined in Chapter III. Attention therefore turns to fiscal measures.

The most significant is the operation of the Commonwealth Grants Commission which since 1933 has enquired into applications by states for federal grants or special financial assistance. Its has traditionally aimed to alleviate financial stress to enable states efficiently to discharge their functions in parallel with others as members of the federation. More recently, this principle has been expanded to provide that each state should be able to offer similar standards of government service without imposing taxes and charges appreciably different from those of other states. In this way the Grants Commission has become a major vehicle of spatial redistribution, redressing inequalities extant at state or local levels in capacities to raise revenue, in relative costs of providing services, and in accomodating the budgetary impacts of the operations of business undertakings. The extent of fiscal equalisation is significant. The difference between the actual distribution of funds and that which would have occured in 1984-85 on the basis solely of population has been estimated as $A825 million, transferred from New South Wales and Victoria to other states (McAuley, 1984: 5). To O'Connor (1984: 130) the Grants Commission's work is the major reason for the lower interregional disparities, quoted earlier, within Australia relative to other countries.

Another macroeconomic measure is the tariff, designed to provide industry-specific assistance. For much of the postwar period, Australian industrial policy favoured import-competing activities and protection was used to direct resources to the relevant sectors. A chief beneficiary was manufacturing though within the secondary sector there are wide variations in tariff levels and in the location of recipient industries. Historically, Victoria and South Australia, which tend to specialise in labour-intensive industries, have received relatively greater protection than other states [Australia (Industries Assistance Commission), 1981b: 12]. Correspondingly, larger urban areas may generally be favoured over rural regions where less manufacturing exists. But since the 1970s federal policy has been to promote the development of industry which is more competitive, specialised, export-oriented, flexible and adaptive. Part of such a move has involved a gradual reduction of tariffs by levels of up to a third during the last decade. As Filmer and Foster (1977: 95) remark, tariffs are an "extremely blunt" spatial instrument. It is doubtful that they have ever been regarded as a regional policy tool in Australia but indications are that what bearing they had is likely to lessen in future.

Related to tariff questions are special assistance and adjustment initiatives as in the recent Steel Industry Plan. To avoid severe social and economic burdens in the steel regions of

Wollongong and Newcastle (New South Wales) and Whyalla (South Australia), the federal government offered over $A100 million over five years to stimulate economic development and provide additional employment and training (Figure 6.3). These funds, disbursed under an agreement with the national monopolist producer, the Broken Hill Proprietary Co. Ltd, are designed to restore long-term industry viability. The plan recognises the strategic and economic importance of maintaining a steel industry in Australia and, in terms of federal actions, proposes unusually specific spatial repercussions.

Other interventions straddle the boundary of macro and microeconomics. The Commonwealth administers the vast majority of social welfare and income-maintenance programmes in Australia and distributes funds without particular focus on the fiscal capacities of regions. This practice contrasts with those adoopted in other OECD federations such as the United States. Other cross-subsidies are incorporated into various utility charges, particularly in posts and telecommunications and also in regulated transportation industries. Taxation concessions have been offered the mining industry which, because of its decentralisation, benefit non-metropolitan areas. Concessions have similarly been extended to petroleum exploration and development companies, this having a positive impact on remote areas such as northwestern Australia. Overall, the continent is differentiated with respect to personal income tax liability and concessions are available for inhabitants of remote regions. Such areas have also from time to time received targetted structural adjustment assistance when key employing industries have encountered difficulties. Various forms of aid are regularly offered to primary industries in rural areas for product research and development, restructuring or marketing. Finally, infrastructural projects may be noteworthy, including irrigation schemes, railway and road construction, the placement of military and educational institutions and the development of the decentralised national capital, Canberra. Yet in a country as large as Australia it would take many such initiatives to sum to a centralised regional policy. Given the constitutional constraints to individual interventions, the corollary is decentralised decision-making via the states and territories.

State Government Initiatives

"Regional policy" in Australia has traditionally been effected at the level of the states and, to the extent that each has an industrial development programme, factory placement is dispersed around the nation. There are, however, differences among states in economic bargaining power and they affect quite markedly the intrastate application of regional industrial policy. To clarify, the dispersion of manufacturing beyond the major metropolis has not been strongly emphasized in economically peripheral states (cf. Loveday, 1982: 147). In core regions of New South Wales and Victoria, by contrast, far more active regional policy has appeared in the form of a "decentralisation" effort to encourage economic activity away from primate capital cities. The rationale has included the alleged lifestyle advantages of non-metropolitan living, negative externalities in the large cities and the apparent strategic advantages of a more dispersed pattern of settlement (cf. Carter, 1983: 1). Metropolitan dominance is thought to truncate the development of alternative centres and may also be associated with inequalities in income distribution. In general, distributional as opposed to other aims have dominated regional initiatives at state level in Australia (cf. Schofield, 1979: 251).

Programmes have featured microeconomic instruments and have been very broad in application. Though usually only manufacturing or tourist development has been eligible (and some would criticise the neglect of service industries), assistance has been economically

136

automatic on most parameters and spatially expansive in that virtually all but the metropolitan locations have been considered. Carter (1983: 8) speaks further of "blanket" policies in that, within non-metropolitan areas of states, aid has not been strongly targetted, though this is gradually changing.

While successive federal governments have adopted rather indirect regional measures, the states have been quite interventionist and would probably have spent more had funds been available. This may be a characteristic of regional development in some federal systems though the possibility of a unanimous interventionist response among states is reduced in countries like the United States which have not several but many constituents. Australia's states have emphasized capital reallocation (Figure 3.1). External adjustment techniques, especially relocation, dominate: they are positive (involving incentives) rather than negative (controls). Most states specialise in offering assistance with economic inputs and, in this limited domain, strive to promote their packages. To enumerate them all is a big task and Australia has no annual recording system of the Yuill and Allen (1980-84) model. A list prepared in 1981 is the best starting point (Table 6.3).

All states have been active in providing the general infrastructural elements of roads, railways, water supplies, communications and so on, though the process obviously has further to go in Queensland, Western Australia and the Northern Territory than in the more densely-settled south. Levels of capital or operating assistance vary depending on the proclivities and capacities of the states. As regards the development of land, factories and industrial estates, Queensland and New South Wales (in its regional growth centres) have led expenditures. The former in fact increased both its number of factories and manufacturing employees during the depressed later 1970s (Wadley, 1986), so perhaps the heavy involvement as a property developer paid off. It has been estimated that among the states, the reduction of occupancy costs in public as opposed to private estates ranged from 20 to 80 per cent [Australia (Bureau of Industry Economics), 1985: 140]. Victorian policy has not favoured estate-building and amounts advanced in Western Australia and Tasmania are negligible (Table 6.4).

By one means or another, all states offer housing assistance for key employees of decentralising firms. Loans may be provided at below-market rates, or properties may be rented preferentially to companies or their staff. The former approach is that of New South Wales, Victoria and Tasmania (though the expenditure of the last has been only nominal in recent years). Remaining states (and also New South Wales) engage in the construction, leasing and renting of houses: difficulties exist in estimating the extent of benefits offered but they are thought small (Table 6.4).

All states offer financial assistance to manufacturers for specific projects or general purposes by way of loans or loan guarantees. Such offers are made only after finance from commercial sources has proved unavailable or prohibitively expensive. Other forms of aid may include expansion or establishment grants or subsidies and lease/purchase arrangements. In New South Wales, Victoria and Tasmania, preference is given to high technology industries, those which are export-oriented or will require a large workforce. Queensland and Western Australia favour new or "pioneer" industries. Although interest rates charged by authorities vary from state to state, financial assistance to industry usually contains a subsidy *vis-à-vis* commercial sources and in 1980-81 this was estimated nationally to be around $A0.65 million [Australia (Bureau of Industry Economics), 1985: 136].

Payroll and land taxes are fiscal measures open to Australian states: equally, rebates can be offered to manufacturing firms. Such incentives have been of major importance in the decentralisation packages of New South Wales and Victoria and, latterly, South Australia. By contrast, they are unavailable in Queensland and a rarity in Tasmania. Where offered, the

Table 6.3. State government assistance measures for industry[a], Australia, 1980

Assistance type	Measure	State[b]					
		New South Wales	Victoria	Queensland	South Australia	Western Australia	Tasmania
Infrastructure	Various types of projects	X	X	X	X	X	X
Capital or Operating	Provision of industrial estates, land and/or factories	X	X	X	X	X	X
	Housing						
	Loans	X	X				X
	Government provided	X				X	
	Loans and loan guarantees	X	X	X	X	X	X
	Interest payment subsidies			X	X	X	
	Expansion or establishment grants or subsidies						
	Other grants and subsidies	X	X	X	X	X	X
	Specific industry assistance	X	X	X	X	X	X
	Payroll tax rebates	X	X		X	X	X
	Land tax rebates	X	X		X	X	X
	Purchase of shares			X	X		X
	Relocation and removal assistance						
	Equipment	X	X	X	X		
	Personnel	X	X		X		X
	Regional significance grants					X	
Labour	Grants or subsidies to employers for labour costs	X	X		X		
	Training						
	Assistance to country apprentices	X		X			
	Government training courses						X

Table 6.3. **State government assistance measures for industry**[a], **Australia, 1980** (continued)

Other Inputs							
Energy, etc.							
Subsidies for water supply, sewerages, electricity and other services			X	X		X	
Transport							
Rail freight concessions or subsidies	X	X	X		X	X	
Road transport concessions	X		X				
Subsidies for demurrage and warehousing	X		X				
Special primary producer freight subsidies	X		X	X		X	
Marketing							
Government purchasing preferences	X	X	X	X	X	X	
Export marketing assistance	X	X	X	X	X	X	
Promotion schemes	X	X	X	X		X	
Market research	X	X	X	X		X	
Technology							
Subsidies to engage technical consultants	X	X		X		X	
Industrial design grants or subsidies	X		X			X	
Subsidies for feasibility studies	X					X	
Provision of technical services	X	X	X	X	X	X	
Pest and disease eradication assistance	X	X	X	X	X	X	
Grants for research and development	X	X	X	X	X	X	
Government research and development	X	X	X	X	X	X	
Special services							
Small business advisory services	X	X	X	X	X	X	
Tourist agencies	X	X	X	X	X	X	
Funding development agencies or committees	X	X	X	X	X	X	

a) While these measures were offered by the States, assistance may not have been provided in each case during 1980.
b) Data for Territories unavailable.
Source: Adapted from Australia (Industries Assistance Commission) (1981a: 213-14).

139

rebates are graded spatially on a percentage basis to take account of disadvantaged areas or those with special claims (Table 6.4).

The purchase of shares is an "intervention" which in the Australian context warrants certain attention. This measure has been used in the 1980s as a protectionist strategy by the peripheral states to ward off takeovers by Sydney or Melbourne-based companies. This is done not on purely sentimental or parochial grounds but because takeovers often mean if not outright asset stripping by raiders then the removal of corporate head office functions and downgrading of facilities to branch status. Such intervention by the state is assuredly controversial and may be costly if stocks fall (whether such partial nationalisation depresses prices in the short-term is another matter). Although the ability of the state to buy into local firms is obviously limited by a lack of funds, the process is notable as a possibly undesirable manifestation of regional policy in decentralised decision-making conditions.

Most states offer removal and relocation assistance to firms newly-establishing from elsewhere. New South Wales, Victoria and Queensland have additionally made grants available to companies about to decentralise within the respective states. Awards cover principally plant and equipment but, with discretionary approval, may be extended to include personal effects of key employees. Sums put forward have been significant in the case of New South Wales and Victoria but less so elsewhere (Table 6.4).

Table 6.4. **Expenditures on major identifiable forms of assistance
for regional and state development, Australia, 1980-81**

$A '000

Form of assistance	State[a]					
	New South Wales	Victoria	Queensland	South Australia	Western Australia	Tasmania
Industrial estates						
Land	2 237	–	5 268	nd	34	120
Buildings	–	–	2 451	nd	–	–
Housing						
Loans	2 166	3 500	–	nd)	1 001	–
Construction	337	–	24	nd)		–
Financial assistance – manufacturing						
Loans	10 166	10 288	–	280	40	1 444
Loan guarantees	190	(b)	4 010	11 900	2 560	3 241
Capital establishment grants	–	–	–	1 043	–	–
Financial assistance – tourism						
Loans	794	3 700	–	na	na	30
Loan guarantees	–	–	–	na	na	1 000
Payroll and land tax rebates	10 061	25 426	–	2 746	278	161
Relocation and removal cost subsidies	1 274	932	16	(c)	–	–
Power, light and fuel subsidies	–	3 045	–	na	na	na
Freight subsidies	610	2 755	70	–	25	–
Preference schemes	8	37	na	na	na	na
Payment of interest subsidy	–	–	–	–	63	–

a)   Data for the territories not available.
b)   Included with loans.
c)   Included with capital establishment grants.
na   Expenditures not available.
Source : Australia (Bureau of Industry Economics) (1985: 131).

State government assistance to labour has been relatively small. The Australian Industries Assistance Commission (1981a: 211) has reported that New South Wales and Victoria confined such aid to decentralised firms for training or recruitment purposes to a limit of $A200 per employee. Schemes in other states were more piecemeal in nature, illustrating the general reluctance of governments to participate in this type of subsidisation, for reasons outlined in Chapter III.

Many "other inputs" are covered under state industry incentive schemes (Table 6.3). Victoria and South Australia have offered power and fuel subsidies as part of the decentralisation initiative (cf. Table 6.4), but overt and *ex ante* proposals to small firms are, in the Australian scene, generally of less significance than arrangements with large energy-intensive factories in fields like metals smelting. In certain cases, analysts have been unable to establish from published sources whether electricity, for example, is being supplied to major undertakings at prices which cover marginal supply costs. Obviously, preliminary negotiations and eventual agreements are highly sensitive matters for governments and corporations alike (Loveday, 1982: 157-58), not only in the framework of interstate competition for factory placement but also in the decision by corporations of where they will pay tax and in their international pricing and competitiveness. The subsidisation of reticulated services is "buying jobs" in the manner described by Blair *et al.* (1984): the only difficulty is that, at the scale outlined above, the subsidy is ongoing and may be kept covert. The public is not told the past or present "cost" of a job, whether the subsidy is efficient, or its likely size in the future. Capital establishment grants, a one-off payment, are obviously much more transparent.

Transport and freight concessions form another, sometimes problematic, operating subsidy. In Australia they have been offered to country firms in New South Wales, Victoria and Queensland to reduce cost disadvantages which accrue *vis-à-vis* metropolitan locations (Table 6.4). Invariably they apply only to transportation using state government railway systems which, as elsewhere in the world, have difficulty in maintaining profitable operations. The concessions may be teamed with the negative incentive (control) of road tax on private hauliers. The efficacy of such a situation can be questioned: is the policy aim to assist firms or to maintain freight volume on the railways? Are the two ends reconcilable or incompatible? Do railway subsidies take account of modal preference in goods transport in which rail appears now to exercise comparative advantage chiefly with respect to bulk commodities rather than finished goods? These issues are raised not as a specific critique but to point up possible problems with particular types of transport subsidies in regional policy. Further potential difficulties are set out by Vanhove and Klaassen (1980: 331).

Among all the other incentives, government purchasing policy draws most attention in the recent Australian Bureau of Industry Economics (1985) report. All state governments assist industry within their own borders by granting local manufacturers preference when tendering for public contracts. Preference is expressed usually as a percentage margin below the lowest tender submitted by a non-domestic firm (Table 6.5). In some states, additions to the margin may be available for decentralised companies or to those directly competing with overseas tenderers. From state to state, the administration of the schemes becomes extremely complex when variations in practice on several parameters are considered but the overriding influence remains the ministerial discretion to accept a local tender regardless of its price parity with competitors. This is a very significant power given the importance of state governments as markets. In 1983, both New South Wales and Victoria introduced schemes whereby, if a local firm's initial tender was not competitive with an interstate or local one despite the preference margin, negotiations could be commenced to allow another bid.

Though state governments form only a fraction of an overall state market, these anti-competitive practices are clearly disturbing from the viewpoint of coherent regional policy. However, they will not expand into full-scale market protectionism among states since that was abolished under the Commonwealth constitution at federation. The chief economic problem is that governments (taxpayers) are paying more for goods and services than they need. The latest developments encourage local producers to increase the price of their tenders, safe in the knowledge that a second chance is available. If, however, the first tender is accepted, the margin above "normal" profits becomes a straight transfer payment (of indeterminable size).

Strong interstate and federal efforts are now being applied to abolish local preference schemes which are increasingly seen as an aberration of a decentralised regional policy system. It is pointed out that at the national level interstate discrimination does nothing to create employment: the effects in one State cancel those in another. State governments can afford fewer goods and services because of the price inflations and so some margin of funds ends up as retained earnings in firms rather than as a payment to them to produce an employment flow-on. The policies encourage further fragmentation of an already small and fragmented market, reduce economies of scale and so lower international competitiveness. The severity of such effects depends, of course, on the size of respective government markets and the extent to which protective policies are applied.

The other incentives to do with technology and special services in Table 6.3 have been of relatively minor scope. This situation is likely to change as the focus of interstate competition shifts to the attraction of high technology industries. A conference among state ministers in June 1983 did not secure a basis for co-operative allocation of advanced firms, and competition for plant location, as per the general postwar model, seems the likely course. The states have set about producing individual technology development plans [cf. Queensland (Premier's Department), 1983] and establishing public or private technology parks. Although it is not yet clear to what extent technology and regional policy will be integrated, departures from past practice appear likely. A related point concerns small business development through the financial incentives just described or through special advisory services (Table 6.3). Such services are attaining statutory authority in various states and are likely to be an important adjunct in sectoral or regional development policy in future, not least because of the electoral muscle which entrepreneurs have mustered in the last few years.

Conspectus

Analysts in Australia recognise that the country's industrial economy is semi-peripheral in the global context, being small and far removed from core markets. Deleteriously affected by the recession of 1974-83, the manufacturing workforce has shrunk to around 1.05 million and the nation has witnessed recent falls compared with other OECD Members on various aspects of economic and technical performance. Truncation of corporate activity caused by quite high levels of foreign direct investment may express itself in fields such as research and development. Apart from the external handicaps the internal market is fragmented and spatially diffuse. Rather than instilling pessimism, these factors should underline the need for a well organised secondary sector, if not to achieve comparative advantage then at least to minimise comparative disadvantage. In this regard, the successes of small, resource-poor European OECD Members are often recounted in Australia.

Can regional, industry and incipient technology policies respond to the challenges presented? To some the key may lie with federal industry policy which in the past has been interventionist, using the tariff and other means of regulations. It may be difficult now to dismantle protectionist structures without major employment dislocations in a trade-off

Table 6.5. **Level of preferences, Australia, September 1983**

State or Territory	Level against the rest of Australia	Extra margin against overseas	Extra margin for decentralised industries
	%	%	%
New South Wales	10	0	2.5-5
Victoria[d]	10	0	5
Queensland	15	5[a]	5[b]
South Australia[d]	10	0	10
Western Australia	10	5	0
Tasmania	10	5	0
Northern Territory	5-10[c]	0	0

a) No additional preference applies against tenders from New Zealand.
b) This additional preference only relates to competitive tenders between Queensland manufacturers in and outside Brisbane. The extra preference is not added to tenders from the rest of Australia or overseas, as it is in all other States.
c) Made up of five per cent to local suppliers and five per cent to local manufacturers.
d) In January 1981 the Victorian and South Australian governments abolished preferences applying between themselves.
Source: Australia (Bureau of Industry Economics) (1985: 146).

which Warhurst (1982) sums up as "jobs or dogma". Yet even if structures were removed, the national government is limited constitutionally in the extent to which it can intervene in regional affairs. Assuming the *status quo* in intergovernmental powers and relations, the longer term welfare of the nation, founded on industry and economic competitiveness, thus relies importantly with the states. So much is supported by O'Connor (1984: 130) in arguing that:

> We really do not need a federal initiative in regional policy, directed toward states. The appropriate scale of operation of regional policy is within a state because it is there that the day-to-day networks of labour, information and contact between firms work themselves out, and it is in these networks that these initiatives can bear most fruit.

Co-ordination of regional policy at all levels has been of concern since first examined by the Australian Study Group on Structural Adjustment in 1979. Federal policy has the political objectives quoted earlier but is diffuse and seldom presented as a package. On the other hand, it is scarcely possible to suggest a national goal for the several co-existing state policies. Conclusions to the recent Australian Bureau of Industry Economics (1985: 172-79) report tend not to address the coherence of Commonwealth policy but rather to point out undesirable effects of competition among the regional policies of the states. It is not immediately clear how the dissipation of competition would benefit federal policymakers or whether it would allow them to vary their focus. At present that focus appears concerned with maintaining broad relativities among states and where possible exercising an influence at lower spatial levels with respect to structural adjustment. As opposed to concentrating on federal-state co-ordination the same report demonstrates significant interest in region-specific policies, if necessary at quite a fine scale. This seems much in accord with the conclusions and suggested foci offered by both Carter (1983) and O'Connor (1984).

Such attention to state programmes is obviously well placed and timely. Over six years ago, Logan (1979: 158) put forward the following controversial perspective:

> Economic and social linkages between (state capital) cities appear to be more significant than the interaction between each capital and its hinterland. Recent census data indicates that the volume of inter-metropolitan migration is large. It appears, also, that the growing concentration of ownership within the private sector leads to a situation in

which the large firms primarily serve local metropolitan demand and markets in other metropolitan cities, rather than an intrastate non-metropolitan market ... Thus it can be argued that the state governments are relics of a past system of spatial organisation and no longer the most appropriate level for regional planning.

Structural impediments may indeed have limited the effectiveness of regional planning in Australia. Both Carter (1983: 14) and the Australian Bureau of Industry Economics (1985) have disputed the effectiveness of certain state initiatives. Quoting a micro study in Victoria, the former argued that the decentralisation package was of critical importance in influencing the location decision of only 22 per cent of firms. Many non-metropolitan manufacturers are dependent on proximity to natural resources and are consequently not footloose in terms of location. Moreover, no tests of industry viability were necessarily applied, resulting sometimes in the placement of firms that shortly afterwards may have been restructured out of existence. Carter (1983: 14-15) thus concluded:

> Not only are the current decentralisation packages in Victoria and New South Wales likely to be ineffective and wasteful in achieving their objectives, they are not tackling some of the major problems faced by firms in non-metropolitan locations ... Meanwhile, in rapid growth regions, the decentralisation package remains irrelevant to problems of skilled labour shortages and pressures on housing markets and community services.

The Australian Bureau of Industry Economics (1985: 156) takes different examples concerning payroll tax rebates (rebated by the state, regarded as income and taxed by the Commonwealth) to suggest that State initiatives may have little effect on decentralisation. It maintains that insofar as incentives are used as a means of competition between states, they have a negative economic impact from a national viewpoint. Either they distort the location decision of firms, resulting in their failing to establish where costs are minimised, or they are simply unnecessary transfers to these companies. This reminds one of a comment by Rasmussen and Ledebur (1983: 752) on the decentralised regional policy delivery system of the United States:

> State and local programs are "rationally parochial" in that their purpose is served equally well with the creation of a new job as with the pirating of a job from a neighboring jurisdiction. If state economic development programs are to be integrated into a sub-national industry policy, these programs must be targeted to promote projects that are likely to increase economic activity in the nation rather than simply re-arrange the location of a fixed amount of activity. A locally based industry policy must focus on the issues of increasing productivity, increasing competitiveness *vis-à-vis* our international trading partners, spurring technological advance and revitalizing distressed industries. In short, the programs at the state level must be oriented to serve the national interest as well as those of the state and local jurisdictions.

Very recently one state has acknowledged certain criticisms and completely reformulated its industry-regional policies. Affected by the manufacturing recession due to its concentration of protected, labour-intensive industries, Victoria overturned its previous policies "designed to address a completely different set of problems" [Victoria (Treasury), 1984: 73]. The decentralisation programme is to be phased out, one-off measures ceasing from April 1984. Rail freight subsidies were discontinued in July 1984 and payroll tax rebates (cumulative cost, $A350 million; effectiveness, uncertain) will be dropped by June 1989. New policies aim at maximising long-term economic and employment growth in the state as well as achieving the government's broader social goals through business revival. A key aim is to make the trade-exposed sector of the economy more competitive in the belief that growth here will attract related development in "follower" industries. On one hand this will involve macroeconomic measures, industrial relations, improvement of capital markets and a reconsideration of regulation and the efficiency of the public sector. On the other it requires identification within the economy of areas of comparative advantage so that specific incentive policies can be developed.

Assistance programmes will no longer favour decentralised industries, a radical break with past practice. However, targeted aid will be provided to any Victorian industry identified as being of strategic importance in terms of growth potential, need for structural adjustment, and regional significance. In this way dynamic firms can be introduced to regions, regional economic bases which are dependent on declining production can be reorganised and additional infrastructure can be provided where necessary. In all cases, short-term or one-off grants will be preferred to ongoing subsidies, instruments such as loans or guarantees, grants, infrastructural investment and advisory services being emphasized.

These moves represent a bold swing to the aggregative rather than the distributional aims of regional policy and they will pay far closer attention to exchequer implications. They reflect a more sectoral approach to industry policy based on exploitation of comparative advantage in the major metropolis, Melbourne, and elsewhere. The possibility of such a strategy was examined by Wadley and Bentley in 1981 with the conclusion that metropolis-led industry development policies could intensify interstate rivalry for factory placement in Australia. In one sense, the previous accord has been breached and now it remains to be seen how other states, particularly the less advantaged ones, will respond to the Victorian initiative. If Victoria in fact manages to differentiate its competitive advantages, effects should be less severe. As to intrastate repercussions within Victoria, the implicit controls of the previous policies in providing alternatives to location in the state capital may have been diluted. While, in general, Australian cities can stand some intensification of land-use, care will be required to ensure that negative externalities within Melbourne do not outweigh the perceived benefits of the new policy.

Parallels appear to exist between the Victorian resolution and moves in other OECD countries which have reduced incentive levels and/or spatial coverage (cf. Chapter III). Yet is Victoria only undertaking in a microcosm what should happen in Australia as a whole if spatial relativities were used to maximise comparative advantage? The country is strongly oriented towards exogenous capital (Crough and Wheelwright, 1982: 1-2) and has experienced problems in encouraging high levels of research and development from private industry. In fact, according to Grant (1983: 239), it is lacking in technological sovereignty. A competitive decentralised regional policy may spread new growth but will this be done productively or so as to fragment and diffuse momentum? In all probability, Australia's pattern of control and technological capacity puts it in an indeterminate area of the policy model developed in Chapter IV and time alone may provide the answer to the question. McAuley (1984: 10) contends that notions of regional equity are time honoured and deeply ingrained and that it is unlikely that such differentials as exist in overseas countries would be acceptable. If so, then the maintenance of a capacity to resist such differentials could be more fully debated since regional economics has not been a particularly prominent discipline in Australia.

This country cameo points up intrinsic strengths but also problems which can emerge when states start actively competing under decentralised decision-making. The relatively small number of states also adds potential risks of synchronisation which may not exist in more extensive federations such as the United States. Competition is undertaken with public funds even though profits derived may not be returned locally. As an island nation, Australia has every capacity to determine and achieve a rational internal economic land-use pattern. The problem in spatial and economic planning is to ascertain whether the island hosts one nation or several sovereign entities, the patterning and delimitation of which has not been reassessed for the best part of a century.

CONCLUSIONS

Preceding case studies highlight the very different regional problems and responses in OECD countries as they adapt to the changed conditions of the 1980s. The detail has intrinsic interest and has been presented to demonstrate points at issue. A broad theme is the congruence of evidence with the policy model of Chapter IV. International influences acting upon economies and their competitiveness as reflected in industry control and technological capacity clearly had a bearing on the direction of regional policy, under whichever auspices it was pursued. At the scale of 24 OECD nations, a precise model may be elusive but the conceptualisation offered is sufficient in ordering and directing initial enquiry. At very least it provides a basis for considering the complexity likely to be associated with regional policy in the future.

NOTES

1.   The Commonwealth government is shorthly to join New South Wales and Cictoria as equity partners in Albury Wodonga and will share any surplus generated by the growth centre; both Bathurst Orange and Macarthur are supported by the New South Wales government.

Chapter VII

PROGNOSIS FOR REGIONAL POLICIES

A dozen years ago, Allen (1973: 35) was stressing the 3R's of regional policy – rationality, realism and relevance. Simultaneously, the OECD's (1974: 137-43) *Reappraisal* concluded that the definition of regional objectives in many countries could be tightened to achieve greater application and precision. These calls have stood the test of time. Future policy may involve different combinations of macro and micro instruments from those presently popular. Yet its success will rest not solely on its design and implementation. As important will be its integration with sectoral economic initiatives and its foundations in databases derived from research.

This chapter concerns the effectiveness and efficiency of future regional policy in light of the empirical circumstances outlined in Chapters I and II, the range of tools set out in Chapter III, the policy model and development options (Chapter IV), the impact on regions of technology (Chapter V), and the responses of selected OECD countries just reviewed. In determining futures for regional policy, the course now is to examine its context, focus, integration and the support required from research activity.

POLICY CONTEXT

The model used here has stressed the importance of international influences of various types on regional policy and it follows that they dominate discussion of its future context. At the broadest level, positive structural adjustment is a force to be reckoned with: it will translate into more specific issues impinging on the major blocks forming the OECD. These elements are examined in turn.

International Framework

In late 1983, a view expressed by Professor Franco Fiorelli, the Italian delegate, found wide acceptance among the OECD Working Party. He argued that the situation of regions now depends more on international or national factors than on the exercise of regional policy itself. In the OECD, the guiding principles of national development are, first, a desire to reduce protectionism and, second, the need for positive adjustment (cf. Chapter I). Clearly, these matters have important implications for regional development since the relevant report (OECD, 1983a: 75) argues that "regional policies and positive adjustment policies should and can be designed to be mutually supportive". Although the Working Party has not published a detailed response to the positive adjustment thesis, certain points are usefully raised in the present discussion.

There can be no doubt of the potential of positive adjustment to instil massive change through the internationalisation of production. The case appears based on an assumption of continuing and marked technological change which would presumably allow already developed nations to specialise in higher technologies, early stages of the innovation cycle or those fields in which high productivity offsets labour costs. A "trickling down" process could be envisaged in which productive functions are transferred from one set of nations to the next, as is already happening now. Perhaps the relative ranking of nations would not alter much: production sophistication would simply pass down the line.

The linearity implied in this process seems important to OECD and any other developed countries. Otherwise, the question "positive adjustment to what" could be raised (cf. Et-zioni, 1984). There must be presumably adequate product innovation and sufficiently long innovation cycles to allow ongoing adjustment. A radical restructuring of the international order could occur if barriers to entry in technology fall, innovation cycles shorten (cf. the Atari case in Chapter V) or there is acceleration in technology transfer. An outright technological challenge from a newly-industrialising or some other country is another possibility.

The positive adjustment case is thus radical in proposing ongoing change but it would arguably occur according to a particular set of precepts. The time horizons of positive adjustment are not presently clear. For the regional policymaker it will be important to know whether this accord is to be seen as more than a short-term response to recession: it may, instead, be a guiding multilateral position till the end of the century. If so, it would seem necessary to work towards some general statements on research and development and technological advance and transfer to ensure the continuation of the "front-end" innovations which would keep the adjustment process alive. If positive adjustment is in fact an implicit technology strategy which would in the long run define and exploit certain areas of comparative advantage for OECD Members, facilitating social and economic responses will be required from national governments. Many of these will have to come from the regional level. Further, the commitment of countries to positive adjustment has implications for nations' internal blend of sectoral and spatial economic policies. A scenario analysis permits some explication of a likely milieu.

Scenario Analysis

In as much as the past can predict the future, the first component of a likely milieu for regional policy lies in Tables 1.1 to 1.4. Broadly they suggest the continuing relative contraction of manufacturing (and, hence, expansion of services), unemployment probably remaining higher than in the 1960s and 1970s and moderate but variable inflation across the OECD. Yet the tables pinpoint nothing concerning the key global macroeconomic events – the shocks, and synchronisations which can develop and become difficult to manage. Any such eventualities, scarcely apparent in advance, could more influence regional policy than overall trends anticipated from past data.

OECD economic projections normally extend for two years beyond the time of publication. This is of limited use in regional development which characteristically involves five or ten year planning. Yet extenuated economic projections are often unreliable and are prone to unforeseen shocks. One thus seeks the best predictors available and deals in general aggregates rather than accuracy to two decimal points.

A European example of the analysis indicated is provided by Camagni and Cappel-lin (1981a, 1981b, 1982) (cf. Chapter II). It concerns scenarios for Community countries.

The authors note first that a high international growth rate can greatly assist the interregional diffusion process, offering increased industrial mobility and higher capital availability for foreign and interregional investments, diminishing concern for balance of payments equilibrium and greater possibility of international and interregional transfers both on the capital and income account. In their view, future community growth should be predicated upon productivity gains as many doubts persist with regard to employment expansion. In the latter 1980s, some generalised variation in weekly working hours, the appearance of new jobs in sectors linked to electronics and biotechnology and the end of the strong effects on labour supply exerted by the baby boom of the 1950s and early 1960s will probably reduce social resistance to change and allow higher productivity gains. Accordingly, assuming continued checks on inflation and a pick-up in investment, possibilities may emerge for more rapid reallocation of resources within countries according to regions' productive aptitudes.

Macroeconomic monetary influences will remain important. Monetary and exchange rate stability tends to help international convergence but hinders employment growth in the most disfavoured regions. Alternatively, an increasing divergence in exchange rates (as evident at present) works as a hidden employment advantage for weaker countries though, equally, it may widen inflation rate differentials and increase international instability. Such processes must be examined not simply within a economic grouping such as the European Community or the OECD because they apply in the same way to relations between block members and other nations. Thus a factor of considerable significance in future regional development within the OECD could be exchange differentials between Members and newly-industrialising or developing countries. They could be expected to have a major bearing on corporate decisions to invest in global core or peripheral regions.

Probable convergence of objectives in economic policy among countries of the European Monetary System lead Camagni and Cappellin (1981a: 165-66) to expect some reduction of international disparities within the Community. At the interregional level, they see renewed possibilities for decentralisation and diffusion based largely on technological developments. Electronics and control systems, for instance, may reduce the optimum minimum scale of production in certain industries allowing fragmentation of manufacturing activity. Transport and communications in relation to total costs are likely to fall, to the advantage of peripheral areas. The market will emphasize the importance of differentiated, customised and personalised goods and services which may benefit small or medium enterprise and offer greater opportunity for higher value-added production.

Yet, how far will these decentralising tendencies go? Are peripheral regions of OECD countries likely to attract investment or will the forces of deconcentration be sufficiently strong to leapfrog them in favour of other, even more peripheral nations? Though the answer may not be immediately evident, debate at this general level is more apposite than excessive reliance on econometric modelling. And what of likely counter forces? Camagni and Cappellin (1981a: 166) discuss industrial concentration and merger which would reinforce existing concentration in core regions, particularly in respect of headquarters and administrative functions. Similarly, unless radically different spatial trends emerge, renewed emphasis on research and development will exert a centralising effect within regional systems. Political pressures to preserve or enhance existing structures could work in a similar way to fortify old centres of production, but the effects may well be only of short-term duration. Finally, severe deflationary policies, rising interest rates and high exchange rates, and extreme interpretations of monetarism are likely to "reduce the possibility of autonomous growth in periphery regions ... and to raise the financial role of central areas" (Camagni and Cappellin, 1981a: 167).

Evidence just presented suggests ongoing pressure within the OECD for product and process technological change and the emergence within the major country groupings of both centrifugal and centripetal tendencies in location. It has also been argued that economic growth in Member nations might rely increasingly on endogenous enterprise and higher technology production. The latter is likely to impinge directly on the focus and bearing of regional policy. Of particular importance could be its posture to risk and concentration on employment generation.

Risks of Intervention

In the 1970s, the potential arose for mistakes in regional policy to become really costly, as much in retaining ailing enterprises as in losing new investment either through inadequate offers, delays or other factors. By the end of the decade, after the microelectronics and incipient biotechnology revolutions had been acknowledged, another element was added to the policy dilemma – potential help for new, high technology firms. This was perhaps one way out of the recession but raised the stakes of intervention because of the risks in this type of business (Macdonald, 1983: 331). Policymakers used to dealing with subsidiaries of well established conglomerates were forced to turn their attention to a new breed of entrepreneur whose technical ideas and managerial experience often had yet to be tested in the marketplace.

In these circumstances one must question the ability of regional development authorities to assess assistance proposals. Blair et al. (1984) underscore the fact that the government which supports industry with funds is, in effect, a joint venturer entitled to some return on investment in terms of a tax take, jobs created or other parameters. Not only must the right sectoral foci be chosen but investment assessments must be conducted with acceptable accuracy. One would guard against hasty support of high technology for its own sake. It can be a field with high non-systematic variation in rates of return: to what extent should the state become a business speculator (Brody, 1985: 17)? While different administrations will hold varying ideological positions on this issue and exhibit disparities in risk aversion, a key point is that regional policymakers should be supported by expert advice. What is indicated may be a joint approach to assessment by departments of regional development and technology. Also presumed would be some sort of national technology policy lest the relevant choices be simply left to field officers.

This new milieu underlines the fact that, in the past, regional policy has not been sufficiently recognised as investment activity under conditions of risk and uncertainty. A strategic outlook with careful monitoring of one-off and ongoing public investments is required today. Departments possibly need additional highly trained financial analysts with the flexibility to act quickly when required: a private sector background is increasingly appropriate. Agencies relying on incentives might come to see themselves more as a finance house than a public sector welfare operation. At least in the cases of research and development and high technology, regional policymakers should note the hard-nosed approach of the venture capital industry which some countries would see anyway as the body best placed to foster new types of production.

Issues of Employment

Among the inputs of labour, land, capital and management, the purpose of policy has become oriented largely to labour since 1974. Yet, one could equally focus on output measures such as levels or rates of production, or composite measures (productivity quotients) or derivatives of inputs and outputs (aggregate or relative income). With all this choice, is there a danger that policy formulation could become too narrow?

At the outset, such a possibility is less likely in decentralised delivery systems, particularly if competitive relations exist among member states. One can imagine loose and tight policies and, among the latter, foci could vary. Over a country, a diversity of aims could thus be expressed. It remains to be investigated whether the process is more effective in multi-state federations such as the United States (50 members) or the more "oligopolistic" situations represented by Canada and Australia with far fewer components.

Centralised delivery systems effectively run greater risks in nominating a focus or basis for evaluation. Here it is perhaps worthwhile to note that regional like most economic policy is ultimately about income and purchasing power, not input measures *per se*. In this light employment is important but remains an intermediate end. The feasibility of a full employment policy is widely doubted and the view has been advanced of six per cent joblessness as normal (Bartels and van Duijn, 1982: 103; Gartner and Riessman, 1984: 24). The point now is to examine the congruence of regional policy, possibly strongly employment-oriented, with a national outlook which, in some cases, might have conceded that total employment is a remote possibility.

In aggregate, the OECD (1984*f*) is unable to express any particular optimism on the jobs issue. Even to reduce unemployment to its 1979 level of 19 million would require the creation of 20 000 positions a day. Recently, only the United States and Japan have approached the necessary job creation targets: Europe has fallen seriously behind. The strength and durability of the current recovery will be a crucial determinant of future employment prospects. Further, there is a growing realisation that generating sufficient new jobs to counter unemployment is likely to remain a key problem in the medium term.

This structural and technological backdrop moves Bartels and van Duijn (1982: 106) to challenge regional policies focused mainly on employment. From Dutch evidence they argue that:

> Our main objections against this employment (distributing) orientation are that it may be detrimental to the attainment of important national economic objectives ... that it rests on some old-fashioned ideas about the determinants of personal welfare and the patterns of regional development, and that it cannot guarantee attainment of the full-employment objective.

Their response is twofold. First, they would adopt a more direct method of redistributing personal incomes. Preferred is a national economic policy that maintains the present relative level of welfare by stimulating promising new initiatives at appropriate locations. This measure, and carefully designed interpersonal income transfers, does not specifically invoke regional policy.

The second proposal manipulates the labour supply to accord with demand. It is said to offer better possibilities for an effective attack on labour market discrepancies and interregional differences in economic welfare than can be provided by traditional regional economic policy. It could also be brought to bear heavily on initiatives supporting endogenous enterprise. Policy foci would thus involve:

a) Extension of general education in problem areas in an attempt to enhance the functional and spatial mobility of labour;

b) Provision of more opportunities for recurrent education in order to both restrict and enhance the labour supply;

c) The setting of regionally differentiated retirement ages;

151

d)　The creation of a regionally differentiated average working time; and

e)　Introduction of selective incentives for the spatial mobility of labour.

Such initiatives have been conceived in and are obviously most relevant to a single country. The second set, at least, can be accommodated within the framework of Figure 3.1. While perhaps not inclusively applicable within the OECD, they raise interesting viewpoints, challenge orthodox policy (which in the event may no longer be overwhelmingly successful) and accord with a current school which holds that populations bearing the burden of structural adjustment deserve a disproportionately bountiful welfare reallocation. In future, therefore, *less* direct regional policies could be examined as to their potential effectiveness.

POLICY INTEGRATION

Adjustment among the macro and micro instruments of regional policy or to its focus will inevitably change its form. At the same time, related sectoral policy is also likely to alter. Co-ordination and integration will thus become as significant as the regional initiatives themselves. Recently, the rationale for sectoral intervention has been contested in the industrial policy debate in the United States but, beyond this, the nature of incipient technology policy requires attention. The issues are complicated enough in unitary governmental systems but will become moreso in decentralised ones. This section views regional initiatives in the evolving framework.

The Industrial Policy Debate

For those countries which choose to positively adjust away from older "smokestack" industries to newer and more viable modes of production, the question of intervention in sectoral development arises. It is largely coextensive with the arguments surrounding intervention in regional affairs. Yet the debate on "industrial policy" is presently much more focused and was both politicised and publicised in the lead-up to the United States Presidential election (6th November 1984). Merrill (1984: 447) explains that the concept of an industrial policy arose outside government. Various academics lent weight to the case after 1981, but they were principally lawyers, sociologists and political scientists rather than economists. As encapsulated in Reich's (1983) book, *The Next American Frontier*, the concern was both economic and political. Many observers were troubled by the federal response to industries' calls for assistance and impressed by the apparent foresightedness of other countries in reallocating resources to productive activities. Others viewed industrial policy as a means of arresting the outflow of capital from existing businesses and regions. Overall, the movement became identified strongly with the Democratic Party and was generally eschewed by Republicans. In the event, the case for and against specific public involvement has been put in a sufficiently generic way that broad outlines are relevant also to other nations.

For the industrial policy school, conventional fiscal, monetary and regulatory (i.e. macroeconomic) tools of the federal government are of limited assistance in dealing with the structural problems identified. It would place greater emphasis on infrastructural supports such as manpower training and retraining, research and development, scientific education, deregulation initiatives and so on. These measures would generally assist in making the economy more flexible, productive and capable of adjustment. At the heart of the movement, however, is a concern with systematic, largely microeconomic measures designed to produce an economic structure different from what the market would have created. It requires a strategy to deal in some way with the losers (i.e. to protect or dismantle them) while at the same time aiding leading-edge industries judged to have the potential to contribute to employment, technological advance or exports (Schultze, 1983: 6-7). Such industrial "targetting" is regarded as preferable to the seemingly *ad hoc* and unco-ordinated industrial policy produced by macroeconomic measures designed to produce a healthy "climate" for economic activity.

For the targetting to proceed, an umbrella industrial policy agency would be required which could implement a vision of the future by dispensing loans and subsidies, devising import and export strategies, altering regulations and so on. The outlook adopted would be based on consultations and perhaps consensus among industrialists, unionists, government officials and special interest groups. Their decisions would be effected by the agency's executive.

It is the sectoral discrimination and the idea of a government-led industry agency which has disturbed the many critics of industrial policy. First, various papers challenge the empirical evidence about the United States' economy upon which the industrial policy movement is founded [e.g. Schultze, 1983: United States (Congress), 1984: 25-39]. Of greater interest here are the theoretical and practical objections to the proposal which offer insights for other economies. McCracken (1984: 12) charges that the movement is "fundamentally weak in its theory of progress". A liberal economic order contains a well developed mechanism for generating and diffusing progress. To McCracken, further direct intervention by government would simply shrink the generation of new ideas to people with a view from the top. There would be less opportunity to use creativity which emanates from unexpected places: the bureaucracy opts for the familiar and comfortable instead of the new and upsetting. He recommends that instead of embarking on a new industrial policy, political inability to follow sufficiently disciplined macroeconomic policies is the matter requiring attention (cf. Badaracco and Yoffie, 1983; Levitt, 1984).

Schultze (1983: 10) worries equally about the difficulty of picking winners in advance. "Beyond a few broad characteristics, it is not really possible to set the criteria for identifying comparative advantage in specific lines of endeavour in advance of the fact". The knowledge, skills and ability attending successful innovation, marketing and export capability are narrowly-defined, idiosyncratic and specialised. They come from a decentralised search by firms seeking to exploit a particular advantage. Intrusion into this process by a government agency is likely to be positively harmful.

The difficulties of invidious choice in the United States' context are amplified by Badaracco and Yoffie (1983). To them, the obstacle resides in interest-group and partisan politics: the industrial policy idea is practically infeasible. Public attempts to reallocate resources on the scale envisaged would inevitably trigger major confrontations, even despite the existence of a politically independent policy institution. The difficulties can be imagined in a proposal such as one to penalise an ailing steel firm and instead subsidise the research and development of a computer manufacturer. Modern democracies are supposed to offer not just efficiency but also social and economic equity and, of the latter, government is seen as the chief arbiter. Thus, even if an industrial policy agency did successfully pick winners and losers, its implementations might be confounded by public expectations of government as a whole. Postwar notions of welfare and equality will not be easily overcome. The alternative, as conceived by Stein (1983: 66), is that the agency would effectively pick losers and then succumb to popular pressure to protect them at considerable cost to long-term national interests.

From this debate it is apparent that intervention in industrial policy has been re-examined probably with greater vigour than has regional intervention. The debate spills over into incipient technology policy insofar as technical change is a means of enhancing productivity and international competitiveness (Merrill, 1984: 445, Roessner, 1984: 430). Rothwell and Zegveld (1984: 438-40) examine innovation initiatives in several European OECD nations, Japan and North America. They write:

> Perhaps the most significant difference ... is between those nations that have a clear-cut, long-term strategy towards the development and exploitation of specific high technology product groups and new technologies and those that do not. In Japan and France and to a lesser extent in Sweden, Canada and West Germany, there is a clear emphasis on attempting to identify potentially important *new* industrial sectors. More recently Britain has joined this club with its emphasis on information technology ... In the United States strategy appears to be left largely in the hands of private companies. Policy tools are available to assist would-be innovative firms, but technology choice is determined mainly by market forces (original emphasis).

These alternative positions correspond roughly to the interventionist and non-interventionist strategies outlined in Chapter V. Indeed, the latter is strongly defended by the Chairman of the Republican Task Force on High Technology Initiatives in the United States Congress. Zschau (1984: 6) closely follows the critics of "industrial policy" by maintaining that "Congress must avoid the temptation to promote direct government involvement in tartetting 'winners' and 'losers' in American industry". His task force instead argues that targetting the *process* of innovation is the appropriate role for public authorities. This has four facets:

a) A strong commitment to basic research;
b) Incentives for investors, entrepreneurs and innovators;
c) A strong educational capability; and
d) Expanding market opportunities.

Admissable measures for Zschau (1984: 7-8) include research funding, reduction of the risk of anti-trust action against large-scale research consortia, tax incentives for individuals and enterprises, expansion of tertiary teaching and tax credits for contributions to education. The aim is to foster innovation: it cannot be forced. The role of the national government is to create a conducive environment for high technology development.

Technology and innovation policies have, to date, been less at point than industry measures. In the United States they have not generally been a partisan issue (Merrill, 1984: 447). This may relate to the fact that in innovation the business of selecting losers for public support is not entertained. Yet interventionist technology policies may in future select losers by mistake and will then have to account for themselves more fully. They have previously been rather loose in nature and often inadequately evaluated (Roessner, 1984: 433). As structural change continues and prospective rather than reactive measures become more important, this situation is likely to alter and technology policy could well lead industrial policy and thus become a key factor in regional matters.

Position of Regional Policy

Implications for regional policy of the above discussion are complex. Ideally, a congruence of industrial, technology and regional policies would exist: various possibilities are outlined in Table 7.1. It arrays the three types of policy in terms of their interventionism or

Table 7.1. **Industrial, technology and regional policies**

Code	Description	Policy type			Comment
		Industrial	Technology	Regional	
A	Interventionism	I	I	I	v
B	Non-spatial interventionism	I	I	NI	v
C	Technology only	NI	I	NI	?
D	Pre-technology	I	NI	I	v
E	Regional only	NI	NI	I	?
F	Non-interventionism	NI	NI	NI	v
G	Industrial only	I	NI	NI	v
H	Technology/regional	NI	I	I	?

I : interventionism
NI : non-interventionism

non-interventionism. The purpose of the exercise is not to be prescriptive about the several viable options but to underscore those which, for various reasons, do not appear viable.

Pure interventionism (A) is a congruent policy set practised by several European OECD countries. Non-spatial interventionism (B) is also possible and could characterise a federation which is unable to act directly at the regional level. The option of having solely a technology policy, however, appears questionable since, in general, a nation with a technology policy appears best served by applying the same level of intervention in its industrial policy. Option D could represent a situation in which a country has yet to develop a technology policy: it is certainly possible, though perhaps of greater application outside than inside the OECD. Solely regional policies (Option E) are questioned since it is difficult in the event to countenance an interventionist regional without a similar industrial stance. This possibility, however, is relevant in decentralised decision-making systems in which states have considerable autonomy.

Option F is complete non-interventionism which is consistent and evidenced in some parts of the OECD. So too is the course of having only an industrial policy: perhaps the regional outcome is regarded of less importance than aggregate or targetted growth. Finally, the case of a nation with a regional technology policy might appear somewhat inconsistent based on the need for congruence from technology to industrial policy.

From this depiction, it seems desirable for regional policy to integrate with the two sectoral-level policies. The majority of the options are currently observable in the OECD, indicating on one hand differing responses toward positive adjustment and, again, to the extent of regional policymaking. Some recent literature has suggested a direct link *from* regional *to* technology policy (cf. Option E): the question here is whether the direction of that argument is correct. Given the attendant risks, new technological development could see regional policy more closely integrated than before with other initiatives: as argued in Chapter V, its potential and success may well be foreshadowed by sectoral performance.

Governmental Systems

Only certain strategies in Table 7.1 appear to offer coherence and consistency and this depiction relates essentially to an unitary governmental system. Relations in decentralised administrations may be still more complicated. Situations can be imagined in which either the national or state partners are constitutionally dominant and they could enforce interventionism or non-interventionism throughout the system. Whatever its complexion, the operations of a federation will require close study at various levels. In the United States, despite all that has just been reviewed concerning the federal attitude to industrial and technology policy, some of the 50 states are prepared to intervene very directly and have adopted specific measures to attract high technology industry. Others have realised a need to overhaul their educational systems from kindergarten upwards, focus education towards technology and expand relevant tertiary faculties (Babbitt, 1984; Dubnick, 1984; Rosenberg, 1985).

Independent actions of this type may not be intrinsically undesirable in the push for enhanced technological development. From a background of finance theory, Rasmussen and Ledebur (1983: 756-77) discuss the portfolio balance and political dispersion problems. The former concerns the federal (or unitary) governmental management of a risk neutral investment pool. Herein, the riskiness of investments (i.e. direct financial interventions) may become correlated. Hence, the pool may not have the desired property of reducing variance in return by virtue of the large number of investments. In addition, the tendency to follow each other among governments which intervene in industrial and technology policy simply raises the spectre of excessive competition as a reason for failure. Clearly, these are points for interventionist unitary and strong federal governments to watch. Yet, the political dispersion requirement further complicates the attainment of centralised portfolio balance. Weighing against deliberations on risk versus expected rates of return is the necessity for administrations to distribute "investments" over the landscape in a satisfactory way.

Extensive federally-led decentralised systems of government may be capable of solving both problems simultaneously. In the United States context of high technology development, Rasmussen and Ledebur (1983: 757) maintain that

> With 50 states supporting the high risk/high return opportunities that exist within their boundaries, the probability that all 50 states will support the same industries will be diminished. Fifty independent investment pools are likely to follow various allocation strategies that will reduce the variance of return among the many projects undertaken. While any state may have a disproportionate number of lemons because its share of the investment is too small to guarantee realization of the expected rate of return, from the viewpoint of the federal financier of the program, independence of outcomes is likely and the many investments made by relatively risk neutral state and local agencies should offer a higher rate of return than is typically earned in the private sector.

This view bears interestingly not merely on the arguments about United States industry policy related previously but also on its rationale and strengths in the higher risk environment likely to be created by advanced technologies. Key aspects concern the number of states (within the OECD, this is maximised in the United States and Japan) and the autonomy they have. Whether regional policy is "derived" or not depends on these factors. Perhaps decentralised systems are administratively clumsier but they can spread risk. Centralised administrations can be highly efficient but risk channelling resources in the wrong direction. Both have, and are likely to retain, their fervent supporters.

POLICY SUPPORT

A vital ingredient for regional policy in OECD countries as it embraces the challenges of the 1980s will be the development of databases detailing conditions from the local to the international level. Apart from work undertaken by regional or national authorities, assistance can come from two further sources. The OECD Working Party from time to time provides reports on countries or multilateral regional affairs. Similar foci are apparent in the work of academic and other analysts. Ways in which the research of these two groups could be channelled are now discussed.

OECD Work

The object of the OECD is to provide a forum for the exchange of views and experience among Members, rather than to engage in research for its own sake. On this basis, the Organisation's strengths lie in empirical studies, particularly those requiring information from the 24 countries in a short space of time. Work of this nature can be both operational and substantive.

In the first area, the present enquiry has pointed up significant gaps in knowledge of regional conditions and even policies in Member countries. There currently exists no overall regional statistical framework for the OECD, as applies in the European Community. The Community's tabulations, however, provide an excellent starting point. Some work would be required to outline the regions of non-Community European members of the OECD, though Council of Europe (1983) regional statistics have already provided useful data for most such areas. In the rest of the OECD area the situation appears fairly straightforward: Japan has its prefectures, Australia and the United States their states, and Canada and New Zealand their provinces. An attempt would be worthwhile to compile a complete regional map of the OECD which might cover, for instance, workforce size, absolute and relative unemployment and absolute and relative employment size by sector. Though basic, these data would be a lynchpin for other work but the difficulty in compiling them should not be underestimated. Once a system existed, it could be updated annually.

A similar initiative could be adopted to establish a regular policy monitoring system. Already a solid foundation exists in the regional incentive yearbooks from the University of Strathclyde (Yuill and Allen, 1980-1984) which cover 13 European OECD Members. With the recording technology and means of collection established, any extension of coverage would be welcome, or perhaps the same methods could be applied by other workers to survey the rest of the OECD. The aforementioned statistics and proposed policy recording seem key elements to underwrite further OECD enquiries and would be of significant use to outside researchers.

Given the potential importance of technologically-instigated and endogenous forms of economic growth in future regional development, various major themes for the OECD Working Party arise from the present and foregoing studies. Four aspects of a medium term programme discussed in May 1983 should be pursued. They are: the stimulation of endogenous regional economic potential; technological innovation and regional development; the restructuring of lagging economies; and co-ordination of regional and other public policies.

Study of endogenous potential would assess new approaches to economic development which might enhance existing programmes. Under consideration would be the upgrading of technological and entrepreneurial capability, promotion of small and medium enterprises, improvements in management and vocational training, development of agricultural and agro-industrial resources and the exploitation of energy sources. Case studies are one approach. But wider enquiries can be contemplated, too, particularly in respect of small and medium enterprise which is a topic of interest to other committees of the OECD. Attention would focus on concrete instruments to encourage entrepreneurial or small business starts in regions and to generate export activity. Private/public sector co-operation is another legitimate object of study, especially insofar as financing arrangements are concerned. Interest further centres on strategies to retain existing regional business, sometimes involving new institutions at the national and regional level.

Additional work on technological innovation following the October 1983 workshop could centre on several topics. Assuming progress with the abiding definitional problems, the locational tendencies of research and development and high technology plants and incipient technopoles could be pursued. This would form a bridgehead for consideration of the employment impacts of such activities. Monitoring of assistance measures to entrepreneurs and small business in these fields will be of general interest to the Working Party which may also involve itself in developments in the venture capital market in Member nations. Another aspect is the enhancement of training facilities for technology workers and managers. Innovative forms of industry-university co-operation should continue to be recorded.

The restructuring of lagging regional economies will remain a thorny theme in research for the next few years, particularly *apropos* areas with high concentrations of stranded activities. The problem is both chronic and acute as witnessed by present adjustment problems in parts of Europe which continue to produce confrontations. Diversification is concerned with expanding non-manufacturing (or non-mining) activities and encouraging technological advance in order to produce a sounder base for economic growth. Some study should be devoted to the private service sector including financial, legal and advertising services and corporate head offices which may be sufficiently mobile to be steered to lagging regions. Monitoring will thus continue of programmes to restructure and modernise regional industry with particular note of innovative measures.

The importance of the co-ordination of regional and other governmental policies has been underlined in this chapter. Account is required of the relation of existing or developing national technology policies, industrial policy and regional policies since each is a dynamic arena in the current milieu. The spinning off of small and medium enterprise, employment schemes, measures to stimulate entrepreneurship, student awareness programmes – in fact, any sectoral approaches which bear on regional development will require attention. The complementarity of regional and manpower policy now appears more significant than ever.

Other Research

Academic and other researchers have different capabilities which can benefit from and simultaneously enhance work done in the OECD. Interest centres on several facets of their work: philosophical and theoretical progress; policy evaluations; and substantive studies.

Various critiques of regional development have been referenced in this study and they have a valuable role in balancing the activities of practitioners. After the shocks of the 1970s, many parts of the economics discipline are now "feeling their way" such that there exists something of a reluctance to be prescriptive on aspects as specific as regional development. Work in understanding the relevant national economic aggregates will remain of interest as will fledgling attempts to gauge differing international competitiveness in high technology and other fields. Leftist analyses have made some useful contributions in interpreting the internationalisation of production but may require a greater predictive thrust to be of general application. On the other hand, some conservative critiques might seek radical alteration or even the elimination of regional policy for the cause of efficiency: it remains for them to explain how welfare aspects are to be handled.

Evaluations of regional policy, both by academics and government agencies, are becoming increasingly sophisticated and now offer a viable means of choice among programmes and instruments. In view of the expenditures involved in regional policy, the pursuit of such work can only be applauded. Periodic audits are useful in keeping policy on track and may help to instigate the time-referenced and strategic framework which may be conducive to greater success.

The substantive enquiries are invariably undertaken within, rather than among, countries. Much evidence thus remains fragmentary but its potential is illustrated by the extensive use of academic and other studies in the present report. Unavailability of suitably detailed and totally up-to-date statistics often bedevils this type of research, a point individual governments might consider in their budgetary allocations.

Assuming sufficient data, various empirical analyses would contribute usefully to ongoing work in regional development. First, the behaviour of multi-plant and foreign firms appears of continuing interest. Researchers in the 1970s were slow to realise that such firms could close as well as open plants and, even now, recording at the regional level could be better developed. More is understood of the management and locational outlook of corporations but they are highly dynamic both in the product and spatial sense and it is erroneous to think that work completed before 1980 is still valid.

Regional policy analyses in the OECD, it is fair to remark, are disproprotionately European-oriented. A particular role thus applies for North American, Japanese and Australian/New Zealand researchers in economics, geography, management and related disciplines to contribute to the ongoing work. In particular, knowledge of Japan, the second largest economic entity in the OECD, is limited. This is mainly a function of the language barrier and it is hoped that economic analyses of domestic conditions can increasingly be translated for the elucidation of outside observers.

Greater attention to the service sector is indicated from this study. The first problem will be to obtain adequate statistical data since the two-thirds of most economies in services has been usually the worst recorded of all segments. Processes of firm formation, entrepreneurial experience and spinoffs would be useful topics for study, as would consideration of new work and remuneration patterns pioneered in services. The bearing of unionisation warrants enquiry. In the longer run, one must tackle the issue of whether services will be able to compensate for the employment shake-out in manufacturing. If not, research shifts onto an entirely new basis: what to do with stranded regional populations beset with an excess of involuntary leisure time. This is a question only whispered about at present: the strategic approach is to admit it exists and consider it before the situation, if it will, becomes worse.

CONCLUSIONS

The formal development of this project, presented at the outset in the executive summary, need not be repeated here. It suffices to note that the regional policy environment of the mid-1980s is not that of a decade earlier and, atop the previous problems, new sectoral and spatial dilemmas have greatly complicated the policymaker's work. Yet knowledge is now such that the framework of intervention is well established and there is no excuse for the application of blunt instruments. The 1980s have seen a willingness of authorities to discard old measures and constantly to try new techniques of adaptation. The future environment remains uncertain but, with constructive work, some progress in the aims of policy might be forthcoming from the growth avenues identified here.

Their analysis has been a key aspect of this report. Its central theme, from the model developed in Chapter IV, is that opportunities for mobile investment in OECD countries in the foreseeable future will be limited. Accordingly, development opportunities could be more satisfactorily pursued in the nexus of endogenous growth and higher technology production. For those nations which wish to pursue an interventionist regional policy, access to distributional (equity) as opposed to solely aggregative (efficiency) aims might be more forthcoming if endogenous, high technology as opposed to exogenous, lower technology investment is sought. Such a distinction is, of course, less important to countries adopting a non-interventionist stance. Unless they operate a decentralised delivery system, it is rather unlikely that the market will allocate economic growth in a very equal way of its own accord.

The current position appears one of increasing heterogeneity in philosophy and practice among countries. It has not been possible to suggest that all OECD nations will be able to undertake the distributional role of regional policy. Some may no longer want to try. Herein they would be supported by analysts such as Chisholm (1984: 352) who (for the United Kingdom) urges aggregative aims as follows:

> Reduction of regional disparities should not be the primary aim of regional policy. Instead, for the foreseeable future the focus should be on creating the conditions for adaptable local economies, and local economies which will foster local initiatives, as a necessary means to faster national growth.

So much challenges the view put three years earlier by his countryman Manners (1981: 298) that:

> Central government cannot indefinitely remain indifferent to the changing economic geography of the country, to the consequential problems that arise, and to the economic opportunities that might be foregone without its intervention. This applies both locally and over wider geographical areas. No government, in other words, can long escape its responsibility to take a strategic view of the interrelationships between its international and national policies on the one hand, and local, sub-regional and regional development issues on the other. Even the least interventionist administration requires the means to interpret these interrelationships through a formal dialogue and information exchange. It also needs the ability to reconcile those elements that are contradictory.

A means of synthesizing these alternative viewpoints has been outlined in the policy model. A further note will here suffice that in the past regional initiatives have moved in congruence with a desire for equilibration in modern society. They have reflected not only efficiency but also equity aims and the latter, if long neglected, tend to reassert themselves in the political arena.

Possibly politicians and policymakers have over-reacted to the setbacks after 1974. One could argue, indeed, that the decade before then was not really the norm but a period of aberrantly strong growth such that the later difficulties become more normal in long-run terms. The suggested reorientation to endogenous growth is now a harder but perhaps more stable road. Technological advance remains a rather unknown quantity but may offer some possibilities for reversing the preponderance of centralising tendencies evident to date. One might close with a vision of a perfectly competitive economy in which economic and spatial elements assume an equilibrium. In such a world equity and efficiency could coexist and it would not be necessary for taxpayers to subsidise private enterprise as now obtains. Regional policy would not need to exist because equimarginality would everywhere prevail. Against this ideal, it emerges that the ultimately successful development agency is one which presides over its own dissolution.

BIBLIOGRAPHY

Allen, K. (1973), "When Will We Learn?: A Critique of British Regional Policy", pp. 23-36 in Neil, A. (ed.), *Priorities in Regional Development*, Peterlee Development Corporation and IBM (United Kingdom) Ltd, Peterlee.

Allen, K. *et al.* (1977), *Options in Regional Incentive Policy*, Wissenschaftszentrum, Berlin, 48 pp; see also in final form as Chapter 1, pp. 1-34 in Allen, K. (ed.) (1979), *Balanced National Growth*, Lexington Books, Lexington (Mass.).

Anderson, A. (1984), "Japan's Tomorrow Here Today", *Nature*, 310 (No. 5972, 5th July), p. 5.

Antikainen, A. (1981), "The Regional Impact of Universities in Finland", *Higher Education*, 10, pp. 437-48.

Armstrong, H.W. (1978), "Community Regional Policy: A Survey and Critique", *Regional Studies*, 12, pp. 511-28.

Armstrong, H. and Taylor, J. (1978), *Regional Economic Policy and its Analysis*, Philip Allan, Oxford, 335 pp.

Ashcroft, B. (1982), "The Measurement of the Impact of Regional Policies in Europe: A Survey and Critique", *Regional Studies*, 16 (4), pp. 287-305.

Ashcroft, B. and Taylor, J. (1979), "The Effect of Regional Policy on the Movement of Industry in Great Britain", Chapter 2, pp. 43-64 in Maclennan, D. and Parr, J.B. (eds), *Regional Policy: Past Experience and New Directions*, Martin Robertson, Oxford.

Australia (Bureau of Industry Economics) (1985), *The Regional Impact of Structural Change: An Assessment of Regional Policies in Australia* (Research Report No. 18), Australian Government Publishing Service, Canberra, 182 pp.

Australia (Industries Assistance Commission) (1981a), *Annual Report 1980-81*, Australian Government Publishing Service, Canberra, 284 pp.

Australia (Industries Assistance Commission) (1981b), *The Regional Implications of Economic Change*, (Approaches to General Reductions in Protection, Discussion Paper No. 3), Australian Government Publishing Service, Canberra, 70 pp.

Australia (Study Group on Structural Adjustment) (1979), *Report* (Vol. 1), Australian Government Publishing Service, Canberra, n.c.p.

Australian Labor Party (1984), *Platform, Constitution and Rules as Approved by the 36th National Conference, Canberra, 1984*, Party Publication, Canberra, 258 pp.

Australian Science and Technology Council (1983), *Technological Change and Employment*, Australian Government Publishing Service, Canberra, 168 pp.

Aydalot, P. (1984), "Questions for Regional Policy", *Tijdschrift voor Economische en Sociale Geografie*, 75 (1), pp. 4-13.

Babbitt, B. (1984), "The States and the Reindustrialization of America", *Issues in Science and Technology*, 1 (1), pp. 84-93.

Badaracco, J.L. and Yoffie, D.B. (1983), "Industrial Policy: It Can't Happen Here", *Havard Business Review*, 61 (6), pp. 97-105.

Bartels, C.P.A. and van Duijn, J.J. (1982), "Regional Economic Policy in a Changed Labour Market", *Papers of the Regional Science Association*, 49, pp. 97-111.

Bartels, C.P.A. *et al.* (1982), "Estimating the Impact of Regional Policy: A Review of Applied Research Methods", *Regional Science and Urban Economics*, 12, pp. 3-41.

Beaumont, P.B. (1979), "An Examination of Assisted Labour Mobility Policy", Chapter 3, pp. 65-80 in Maclennan, D. and Parr, J.B. (eds), *Regional Policy: Past Experience and New Directions*, Martin Robertson, Oxford.

Belassa, B. (1979*a*), "The Changing International Division of Labor in Manufactured Goods", *Banca Nazionale del Lavoro Quarterly Review*, 130, pp. 243-85.

Belassa, B. (1979*b*), "World Trade and the International Economy: Trends, Prospects and Policies", Part 4 in Belassa, B. *et al.*, *World Trade: Constraints and Opportunities in the 80's*, Atlantic Institute for International Affairs, Paris.

Belassa, B. (1983), "Industrial Prospects and Policies in the Developed Countries", Chapter 13, pp. 257-78 in Machlup, F. *et al.* (eds), *Reflections on a Troubled World Economy: Essays in Honour of Herbert Giersch*, (Trade Policy Research Centre), Macmillan, London.

Belassa, B. (1984), *Trends in International Trade in Manufactured Goods and Structural Change in the Industrial Countries*, (Staff Working Paper No. 611), World Bank, Washington D.C., 32 pp.

Birch, D.L. (1979), *The Job Generation Process*, (Program on Neighborhood and Regional Change), Massachusetts Institute of Technology, Cambridge (Mass.), 22 pp.

Blackbourn, A. (1978), "Multinational Enterprises and Regional Development: A Comment", *Regional Studies*, 12, pp. 125-27.

Blair, J.P. *et al.* (1984), "The Market for Jobs: A New Approach to Solving Unemployment", *Futurist*, 18 (2), pp. 54-59.

Botham, R. and Lloyd, G. (1983), "The Political Economy of Enterprise Zones", *Westminster Bank Quarterly Review*, (May), pp. 24-32.

Braun, E. (1984), *Wayward Technology*, Frances Pinter, London, 224 pp.

Brody, H. (1985), "States Vie for a Slice of the Pie", *High Technology*, 5 (1), pp. 16-28.

Brown, A.J. and Burrows, E.M. (1977), *Regional Economic Problems: Comparative Experiences of Some Market Economies*, George Allen and Unwin, London, 209 pp.

Buswell, R.J. (1983), "Research and Development and Regional Development: A Review", pp. 9-22 in Gillespie, A. (ed.), *Technological Change and Regional Development*, (London Papers in Regional Science No. 12), Pion, London.

Butler, G.J. and Mandeville, T.D. (1981), *Regional Economics: An Australian Introduction*, University of Queensland Press, St. Lucia, 139 pp.

Butler, S.M. (1982), *Enterprise Zones: Greenlining the Inner Cities*, Heinemann, London, 175 pp.

Camagni, R. and Cappellin, R. (1981*a*), "European Regional Growth and Policy Issues for the 1980s", *Built Environment*, 7 (3/4), pp. 162-71.

Camagni, R. and Cappellin, R. (1981*b*), "Policies for Full Employment and More Efficient Utilization of Resources and New Trends in European Regional Development", *Lo Spectatore Internazionale*, 2, pp. 99-135.

Camagni, R. and Cappellin, R. (1982), *Scenarios of Economic Change in the European Regions*, (Studi Economici No. 3, Dipartimento di Economia Politica), Università Bocconi, Milan, 42 pp.

Cappellin, R. (1983), "Productivity Growth and Technological Change in a Regional Perspective", *Giornale degli Economisti e Annali di Economia*, (Nuova Serie), 42, Fasc. 7/8, pp. 459-82.

Carney, J. (1980), "Regions in Crisis: Accumulation, Regional Problems and Crisis Formation", Chapter 2, pp. 28-59 in Carney, J. *et al.* (eds), *Regions in Crisis: New Perspectives in European Regional Theory*, St. Martins Press, New York.

Carter, R.A. (1983), "Debunking Decentralisation Myths: The Case for Region-Specific Policies in Australia", (Paper presented to 23rd European Regional Science Association Congress, Poitiers, France), (Mimeo.), 25 pp.

Chisholm, M. (1984), "Regional Policy for the Late Twentieth Century", *Regional Studies*, 18, pp. 348-52.

Clark, N.G. (1971), "Science, Technology, and Regional Economic Development", *Research Policy*, 1, pp. 296-319.

Collier, D. (1983), "The Service Sector Revolution: The Automation of Services", *Long Range Planning*, 16 (6), pp. 10-20.

Commission of the European Communities (1984), *The Regions of Europe: Second Periodic Report on the Social and Economic Situation and Development of the Regions of the Community*, Commission Publication, Brussels, n.c.p.

Cooke, P. *et al.* (1984), "New Technology and Regional Development in Austerity Britain: The Case of the Semiconductor Industry", *Regional Studies*, 18 (4), pp. 277-89.

Council of Europe (1983), *Compendium of Regional Statistics for Council of Europe Member States and Finland and Yugoslavia*, (Mimeo), Council of Europe, Strasbourg, 130 pp.

Crough, G. and Wheelwright, T. (1982), *Australia: A Client State*, Penguin Books, Ringwood (Vic.), 255 pp.

Cruze, A.M. (1983), "The Research Triangle's Expanding Influence", (Unpublished Paper Presented to Research, Technology and Regional Development Workshop, Paris, 24-27th October), OECD, Paris, 11 pp.

Daniels, P.W. (1983), "Service Industries: Supporting Role or Centre Stage?", *Area*, 15 (4), pp. 301-09.

Diamond, D. and Spence, N. (1983), *Regional Policy Evaluation: A Methodological Review and the Scottish Example*, Gower, Aldershot, 170 pp.

Diamond, D.R. (1984), "Issues in Public Policy Evaluation: The Case of Regional Policy", *Geoforum*, 15 (1), pp. 33-38.

Dorfman, N.S. (1983), "Route 128: The Development of a Regional High Technology Economy", *Research Policy*, 12, pp. 299-316.

Dubnick, M. (1984), "American States and the Industrial Policy Debate", *Policy Studies Review*, 4 (1), pp. 22-27.

Dunford, R. (1983), "Technology: The Contingent Nature of its Impact", *Prometheus*, 1 (2), pp. 290-302.

Eads, G. and Graham, E.M. (1982), "Transparency: A Prerequisite for Positive Adjustment", *OECD Observer*, 119, pp. 8-11.

Emanuel, A. (1973), *Issues of Regional Policies*, OECD, Paris, 274 pp.

Erickson, R.A. (1981), "Corporations, Branch Plants and Employment Stability in Nonmetropolitan Areas", Chapter 9, pp. 135-53 in Rees, J. *et al.* (eds), *Industrial Location and Regional Systems: Spatial Organisation in the Economic Sector*, Bergin, Brooklyn.

Etzioni, A. (1984), "The Two-Track Society", *National Forum*, 64 (3), pp. 3-5.

European Communities (1984), *Yearbook of Regional Statistics (Eurostat)*, Commission Publication, Brussels, 241 pp.

Ezra, E. (1982), "Comparative Trends in Conditions for the Development of Efficient Regional Policies: The Experience of the OECD Countries"; 16 pp. in Instituto di Stude sulle Regioni, *CEE-USA: Istituzioni Regionali e Politiche di Sviluppo*, (Conference of Consiglio Nazionale delle Ricerche and Instituto Internazionale di Scienze Amministrative, Rome, 27-29th January), Institute Publication, Rome.

Filmer, R. and Foster R. (1977), "Economic Policy Instruments and Regional Objectives", pp. 89-103 in Neilson, R. (ed.), *Papers of the Meeting of the Australian and New Zealand Section, Regional Science Association: Second Meeting, Sydney, December 1977*, Regional Science Association, Melbourne.

Firn, J.R. and Maclennan, D. (1979), "Devolution: The Changing Political Economy of Regional Policy", Chapter 13, pp. 273-95 in Maclennan, D. and Parr, J.B. (eds), *Regional Policy: Past Experience and New Directions*, Martin Robertson, Oxford.

Furuki, T. (1983), "The Postwar Development of Capitalism and Regional Problems: A Comparison of Italy and Japan", pp. 179-92 in Fodella, G. (ed.), *Japan's Economy in a Comparative Perspective*, Paul Norbury, Tenterden (Kent).

Gartner, A. and Riessman, F. (1984), "The Service Society: A Revisit", *National Forum*, 64 (3), pp. 24-27.

Gershuny, J.I. (1978), *After Industrial Society?: The Emerging Self-Service Economy*, Macmillan, London, 177 pp.

Gershuny, J.I. (1979), "The Informal Economy: Its Role in Post-Industrial Society", *Futures*, 11 (1), pp. 3-5.

Gershuny, J.I. and Miles, I.D. (1983), *The New Service Economy: The Transformation of Employment and Industrial Societies*, Francis Pinter, London, 282 pp.

Gibson, K.D. and Horvath, R.J. (1983), "Global Capital and the Restructuring Crisis in Australian Manufacturing", *Economic Geography*, 59 (2), pp. 178-94.

Glasson, J. (1978), *An Introduction to Regional Planning: Concepts, Theory and Practice*, (2nd Edition), Hutchinson, London, pp. 422.

Goldsmith, W.W. (1982), "Enterprise Zones: If They Work, We're in Trouble", *International Journal of Urban and Regional Research*, 6 (3), pp. 435-42.

Golt, S. (1979), "The Nineteen Eighties: Constraints and Opoportunities", Part 3A, pp. 28-34 in Belassa, B. *et al.* (eds), *World Trade: Constraints and Opportunities in the 80s*, Atlantic Institute for International Affairs, Paris.

Gordus, J.P. *et al.* (1981), *Plant Closings and Economic Dislocation*, Upjohn Institute for Employment Research, Kalamazoo (Mich.), 173 pp.

Grant, P. (1983), "Technological Sovereignty: Forgotten Factor in the 'Hi-Tech' Razzamatazz", *Prometheus*, 1 (2), pp. 239-69.

Gudgin, G.H. and Fothergill, S. (1984), "The Impact of Regional Policy on the Geography of Employment", *Geography*, 69 (2), pp. 159-63.

Hall, P. (1982), "Enterprise Zones: A Justification", *International Journal of Urban and Regional Research*, 6 (3), pp. 416-21.

Hambrecht, W.R. (1984), "Venture Capital and the Growth of Silicon Valley", *California Management Review*, 26 (2), pp. 74-82.

Hamley, W. (1982), "Research Triangle Park: North Carolina", *Geography*, 67 (1), pp. 59-62.

Harrison, B. (1982), "The Politics and Economics of the Urban Enterprise Zone Proposal: A Critique", *International Journal of Urban and Regional Research*, 6 (3), pp. 422-28.

Hayter, R. (1982), "Truncation, the International Firm and Regional Policy", *Area*, 14, pp. 277-82.

Heaton, G.R. and Hollomon, J.H. (1984), "Technological Diffusion and National Policy", *Research Management*, 27 (1), pp. 5-7.

Henkin, W.A. (1983), "Silicon Valley: Incubator of High Technology", *Economic Impact*, 41, pp. 43-49.

Hesselman, L. (1983), "Trends in European Industrial Intervention", *Cambridge Journal of Economics*, 7, pp. 197-208.

Higgott, R. (1984), "Export-Oriented Industrialisation, the New International Division of Labour and the Corporate State in the Third World: An Exploratory Essay on Conceptual Linkage", *Australian Geographical Studies*, 22 (1), pp. 58-71.

Holland, S. (1976), *Capital Versus the Regions*, Macmillan, London, 328 pp.

Hudson, R. and Lewis, J.R. (1982), "Regional Planning in Europe: Introductory Remarks", pp. 1-6 in Hudson, R. and Lewis, J.R. (eds), *Regional Planning in Europe*, (London Papers in Regional Science No. 11), Pion, London.

Japan External Trade Organisation (1983), *Technopolises Now in Japan*, Organisation Publication, Tokyo, 48 pp.

Japan (Ministry of International Trade and Industry) (1980), *The Industrial Structure of Japan in the 1980s: Future Outlook and Tasks*, Ministry Publication, Tokyo, 110 pp.

Japan (Ministry of International Trade and Industry) (1983), *Small Business in Japan: White Paper on Small and Medium Enterprises in Japan*, (Small and Medium Enterprise Agency), Ministry Publication, Tokyo, 108 pp.

Japan (Prime Minister's Office) (1984), *Statistical Handbook of Japan*, Japan Statistical Association, Tokyo, 158 pp.

Japan Trade and Industry Publicity Inc. (1984), "The Technopolis Plan: Recent Developments", *Digest of Japanese Industry and Technology*, 196, pp. 54-56.

Jenness, R.A. (1984), *Positive Adjustment in Manpower and Social Policies*, OECD, Paris, 88 pp.

Johnson, H. (1973), "Economic Benefits of the Multinational Enterprise", Chapter 7, pp. 165-70 in Hahlo, H.R. *et al.* (eds), *Nationalism and the Multinational Enterprise: Legal, Economic and Managerial Aspects*, Sijthoff International, Dobbs Ferry (N.Y.).

Jones, B. (1982), *Sleepers Wake!: Technology and the Future of Work*, Wheatsheaf Books, Brighton, 285 pp.

Jones, B.G. and Manson, D.M. (1982), "The Geography of Enterprise Zones: A Critical Analysis", *Economic Geography*, 58, pp. 329-42.

Jones, B.O. (1983), "Sunrise Industries: Leading the Revolution", *Human Resources Management Australia*, 21 (3), pp. 42-47.

Joseph, R. (1984), "Recent Trends in Australian Government Policies for Technological Innovation", *Prometheus*, 2 (1), pp. 93-111.

Kavanagh, J. (1984), "Academia Meets Business: Both Profit", *Business Review Weekly*, 6 (28), (14th July), pp. 51-52, 55, 57.

Keeble, D. *et al.* (1982), "Regional Accessibility and Economic Potential in the European Community", *Regional Studies*, 16 (6), pp. 419-32.

Klein, R. (1981), "Values, Power and Policies", pp. 166-77 in OECD, *The Welfare State in Crisis*, OECD, Paris.

Konaga, K. (1983), "Industrial Policy: The Japanese Version of a Universal Trend", *Journal of Japanese Trade and Industry*, 2 (4), pp. 18-23.

Kondratieff, N.D. (1935), "The Long Waves in Economic Life", *Review of Economic Statistics*, 17, pp. 149-58.

Kreile, M. (1983), "Public Enterprise and the Pursuit of Strategic Management: Italy", Chapter 7, pp. 193-219 in Dyson, K. and Wilks S. (eds), *Industrial Crisis: A Comparative Study of the State and Industry*, Martin Robertson, Oxford.

Levin, H. and Rumberger, R. (1983), "The Low-Skill Future of High Tech", *Technology Review*, 86 (6), pp. 18-21.

Levitt, A. (1984), "Industrial Policy: Slogan or Solution?", *Harvard Business Review*, 62 (2), pp. 6-8.

Logan, A. (1979), "Recent Directions of Regional Policy in Australia", *Regional Studies*, 13, pp. 153-60.

Loveday, P. (1982), *Promoting Industry: Recent Australian Political Experience*, University of Queensland Press, St. Lucia, 223 pp.

McAuley, I. (1984), "Federal Perspectives on Regional Policy Development", (Unpublished Paper Presented to Ninth Australian and New Zealand Regional Science Association Conference, 4-6th December), Melbourne, 11 pp.

McCracken, P.W. (1984), "Does the US Need an Industrial Policy?", *Economic Impact*, 46, pp. 8-13.

McKay, R. (1979), "The Death of Regional Policy – Or Resurrection Squared?", *Regional Studies*, 13, pp. 281-95.

McKersie, R.B. and Sengenberger, W. (1983), *Job Losses in Major Industries: Manpower Strategy Responses*, OECD, Paris, 125 pp.

Macdonald, S. (1983), "High Technology Policy and the Silicon Valley Model: An Australian Perspective", *Prometheus*, 1 (2), pp. 330-49.

Malecki, E.J. (1979), "Locational Trends in R and D by Large US Corporations, 1965-1977", *Economic Geography*, 55, pp. 309-23.

Malecki, E. (1981a), "Product Cycles, Innovation Cycles, and Regional Economic Change", *Technological Forecasting and Social Change*, 19, pp. 291-306.

Malecki, E.J. (1981b), "Government-Funded R and D: Some Regional Economic Implications" *Professional Geographer*, 33 (1), pp. 72-82.

Malecki, E.J. (1981c), "Science, Technology, and Regional Economic Development: Review and Prospects", *Research Policy*, 10 (4), pp. 312-34.

Malecki, E.J. (1983), "Technology and Regional Development: A Survey", *International Regional Science Review*, 8 (2), pp. 89-125.

Manners, G. (1981), "Regional Policies and the National Interest", Geo*forum*, 12 (4), pp. 281-99.

Mansfield, E. (1968), *The Economics of Technological Change*, Norton, New York, 257 pp.

Marquand, J. (1980a), *Measuring the Effects and Costs of Regional Incentives*, (Government Economic Service Working Paper No. 32), United Kingdom Department of Industry, London, 118 pp.

Marquand, J. (1980b), "The Role of the Tertiary Sector in Regional Policy: Comparative Analysis", pp. 1-20 in Commission of the European Communities, *The Role of the Tertiary Sector in Regional Policy: Summaries of the National Reports and of Their Comparative Study*, (Internal Documentation on Regional Policy in the Community No. 7), Commission Publication, Brussels.

Marsh, P. (1984), "Cambridge Blossoms as Britain's Silicon Valley", *Science and Government Report*, 14 (1), pp. 6-7.

Martin, R.L. (1982), "Job Loss and the Regional Incidence of Redundancies in the Current Recession", *Cambridge Journal of Economics*, 6, pp. 375-95.

Maruyama, M. (1985), "Report on a New Technological Community: The Making of a Technopolis in an International Context", *Technological Forecasting and Social Change*, 27, pp. 75-98.

Massey, D. (1979), "In What Sense a Regional Problem?" *Regional Studies*, 13, pp. 233-43.

Massey, D. (1982), "Enterprise Zones: A Political Issue", *International Journal of Urban and Regional Research*, 6 (3), pp. 429-34.

Massey, D. and Meegan R. (1982), *The Anatomy of Job Loss: The How, Why and Where of Employment Decline*, Methuen, London, 258 pp.

Mazur, L. (1984), "Boston's High-Tech Highway", *Management Today*, (January), pp. 62-67.

Merrill, S.A. (1984), "The Politics of Micropolicy: Innovation and Industrial Policy in the United States", *Policy Studies Review*, 3 (3-4), pp. 445-52.

Meyers, N. (1984), "Biggest Science Park So Far", *Nature*, 310 (No. 5972, 5th July), p. 7.

Michalski, W. (1982), "Structural Change: Positive Adjustment Policies, Key to Economic Recovery", *OECD Observer*, 119, pp. 6-7.

Moore, B. and Rhodes, J. (1977), "Evaluating the Economic Effects of Regional Policy", pp. 11-82 in OECD, *Report on Methods of Measuring the Effects of Regional Policies*, OECD, Paris.

Moore, B. and Spires, R. (1983), "The Experience of the Cambridge Science Park", (Unpublished Paper Presented to Research, Technology and Regional Policy Workshop, Paris, 24-27th October), OECD, Paris, 33 pp.

Nicol, B. and Wettmann, R. (1977), *Background Notes to Restrictive Regional Policy Measures in the European Community*, (Paper to the Atlantic Conference on Balanced National Growth, Racine, Wisconsin, United States, 4-6th January), Wissenschaftszentrum, Berlin, 103 pp.

Nicol, B. and Wettmann, R. (1979), "Background Notes to Restrictive Regional Policy Measures in the European Community", Chapter 6, pp. 157-230 in Allen, K. (ed.), *Balanced National Growth*, Lexington Books, Lexington (Mass.).

Nicol, W.R. (1979), "Relaxation and Reorientation: Parallel Trends in Regional Disincentive Policies", *Urban Studies*, 16, pp. 333-39.

Nicol, W.R. (1980), *An Appreciation of Regional Policy Evaluation Studies: A Comparative Study, Final Report*, Wissenschaftszentrum, Berlin, 125 pp.

Nicol, W.R. (1982), "Estimating the Effects of Regional Policy: A Critique of the European Experience", *Regional Studies*, 16 (3), pp. 199-210.

Nishioka, H. (1983), "High Technology Industry Location and Regional Development", (Unpublished Paper Presented to Research, Technology and Regional Policy Workshop, 24-27th October), OECD, Paris, 15 pp.

Norcliffe, G.B. and Hoare, A.G. (1982), "Enterprise Zone Policy for the Inner City: A Review and Preliminary Assessment", *Area*, 14 (4), pp. 265-74.

Nord-Pas de Calais (Conseil Régional) (1984), "Traditional Industrial Regions of Europe in the Eighties and Nineties", (Conference, 25-27th April), Lille, n.c.p.

Noyelle, T.J. (1983), "The Rise of Advanced Services: Some Implications for Economic Development in US Cities", *Journal of the American Planning Association*, 49 (3), pp. 280-90.

Oakey R.P. (1979), "Technological Change and Regional Development: A Note on Policy Implications", *Area*, 11, pp. 340-44.

Oakey, R.P. (1983), "New Technology, Government Policy and Regional Manufacturing Employment", *Area*, 15 (1), pp. 61-65.

Oakey, R.P. (1984a), "High Technology Industry", *Geography*, 69 (2), pp. 157-59.

Oakey, R.P. (1984b), "Innovation and Regional Growth in Small High Technology Firms: Evidence from Britain and the USA", *Regional Studies*, 18 (3), pp. 237-51.

O'Connor, K. (1984), "Rethinking Regional Policy", pp. 119-33 in Sorensen, A.D. *et al.* (eds), *Papers of the Eighth Meeting of the Australia and New Zealand Regional Science Association, Armidale, December 1983*, Regional Science Association, Armidale.

OECD (1970), *The Regional Factor in Economic Development: Policies in Fifteen Industrialised OECD Countries*, OECD, Paris, 125 pp.

OECD (1974), *Reappraisal of Regional Policies in OECD Countries*, OECD, Paris, 172 pp.

OECD (1976a), *Regional Problems and Policies in OECD Countries: Volume 1 (France, Italy, Ireland, Denmark, Sweden, Japan)*, OECD, Paris, 125 pp.

OECD (1976b), *Regional Problems and Policies in OECD Countries: Volume 2 (United Kingdom, Belgium, Netherlands, Norway, Finland, Spain, Austria, Germany, Canada, Switzerland)*, OECD, Paris, 213 pp.

OECD (1977a), *Regional Policies: The Current Outlook*, OECD, Paris, 80 pp.

OECD (1977*b*), *Report on Methods of Measuring the Effects of Regional Policies*, OECD, Paris, 118 pp.

OECD (1977*c*), *Restrictive Regional Policy Measures*, OECD, Paris, 34 pp.

OECD (1978*a*), *Regional Policies and the Services Sector*, OECD, Paris, 42 pp.

OECD (1978*b*), *Regional Problems and Policies in Portugal*, OECD, Paris, 69 pp.

OECD (1979*a*), *Regional Policies in Norway*, OECD, Paris, 69 pp.

OECD (1979*b*), *Report on The Role of Industrial Incentives in Regional Development*, OECD, Paris, 92 pp.

OECD (1979*c*), *The Impact of the Newly Industrialising Countries on Production and Trade in Manufactures: Report by the Secretary-General*, OECD, Paris, 96 pp.

OECD (1979*d*), *International Investment and Multinational Enterprises: Review of the 1976 Declaration and Decisions*, OECD, Paris, 67 pp.

OECD (1979*e*), *International Investment and Multinational Enterprises*, (Revised Edition), OECD, Paris, 28 pp.

OECD (1980*a*), *Regional Policies in Canada*, OECD, Paris, 80 pp.

OECD (1980*b*), *Regional Policies in the United States*, OECD, Paris, 97 pp.

OECD (1980*c*), *Technical Change and Economic Policy: Science and Technology in the New Economic and Social Context*, OECD, Paris, 117 pp.

OECD (1981*a*), *Regional Problems and Policies in Greece*, OECD, Paris, 87 pp.

OECD (1981*b*), *Report on the Nature and Modes of Organisations Set Up to Deal with Regional Problems in Countries with Federal-Type Constitutions*, OECD, Paris, 23 pp.

OECD (1981*c*), *Research and Policy Making: The Case of Regional Policy*, OECD, Paris, 105 pp.

OECD (1981*d*), *International Investment and Multinational Enterprises: Recent International Direct Investment Trends*, OECD, Paris, 106 pp.

OECD (1981*e*), *The Welfare State in Crisis*, OECD, Paris, 274 pp.

OECD (1981*f*), "Stimulating Innovation in Small Firms", *OECD Observer*, 113, pp. 21-25.

OECD (1982*a*), *Survey of Recent Developments in Regional Problems and Policies in OECD Countries*, OECD, Paris, 35 pp.

OECD (1982*b*), *Innovation in Small and Medium Firms*, OECD, Paris, 41 pp.

OECD (1982*c*), *Innovation in Small and Medium Firms: Background Reports*, OECD, Paris, 274 pp.

OECD (1982*d*), "The Hidden Economy and the National Accounts", pp. 8-45 in *Occasional Studies*, (June), OECD, Paris.

OECD (1983*a*), *Positive Adjustment Policies: Managing Structural Change*, OECD, Paris, 116 pp.

OECD (1983*b*), *Regional Policies: The Problem of Co-ordination*, (Mimeo.), OECD, Paris, 23 pp.

OECD (1983*c*), *Industry in Transition: Experience of the 70s and Prospects for the 80s*, OECD, Paris, 236 pp.

OECD (1983*d*), *World Economic Interdependence and the Evolving North-South Relationship*, OECD, Paris, 83 pp.

OECD (1983*e*), *The Effectiveness of Regional Financial Incentives to Industry*, (Mimeo.), OECD, Paris, 36 pp.

OECD (1983*f*), *Transparency for Positive Adjustment: Identifying and Evaluating Government Intervention*, OECD, Paris, 257 pp.

OECD (1983*g*), *Managing Urban Change: Volume II, The Role of Government*, OECD, Paris, 114 pp.

OECD (1984*a*), *Historical Statistics: Statistiques Rétrospectives 1960-1982*, OECD, Paris, 166 pp.

OECD (1984*b*), *International Investment and Multinational Enterprises: The 1984 Review of the 1976 Declaration and Decisions*, OECD, Paris, 66 pp.

OECD (1984*c*), *International Investment and Multinational Enterprises*, (Revised Edition), OECD, Paris, 34 pp.

OECD (1984*d*), *The Steel Market in 1983 and the Outlook for 1984*, OECD, Paris, 37 pp.

OECD (1984*e*), "Japan Then and Now", *OECD Observer*, 127, pp. 3-15.

OECD (1984*f*), "The Employment Outlook: Where are the Jobs in Today's Labour Market?", *OECD Observer*, 130, pp. 5-10.

OECD (1986), *The Technopolis Concept in the Regional Development Policy of Japan*, OECD, 1986, Paris, 68 pp.

Oman, C. (1984), *New Forms of International Investment in Developing Countries*, (Development Centre Studies), OECD, Paris, 139 pp.

Pavitt, K. (1983), *Patterns of Technical Change: Evidence, Theory and Policy Implications*, (Lecture at Imperial College of Science and Technology, University of London, 8th February 1983), Science Policy Research Unit, University of Sussex, Brighton, 17 pp.

Peet, R. (1983), "Introduction: The Global Geography of Contemporary Capitalism", *Economic Geography*, 59 (2), pp. 105-11.

Phalon, R. (1984), "Incubator Programme Helps Firms Hatch", *Economic Impact*, 46, pp. 44-47.

Pinder, D. (1983), *Regional Economic Policy and Development: Theory and Practice in the European Community*, George Allen and Unwin, London, 130 pp.

Queensland (Premier's Department) (1983), *Towards a Technology Strategy for Queensland*, Departmental Publication, Brisbane, 116 pp.

Rasmussen, D.W. and Ledebur, L.C. (1983), "The Role of State Economic Development Programs in National Industry Policy", *Policy Studies Review*, 2 (4), pp. 750-61.

Rees, J. (1979), "Technological Change and Regional Shifts in American Manufacturing", *Professional Geographer*, 31 (1), pp. 45-54.

Reich, R.B. (1983), *The Next American Frontier*, Penguin, Harmondsworth, 324 pp.

Reich, R.B. (1984), "Thoughts on Innovation", *Dialogue*, 64 (February), pp. 23-29.

Robert, J. (1984), "Technical Report on What is at Stake in the Traditional Industrial Regions of Europe", Paper Presented to Nord-Pas de Calais (Conseil Régional), "Traditional Industrial Regions of Europe in the Eighties and Nineties", (Conference, 25-27th April), Lille, 20 pp.

Robert-Müller, A. and Robert, J. (1979), *The Impact of International Economic Change on Development Trends in Europe's Regions*, (European Regional Planning Study Series No. 25), Council of Europe, Strasbourg, 34 pp.

Robson, P. (1979), "Technological Change and Employment in the 1980s", *Journal of Australian Political Economy*, 5, pp. 58-69.

Roessner, J.D. (1984), "Innovation Policy in the United States: An Overview of the Issues", *Policy Studies Review*, 3 (3-4), pp. 429-35.

Roger Tym and Partners (1984), *Monitoring Enterprise Zones: Year Three Report*, Company Publication, London, 151 pp.

Rohwer, J. (1984), "The Crest of the Wave", *Economist*, 291 (No. 7342, 19th May), pp. 3-7, 10, 15-18, 21-22.

Rosenberg, R. (1985), "What Companies Look For", *High Technology*, 5 (1), pp. 30-31, 34-37.

Ross, R. *et al.* (1984), "Global Capitalism and Regional Decline: Implications for the Strategy of Classes in Older Regions", pp. 109-29 in O'Keefe, P. (ed.), *Regional Restructuring under Advanced Capitalism*, Croom Helm, London.

Rothwell, R. (1982), "The Role of Technology in Industrial Change: Implications for Regional Policy", *Regional Studies*, 16 (5), pp. 361-69.

Rothwell, R. and Zegfeld, W. (1984), "An Assessment of Government Innovation Policies", *Policy Studies Review*, 3 (3-4), pp. 436-44.

Sawada, J. (1983), "Government Industrial Policy for a Healthy World Economy", *Technological Forecasting and Social Change*, 24, pp. 95-105.

Schnee, J.E. (1978), "Government Programmes and the Growth of High-Technology Industries", *Research Policy*, 7, pp. 2-24.

Schofield J.A. (1976), "Economic Efficiency and Regional Policy", *Urban Studies*, 13 (2), pp. 181-92.

Schofield, J.A. (1979), "Macro Evaluations of the Impact of Regional Policy in Britain: A Review of Recent Research", *Urban Studies*, 16 (3), pp. 251-71.

Schultze, C.L. (1983), "Industrial Policy: A Solution in Search of a Problem", *California Management Review*, 25 (4), pp. 5-15.

Schumpeter, J.A. (1939), *Business Cycles*, McGraw Hill, New York, 1095 pp.

Schumpeter, J.A. (1942), *Capitalism, Socialism and Democracy*, Harper and Brothers, New York, 381 pp.

Secchi, B. (1977), "Central and Peripheral Regions in a Process of Economic Development: The Italian Case", pp. 36-51 in Massey, D.B. and Batey, P.W.J. (eds), *Alternative Frameworks for Analysis*, (London Papers in Regional Science Vol. 7), Pion, London.

Sefer, B. (1981), "The Economic Environment and Social Policy of the OECD Countries in the 80s", pp. 119-36 in OECD, *The Welfare State in Crisis*, OECD, Paris.

Segal, N.S. (1979), "The Limit and Means of 'Self-Reliant' Regional Economic Growth", Chapter 10, pp. 211-24 in Maclennan, D. and Parr, J.B. (eds), *Regional Policy: Past Experience and New Directions*, Martin Robertson, Oxford.

Steed, G.P.F. and DeGenova, D. (1983), "Ottawa's Technology-Oriented Complex", *Canadian Geographer*, 27 (3), pp. 263-78.

Stein, H. (1983), "Don't Fall for Industrial Policy", *Fortune*, 108 (10), pp. 64-66 *et seq.*

Storey, D.J. (1983), "Small Firms Policy: A Critique", *Journal of General Management* 8 (4), pp. 5-19.

Strong, J.S. (1983), "Regional Variations in Industrial Performance", *Regional Studies*, 17 (6), pp. 429-44.

Susman, P.H. (1984), "Capital Restructuring and the Changing Regional Environment", pp. 89-107 in O'Keefe, P. (ed.), *Regional Restructuring under Advanced Capitalism*, Croom Helm, London.

Susman, P. and Schutz, E. (1983), "Monopoly and Competitive Firm Relations and Regional Development in Global Capitalism", *Economic Geography*, 59 (2), pp. 161-77.

Sweet, M.L. (1981), *Industrial Location Policy for Economic Revitalisation: National and International Perspectives*, Praeger, New York, 184 pp.

Taylor, M.J. (1983), "Technological Change and the Segmented Economy", pp. 104-17 in Gillespie, A. (ed.), *Technological Change and Regional Development*, (London Papers in Regional Science No. 12), Pion, London.

Taylor, S. (1981), "The Politics of Enterprise Zones", *Public Administration*, 59 (4), pp. 421-39.

Thwaites, A.T. (1978), "Technological Change, Mobile Plants and Regional Development", *Regional Studies*, 12, pp. 445-61.

Thwaites, A.T. (1983), "The Employment Implications of Technological Change in a Regional Context", pp. 36-53 in Gillespie, A. (ed.), *Technological Change and Regional Development*, (London Papers in Regional Science No. 12), Pion, London.

Todd, D. (1983), "Technological Change, Industrial Evolution and Regional Repercussions: The Case of British Shipbuilding", *Canadian Geographer*, 27 (4), pp. 345-60.

Toffler, A. (1980), *The Third Wave*, Morrow, New York, 544 pp.

Townsend, A.R. (1983), *The Impact of Recession on Industry, Employment and the Regions, 1976-1981*, Croom Helm, London, 225 pp.

United Kingdom (Department of Trade and Industry) (1984), *Regional Industrial Policy: Some Economic Issues*, Departmental Publication, London, 134 pp.

United States (Congress) (1982), *Location of High Technology Firms and Regional Economic Development*, (Joint Economic Committee), US Government Printing Office, Washington D.C., 70 pp.

United States (Congress) (1984), *Industrial Policy Movement in the United States: Is it the Answer?* (Joint Economic Committee), US Government Printing Office, Washington, D.C., 104 pp.

United States (Department of Commerce) (1983), *An Assessment of US Competitiveness in High Technology Industries*, (International Trade Administration), US Government Printing Office, Washington, D.C., 68 pp.)

Van Heesch, T. (1984), "Structural Change and Small and Medium Sized Enterprises", (Unpublished Paper Presented to Conference on "La PME en Devenir dans un Monde en Mutation"), Université du Québec à Trois-Rivières, 45 pp.

Vanhove, N. and Klaassen, L.H. (1980), *Regional Policy: A European Approach*, Saxon House, Westmead, 488 pp.

Vickery, G. (1984), "Some Aggregate Measures of New Forms of Investment", Appendix pp. 119-39 in Oman, C., *New Forms of International Investment in Developing Countries*, (Development Studies Centre), OECD, Paris.

Victoria (Treasury) (1984), *The Economic Strategy for Victoria: Detailed Papers*, Government Printer, Melbourne, 190 pp.

Wade, R. (1977), "Policies and Politics of Dualism: The Italian Case", *Pacific Viewpoint*, 18 (2), pp. 167-200.

Wadley, D. (1984), "Management of Industrial Parks: Australian Perspectives", *Canadian Geographer*, 28 (3), pp. 258-75.

Wadley, D.A. (1986), "Industrial Systems", Chapter 11, pp. 229-47 in Holmes, J.H. (ed.), *Queensland: A Geographical Interpretation*, Boolarong Press, Brisbane.

Wadley, D. and Bentley, L. (1981), "Industrial Restructuring and Metropolitan Planning: Case History of Melbourne", Chapter 8, pp 237-72 in Linge, G.J.R. and McKay, J.S. (eds), *Structural Change in Australia: Some Spatial and Organisational Responses*, (Publication HG/15, Department of Human Geography, Research School of Pacific Studies), Australian National University, Canberra.

Walker, R. (1983), "Research Triangle in the 'Sunbelt'", *Economic Impact*, 44, pp. 42-47.

Warhurst, J. (1982), *Jobs or Dogma? The Industries Assistance Commission and Australian Politics*, University of Queensland Press, St. Lucia, 255 pp.

Weaver, C. (1982), "The Limits of Economism: Towards a Political Approach to Regional Development and Planning", pp. 184-202 in Hudson, R. and Lewis, J.E. (eds), *Regional Planning in Europe*, (London Papers in Regional Science No. 11), Pion, London.

Weiner, S.E. (1984), "Enterprise Zones as a Means of Reducing Structural Unemployment", *Economic Review of the Federal Reserve Bank of Kansas City*, 69 (3), pp. 3-16.

Wettmann, R.W. and Ciciotti, E. (1981), *The Mobilisation of Indigenous Potential*, Commission of the European Communities, Brussels, 142 pp.

Wild, J.P. (1984), "High Technology: Is it the Answer?", *Australian Director*, (June/July), pp. 47-48, 51-52.

Wilson, T. (1979), "Regional Policy and the National Interest", Chapter 4, pp. 81-108 in Maclennan, D. and Parr, J.B. (eds), *Regional Policy: Past Experience and New Directions*, Martin Robertson, Oxford.

Yuill, D. and Allen, K. (eds) (1980), *European Regional Incentives, 1980: A Survey of Regional Incentives in the Countries of the European Community*, University of Strathclyde, Glasgow, 382 pp.

Yuill, D. and Allen K. (eds) (1981), *European Regional Incentives, 1981: A Survey of Regional Incentives in the Countries of the European Community, Portugal and Sweden*, University of Strathclyde, Glasgow, 497 pp.

Yuill, D. and Allen, K. (eds), (1982), *European Regional Incentives, 1982: A Survey of Regional Incentives in the Countries of the European Community, Portugal, Spain and Sweden*, University of Strathclyde, Glasgow, 554 pp.

Yuill, D. and Allen, K. (eds), (1983), *European Regional Incentives, 1983: A Survey of Regional Incentives in the Countries of the European Community, Portugal, Spain and Sweden*, University of Strathclyde, Glasgow, 595 pp.

Yuill, D. and Allen, K. (eds), (1984), *European Regional Incentives, 1984: A Survey of Regional Incentives in Countries of the European Community, Portugal, Spain and Sweden*, University of Strathclyde, Glasgow, 543 pp.

Zschau, E. (1984), "Government Policy for Maintaining US Technological Leadership", *Research Management*, 27 (5), pp. 6-8.

OECD SALES AGENTS
DÉPOSITAIRES DES PUBLICATIONS DE L'OCDE

ARGENTINA - ARGENTINE
Carlos Hirsch S.R.L.,
Florida 165, 4º Piso,
(Galeria Guemes) 1333 Buenos Aires
Tel. 33.1787.2391 y 30.7122

AUSTRALIA-AUSTRALIE
D.A. Book (Aust.) Pty. Ltd.
11-13 Station Street (P.O. Box 163)
Mitcham, Vic. 3132   Tel. (03) 873 4411

AUSTRIA - AUTRICHE
OECD Publications and Information Centre,
4 Simrockstrasse,
5300 Bonn (Germany)   Tel. (0228) 21.60.45
Local Agent:
Gerold & Co., Graben 31, Wien 1 Tel. 52.22.35

BELGIUM - BELGIQUE
Jean de Lannoy, Service Publications OCDE,
avenue du Roi 202
B-1060 Bruxelles   Tel. 02/538.51.69

CANADA
Renouf Publishing Company Limited/
Éditions Renouf Limitée Head Office/
Siège social – Store/Magasin :
61, rue Sparks Street,
Ottawa, Ontario K1P 5A6
Tel. (613)238-8985. 1-800-267-4164
Store/Magasin : 211, rue Yonge Street,
Toronto, Ontario M5B 1M4.
Tel. (416)363-3171
Regional Sales Office/
Bureau des Ventes régional :
7575 Trans-Canada Hwy., Suite 305,
Saint-Laurent, Quebec H4T 1V6
Tel. (514)335-9274

DENMARK - DANEMARK
Munksgaard Export and Subscription Service
35, Nørre Søgade, DK-1370 København K
Tel. +45.1.12.85.70

FINLAND - FINLANDE
Akateeminen Kirjakauppa,
Keskuskatu 1, 00100 Helsinki 10   Tel. 0.12141

FRANCE
OCDE/OECD
Mail Orders/Commandes par correspondance :
2, rue André-Pascal,
75775 Paris Cedex 16
Tel. (1) 45.24.82.00
Bookshop/Librairie : 33, rue Octave-Feuillet
75016 Paris
Tel. (1) 45.24.81.67 ou/ou (1) 45.24.81.81
Principal correspondant :
Librairie de l'Université,
12a, rue Nazareth,
13602 Aix-en-Provence   Tel. 42.26.18.08

GERMANY - ALLEMAGNE
OECD Publications and Information Centre,
4 Simrockstrasse,
5300 Bonn   Tel. (0228) 21.60.45

GREECE - GRÈCE
Librairie Kauffmann,
28, rue du Stade, 105 64 Athens Tel. 322.21.60

HONG KONG
Government Information Services,
Publications (Sales) Office,
Beaconsfield House, 4/F.,
Queen's Road Central

ICELAND - ISLANDE
Snæbjörn Jónsson & Co., h.f.,
Hafnarstræti 4 & 9,
P.O.B. 1131 – Reykjavik
Tel. 13133/14281/11936

INDIA - INDE
Oxford Book and Stationery Co.,
Scindia House, New Delhi 1   Tel. 45896
17 Park St., Calcutta 700016   Tel. 240832

INDONESIA - INDONESIE
Pdin Lipi, P.O. Box 3065/JKT.Jakarta
Tel. 583467

IRELAND - IRLANDE
TDC Publishers – Library Suppliers
12 North Frederick Street, Dublin 1
Tel. 744835-749677

ITALY - ITALIE
Libreria Commissionaria Sansoni,
Via Lamarmora 45, 50121 Firenze
Tel. 579751/584468
Via Bartolini 29, 20155 Milano   Tel. 365083
Sub-depositari :
Ugo Tassi, Via A. Farnese 28,
00192 Roma   Tel. 310590
Editrice e Libreria Herder,
Piazza Montecitorio 120, 00186 Roma
Tel. 6794628
Agenzia Libraria Pegaso,
Via de Romita 5, 70121 Bari
Tel. 540.105/540.195
Agenzia Libraria Pegaso, Via S.Anna dei
Lombardi 16, 80134 Napoli.   Tel. 314180
Libreria Hœpli,
Via Hœpli 5, 20121 Milano   Tel. 865446
Libreria Scientifica
Dott. Lucio de Biasio "Aeiou"
Via Meravigli 16, 20123 Milano   Tel. 807679
Libreria Zanichelli, Piazza Galvani 1/A,
40124 Bologna   Tel. 237389
Libreria Lattes,
Via Garibaldi 3, 10122 Torino   Tel. 519274
La diffusione delle edizioni OCSE è inoltre
assicurata dalle migliori librerie nelle città più
importanti.

JAPAN - JAPON
OECD Publications and Information Centre,
Landic Akasaka Bldg., 2-3-4 Akasaka,
Minato-ku, Tokyo 107   Tel. 586.2016

KOREA - CORÉE
Pan Korea Book Corporation
P.O.Box No. 101 Kwangwhamun, Seoul
Tel. 72.7369

LEBANON - LIBAN
Documenta Scientifica/Redico,
Edison Building, Bliss St.,
P.O.B. 5641, Beirut   Tel. 354429-344425

MALAYSIA - MALAISIE
University of Malaya Co-operative Bookshop
Ltd.,
P.O.Box 1127, Jalan Pantai Baru,
Kuala Lumpur   Tel. 577701/577072

NETHERLANDS - PAYS-BAS
Staatsuitgeverij
Chr. Plantijnstraat, 2 Postbus 20014
2500 EA S-Gravenhage   Tel. 070-789911
Voor bestellingen: Tel. 070-789880

NEW ZEALAND - NOUVELLE-ZÉLANDE
Government Printing Office Bookshops:
Auckland: Retail Bookshop, 25 Rutland Street,
Mail Orders, 85 Beach Road
Private Bag C.P.O.
Hamilton: Retail: Ward Street,
Mail Orders, P.O. Box 857
Wellington: Retail, Mulgrave Street, (Head
Office)
Cubacade World Trade Centre,
Mail Orders, Private Bag
Christchurch: Retail, 159 Hereford Street,
Mail Orders, Private Bag
Dunedin: Retail, Princes Street,
Mail Orders, P.O. Box 1104

NORWAY - NORVÈGE
Tanum-Karl Johan a.s
P.O. Box 1177 Sentrum, 0107 Oslo 1
Tel. (02) 801260

PAKISTAN
Mirza Book Agency
65 Shahrah Quaid-E-Azam, Lahore 3 Tel. 66839

PORTUGAL
Livraria Portugal,
Rua do Carmo 70-74, 1117 Lisboa Codex.
Tel. 360582/3

SINGAPORE - SINGAPOUR
Information Publications Pte Ltd
Pei-Fu Industrial Building,
24 New Industrial Road No. 02-06
Singapore 1953   Tel. 2831786, 2831798

SPAIN - ESPAGNE
Mundi-Prensa Libros, S.A.,
Castelló 37, Apartado 1223, Madrid-28001
Tel. 431.33.99
Libreria Bosch, Ronda Universidad 11,
Barcelona 7   Tel. 317.53.08/317.53.58

SWEDEN - SUÈDE
AB CE Fritzes Kungl. Hovbokhandel,
Box 16356, S 103 27 STH,
Regeringsgatan 12,
DS Stockholm   Tel. (08) 23.89.00
Subscription Agency/Abonnements:
Wennergren-Williams AB,
Box 30004, S104 25 Stockholm. Tel. 08/54.12.00

SWITZERLAND - SUISSE
OECD Publications and Information Centre,
4 Simrockstrasse,
5300 Bonn (Germany)   Tel. (0228) 21.60.45
Local Agent:
Librairie Payot,
6 rue Grenus, 1211 Genève 11
Tel. (022) 31.89.50

TAIWAN - FORMOSE
Good Faith Worldwide Int'l Co., Ltd.
9th floor, No. 118, Sec.2
Chung Hsiao E. Road
Taipei   Tel. 391.7396/391.7397

THAILAND - THAILANDE
Suksit Siam Co., Ltd.,
1715 Rama IV Rd.,
Samyam Bangkok 5   Tel. 2511630

TURKEY - TURQUIE
Kültur Yayinlari Is-Türk Ltd. Sti.
Atatürk Bulvari No: 191/Kat. 21
Kavaklidere/Ankara   Tel. 25.07.60
Dolmabahce Cad. No: 29
Besiktas/Istanbul   Tel. 160.71.88

UNITED KINGDOM - ROYAUME UNI
H.M. Stationery Office,
Postal orders only:
P.O.B. 276, London SW8 5DT
Telephone orders: (01) 622.3316, or
Personal callers:
49 High Holborn, London WC1V 6HB
Branches at: Belfast, Birmingham,
Bristol, Edinburgh, Manchester

UNITED STATES - ÉTATS-UNIS
OECD Publications and Information Centre,
Suite 1207, 1750 Pennsylvania Ave., N.W.,
Washington, D.C. 20006 - 4582
Tel. (202) 724.1857

VENEZUELA
Libreria del Este,
Avda F. Miranda 52, Aptdo. 60337,
Edificio Galipan, Caracas 106
Tel. 32.23.01/33.26.04/31.58.38

YUGOSLAVIA - YOUGOSLAVIE
Jugoslovenska Knjiga, Knez Mihajlova 2,
P.O.B. 36, Beograd   Tel. 621.992

Orders and inquiries from countries where Sales
Agents have not yet been appointed should be sent
to:
OECD, Publications Service, Sales and
Distribution Division, 2, rue André-Pascal, 75775
PARIS CEDEX 16.

Les commandes provenant de pays où l'OCDE n'a
pas encore désigné de dépositaire peuvent être
adressées à :
OCDE, Service des Publications. Division des
Ventes et Distribution. 2. rue André-Pascal. 75775
PARIS CEDEX 16.

69928-07-1986

OECD PUBLICATIONS, 2, rue André-Pascal, 75775 PARIS CEDEX 16 - No. 43627 1986
PRINTED IN FRANCE
(70 86 02 1) ISBN 92-64-12868-9